PSYCHOLOGY RESEARCH PROGRESS

PSYCHOLOGY OF MORALITY

PSYCHOLOGY RESEARCH PROGRESS

Additional books in this series can be found on Nova's website
under the Series tab.

Additional E-books in this series can be found on Nova's website
under the E-book tab.

ETHICAL ISSUES IN THE 21ST CENTURY

Additional books in this series can be found on Nova's website
under the Series tab.

Additional E-books in this series can be found on Nova's website
under the E-book tab.

PSYCHOLOGY RESEARCH PROGRESS

PSYCHOLOGY OF MORALITY

ANGELO S. FRUILI
AND
LUISA D. VENETO
EDITORS

Nova Science Publishers, Inc.
New York

For permission to use material from this book please contact us:
Telephone 631-231-7269; Fax 631-231-8175
Web Site: http://www.novapublishers.com

NOTICE TO THE READER

The Publisher has taken reasonable care in the preparation of this book, but makes no expressed or implied warranty of any kind and assumes no responsibility for any errors or omissions. No liability is assumed for incidental or consequential damages in connection with or arising out of information contained in this book. The Publisher shall not be liable for any special, consequential, or exemplary damages resulting, in whole or in part, from the readers' use of, or reliance upon, this material. Any parts of this book based on government reports are so indicated and copyright is claimed for those parts to the extent applicable to compilations of such works.

Independent verification should be sought for any data, advice or recommendations contained in this book. In addition, no responsibility is assumed by the publisher for any injury and/or damage to persons or property arising from any methods, products, instructions, ideas or otherwise contained in this publication.

This publication is designed to provide accurate and authoritative information with regard to the subject matter covered herein. It is sold with the clear understanding that the Publisher is not engaged in rendering legal or any other professional services. If legal or any other expert assistance is required, the services of a competent person should be sought. FROM A DECLARATION OF PARTICIPANTS JOINTLY ADOPTED BY A COMMITTEE OF THE AMERICAN BAR ASSOCIATION AND A COMMITTEE OF PUBLISHERS.

Additional color graphics may be available in the e-book version of this book.

LIBRARY OF CONGRESS CATALOGING-IN-PUBLICATION DATA

Psychology of morality / editors, Angelo S. Fruili and Luisa D. Veneto.
     p. cm.
  Includes index.
  ISBN 978-1-62100-910-8 (hardcover)
  1. Ethics. 2. Psychology and philosophy. 3. Ethics--Psychological aspects. 4. Psychology--Moral and ethical aspects. I. Fruili, Angelo S. II. Veneto, Luisa D.
  BJ45.P79 2011
  170.1'9--dc23
                2011040314

Published by Nova Science Publishers, Inc. † *New York*

CONTENTS

PREFACE

Based on general attribution principles, much research has focused on the processes involved in making morally relevant trait attributions. For example, it has long been thought that the process by which people make trait attributions is different in the moral domain than in other domains. However, more recent research demonstrates that the story is much more complex than that; there exist multiple attribution processes even in the moral domain. Topic discussed in this book include coping with offline prohibited actions in gamespace; moral thinking vs. moral action; worldview beliefs, morality beliefs and decision-making referents and rational choice, capabilities and morality of human well-being.

Chapter 1 - Psychopathy is increasingly in the public eye.However, it is yet to be fully and effectively understood.Within the context of the DSM-IV, for example, it is best regarded as a complex family of disorders.The upside is that this family can be tightly related along common dimensions.Characteristic marks of psychopaths include a lack of guilt and remorse for paradigm case immoral actions, leading to the common conception of psychopathy rooted in affective dysfunctions.An adequate portrait of psychopathy is much more complicated, however.Though some neural regions and corresponding functions are commonly indicated, they range across those responsible for action planning and learning, as well as emotional processes.Accordingly, a complete fine-grained map of all neural mechanisms responsible for psychopathy has not been realized, and even if it were, such a map would have limited utility outside of the context of surgical or chemical intervention. The utility of a neural-level understanding of psychopathy is further limited by the fact that it is only applicable in the clinical identification of *individual* subjects, and the neuro-chemical/biological correction of those subjects *after* they are positively identified as psychopaths.On the other hand, an information processing model of moral cognition provides for wider-ranging applications.The theoretical and practical implications for such a feasible working model of psychopathic personalities are assessed.Finally, this chapter raises the possibility of directed modification of social-environmental factors (including at the meta-organizational level) discouraging the development of psychopathic personalities in the first place, modifications which are also open to simulation and testing in terms of the same model of moral cognition.

Chapter 2 - Video games provide virtual spaces for the representation and enactment of prohibited offline behaviour, be it in the form of more conventional violence (e.g., assault, killings, murder) or other forms of taboo violation (e.g., torture, rape, even cannibalism). This chapter considers the ways in which gamers cope with the moral freedoms afforded by gamespace and the strategies adopted by gamers to morally manage and otherwise cope with

viii   Angelo S. Fruili and Luisa D. Veneto

virtual behaviours that are severely prohibited offline. The authors argue that virtual acts of violence and taboo (as noted above) should not be judged by a moral system constitutive of our offline world. Instead, the permissibility of virtual representation and interaction should be informed by psychology rather than morality. This chapter therefore provides an overview of psychological research investigating factors which have been shown to impact on gamers' moral-well being, as well as strategies for managing virtual violence and taboos. It also proffers a new direction for research into gamers and game content, in the hope that it will provide further insight into who is more susceptible to the potential negative impact of video game violence on moral well-being.

Chapter 3 – The authors conducted a survey about moral thinking at the abstract level of students of the Faculty of Technical Sciences in Novi Sad, Serbia. Their comprised sample 1.057 students who finished a secondary school and begin their studies. Seven questions which describe their moral thinking indicate to their moral thinking at the abstract level. When they performed the exploratory factor on the randomly selected sample half, analysis showed them the existence of two independent patterns which best describe their moral thinking at the abstract level. The first pattern is called AUTHENTIC PATTERN and the second pattern is called EGOISTIC PATTERN. Also, the authors' results showed them that female respondents have significantly higher second pattern activation level. Performed confirmatory factor analysis on second half of their sample confirmed this factor structure. This research shows that during the process of moral thinking at the abstract level both patterns are activated simultaneously (analogy with the computer dual core processor) and that difference in their activation level determinate direction of someone's moral behavior. Putting in this way this model overcomes gap between moral thinking and moral acting. Research has shown that EGOISTIC PATTERN activation level during the process of moral thinking at the abstract level is more dominant among women of the same age, which means that women's process of moral thinking at the abstract level is prone to the influences of the environment, so they more develop moral thinking that is a product of environmental influences. On the other hand, AUTHENTIC PATTERN activation level during the process of moral thinking at the abstract level is higher among male respondents, whereas their EGOISTIC PATTERN activation level is quite below the average. These findings coincide with the findings obtained so far related to the gender difference in the process of ethical decision-making. These findings also shed a new light on the nature of the difference since women are more ethical with respect to a cultural model or a philosophical construct. The authors have unsolved problem of thinking-acting gap problem. One fresh theory (Belimp theory) created by Petrides (2011) provides them fruitful approach to this problem. Also they conducted an on-line survey to investigate the professor's idea of "morality" and then to compare their moral thinking at the abstract level with their moral thinking in the real life situations by sampling 257 professors from the University of Novi Sad. Their results show (after the authors performed exploratory factor analysis) that the professor's idea of "morality" consists of the three moral thinking patterns which are simultaneously activated during the process of their abstract moral thinking. They have identified these patterns in the following manner: deontological, formal and subjective pattern. In addition, the authors' results show that of the three, the subjective pattern is more activated than the other two during their process of the moral thinking at the abstract level. They also discovered that there is a statistically significant difference (Bandura, 1987) between professor's moral thinking patterns activation level at the abstract level and their moral thinking patterns activation level in the real life situation. The results, thus, confirmed general hypothesis of this research and showed that the investigation of moral thinking, without inclusion of dimension of activation and deactivation of the mechanism of moral control (Bandura, 1986), does not shed adequate light on this aspect of human behavior.

Chapter 4 - Values have been a staple in the study of the psychology of morality, but the construct of worldview, in particular, fundamental assumptions related to personal epistemology, can also shed light on the field. In the exploratory correlational study presented in this chapter, worldview beliefs made a significant contribution, apart from morality beliefs, to explaining an individual's tendency to rely on either intrinsic or extrinsic decision-making referents. Although worldview beliefs and morality beliefs were largely independent, multivariate models that included both types of beliefs often were more predictive of an individual's preference for intrinsic or extrinsic referents. Core worldview beliefs seemed to be foundational to decision-making, and scholarship in the psychology of morality would benefit from considering the influence of worldviews. Also, effective ethics training, in addition to providing instruction in ethical skills, should engage students' worldviews and effect incremental transformation over the course of time.

Chapter 5 - Recently the idea according to which well-being is to be valued in view of the maximization of self-utility, has been challenged by several economic theories as in particular by Sen's capability approach. This has amounted to the view according to which the "rationality" of the rational choice is something much more complex and diverse than what is a mere criterion of self-advantage. With the present essay the author tries to capture first the limits of rational choice theories in order to point to a more complex view of rationality. He will also discuss the role that psychology plays in such criticism and particularly in the problematization of the notion of "utility." The author will then criticize two extreme and mutually exclusive interpretations that consider the capabilities either as an unconstrained list of yet to be defined human potentialities or, alternatively, as a fixed set of capabilities (Nussbaum 2006, 76-78). He will suggest that, differently from Sen's and Nussbaum's views, a third way can be defended as something based on a constrained characterization of the normative role of political judgment in conjunction with the notion of "pluralist universalism." In view of the fact that variation can be placed both across different configurations of functionings − when related to one single capability − as well as across the definition of the same list of capabilities, it follows that any list of capabilities should be contextually relevant without turning into mere relativism.

Chapter 6 - Based on general attribution principles, much research has focused on the processes involved in making morally relevant trait attributions. For example, it has long been thought that the process by which people make trait attributions is different in the moral domain than in other domains. However, more recent research demonstrates that the story is much more complex than that; there exist multiple attribution processes even in the moral domain. The present chapter reviews both the relevant empirical findings and theoretical developments that have contributed to their present understanding.

Chapter 7 - This study examines the effects of self-control and morality on adolescent offending. It is well known that low self-control and low morality increase the risk of offending. The question whether low levels of morality and low self-control *interact* in the explanation of offending, has been recently examined in a test in three countries (Svensson, Pauwels and Weerman, 2010). As outlined by Wikström's Situational Action Theory (Wikström, 2006), it is assumed that self-control has a stronger effect on offending for individuals with low levels of morality than for individuals with high levels of morality. No previous study has demonstrated the stability of these findings in sub groups by gender and immigrant background. To test how similar this interaction effect is, data are used from a sample of young adolescents in Antwerp, Belgium ($N = 2,486$). These data provide strong support for the hypothesis that the effect of self-control on offending is dependent on the individual's level of morality. The results are almost identical in all subgroups by gender and immigrant background. It seems that causal mechanisms of offending operate rather similar than dissimilar for Belgian immigrant and non-immigrant boys and girls.

In: Psychology of Morality
Editors: A. S. Fruili and L. D. Veneto

ISBN: 978-1-62100-910-8
© 2012 Nova Science Publishers, Inc.

Chapter 1

AN INFORMATION PROCESSING MODEL OF PSYCHOPATHY AND ANTI-SOCIAL PERSONALITY DISORDERS INTEGRATING NEURAL AND PSYCHOLOGICAL ACCOUNTS TOWARDS THE ASSAY OF SOCIAL IMPLICATIONS OF PSYCHOPATHIC AGENTS[*]

Jeffrey White[*]
KAIST South Korea

ABSTRACT

Psychopathy is increasingly in the public eye.However, it is yet to be fully and effectively understood.Within the context of the DSM-IV, for example, it is best regarded as a complex family of disorders.The upside is that this family can be tightly related along common dimensions.Characteristic marks of psychopaths include a lack of guilt and remorse for paradigm case immoral actions, leading to the common conception of psychopathy rooted in affective dysfunctions.An adequate portrait of psychopathy is much more complicated, however.Though some neural regions and corresponding functions are commonly indicated, they range across those responsible for action planning and learning, as well as emotional processes.Accordingly, a complete fine-grained map of all neural mechanisms responsible for psychopathy has not been realized, and even if it were, such a map would have limited utility outside of the context of surgical or chemical intervention.

The utility of a neural-level understanding of psychopathy is further limited by the fact that it is only applicable in the clinical identification of *individual* subjects, and the neuro-chemical/biological correction of those subjects *after* they are positively identified as psychopaths.On the other hand, an information processing model of moral cognition provides for wider-ranging applications.The theoretical and practical implications for such a feasible working model of psychopathic personalities are assessed.Finally, this

---

[*] E-mail: kaistethics@gmx.com

chapter raises the possibility of directed modification of social-environmental factors (including at the meta-organizational level) discouraging the development of psychopathic personalities in the first place, modifications which are also open to simulation and testing in terms of the same model of moral cognition.

1. INTRODUCTION

"Psychopathy is a personality disorder manifested in people who use a mixture of charm, manipulation, intimidation, and occasionally violence to control others, in order to satisfy their own selfish needs."

Jim Kouri[1]

Psychopathy can be understood as a family of disorders, as a disorder special unto itself, or as one of a family of antisocial disorders.Risk indicators for antisocial behavior, of which psychopathy is assumed to be a subgroup, are incredibly diverse and surprisingly effective.For instance, exposure to nicotine during gestation doubles incidence of conduct disorder, the pre-adult clinical precursor to antisocial personality diagnoses.[2][1]Other factors range from parental child-rearing styles (including abusive parental models) which fail to positively reinforce prosocial attitudes and actions, to family/parental marital conflict, to socio-economic status, to culture/media presenting models of aggressive behaviors which are not followed by negative consequences.This final factor, when considered across generations of psychological development, invites Lobaczewski's forecast that any socio-economic system sufficiently infiltrated by psychopathic personalities rapidly creates a pathological social environment in the main, a systemic "pathocacy," wherein psychopathic personalities are rewarded and others punished.[3][2]

With the scope of influence on the development of antisocial and the reinforcement of psychopathic psychologies encompassing the whole of social strata, the need for a basic model effective across all such levels in identifying and characterizing both antisocial and prosocial relational modes becomes readily apparent.Moreover, such a model should be popularly accessible, given increasing popular attention to the presence of psychopaths and psychopathic traits in general society, reflecting long-standing traditional moral convictions while serving as a generic model for moral cognition.Though headway is made in identifying some dysfunctions due to neurological defect, this is a cumbersome process and species specific in application, failing to meet other desired criteria, as well.Neuro-physical identification is only feasible after the fact of diagnosis and observation, requiring further apparatus and expertise to generate such, while failing to efficiently capture conventional moral beliefs.As such, there is a need for an approach effective both in identification and in representation of neurological defect, without technically cumbersome imaging, and applicable to other levels of organization outside of the clinical psychological context.A generic information processing model is able to transcend aforesaid obstacles, permitting the

---

[1]Page 443.

[2]Lobaczewski defines "pathocracy" as such: "I shall accept the denomination of **pathocracy** for a system of government thus created, wherein a small pathological minority takes control over a society of normal people. The name thus selected, above all, emphasizes the basic quality of the macrosocial psychopathological phenomenon, and differentiates it from the many possible social systems dominated by normal people's structure, custom, and law." (Page 193, Lobaczewski's emphasis.)

ready analysis of any system in question, through direct observation unburdened by technological machinations.

2. WHAT IS PSYCHOPATHY?

Traditionally, a psychopath is a person without "conscience."Conscience plays a central role in the moral theories of everyone from Kant to Mill, arguably is the 'daemon' motivating Socrates to be the "most just man in Athens," and lately appears in Robert Hare's book title, *Without Conscience: the disturbing world of the psychopaths amongst us,* among others.[4]Conscience, being a psychological construct recently out of favor in moral and psychological theory, is the complex of feelings that guide a person to right actions at right times, most notably in the form of a warning voice that serves as an alert obstacle to the commission of some immoral act.Thus, fully consistent with this understanding, but in contemporary terms - psychopathy is being without conscience, described without *mentioning* conscience – the characteristic marks of the psychopath:

> are linked to a diminished sensitivity of certain emotions that are crucial for inhibiting socially unacceptable conduct. In particular, psychopaths seem insensitive to the suffering their crimes cause. They seem unimpressed by the strong negative feelings normal people generally experience if they commit violent or damaging acts. Psychopaths lack the deep social instincts inhibiting human aggression in normal circumstances. If ordinary men notice people in trouble or perceive signs of submission during a violent encounter, their aggression ceases at once. One does not continue to kick a person who begs for mercy. In normal people, cues of fear and sadness block aggression and violence. It has been hypothesized that psychopaths detect these emotional cues less accurately and, consequently, experience less distress.[5][3]

Should the authors of the above quoted passage have written with conscience in mind, it would have stood in for "deep social instincts," traditionally serving as the vehicle for empathy, "cues of fear and sadness," and the famous "voice of conscience" would have stood in for "sensitivity of certain emotions ... crucial for inhibiting socially unacceptable conduct."[4]

In fact, not only have the modes of its description changed within a brief window of a few decades in this, the English speaking West, the very names for the psychopath have changed over time.[5]"Psychopathy," the term we use today, replaced the older term, "moral insanity" not so long ago, in the late 19th century.During the early part of the 20th century, Freud delivered the basic two-dimensional model of psychopathy still in play, today, consisting of "pathological narcissism" and "cruel aggression."[7]And, long prior to the use of either denominations, and to the modern model itself, the first Western description of the

---

[3]Page 18.

[4]This only goes to show, recalling Husserl, that though bound up in the terminology of the era, we must not lose sight of the thing itself. Though we call it by another name, psychopathy is not a new concept, and we must, recalling Quine, be flexible in our linguistic associations should we wish to make any headway in accurately determining the construct of psychopathy at all.

[5]Different cultures have different terms for the same deviations, as well.[6]

character that we now recognize as the psychopath has been attributed to Theophrastus' description of what he called the "Unscrupulous Man":

> The Unscrupulous Man will go and borrow more money from a creditor he has never paid ... When marketing he reminds the butcher of some service he has rendered him and, standing near the scales, throws in some meat, if he can, and a soup-bone. If he succeeds, so much the better; if not, he will snatch a piece of tripe and go off laughing.[8][6]

Theophrastus did not call this man a psychopath, but his description clearly qualifies.Here is a picture of a man who is apparently remorseless, opportunistic, deceitful and manipulative of other people's good-will, a model from which the current profile of the psychopath has hardly deviated.For example, compare this ancient description with that of psychological scientists Kiehl and Buckholtz:

> One of the most striking peculiarities of psychopaths is that they lack empathy; they are able to shake off as mere tinsel the most universal social obligations. They lie and manipulate yet feel no compunction or regrets - in fact, they don't feel particularly deeply about anything at all.[9][7]

Regardless of the words we use to describe the phenomena, linguistic conventions, the differences in cultures, and the span of two and a half millennia, these two descriptions point to the same thing.Both of the above focus on the lack of remorse, lack of empathy, willingness to prey on others, shirk obligations and to put others into bad situations without reservations typically restraining "moral" agents.These are issues of much importance, to be returned to later on in this chapter.In the words of Robert Hare, what we are dealing with in psychopaths is:

> a class of individuals who have been around forever and who are found in every race, culture, society and walk of life. Everybody has met these people, been deceived and manipulated by them, and forced to live with or repair the damage they have wrought. These often charming—but always deadly—individuals have a clinical name: psychopaths. Their hallmark is a stunning lack of conscience; their game is self-gratification at the other person's expense. Many spend time in prison, but many do not. All take far more than they give.[10]

3. MODELS OF PSYCHOPATHY

The DSM-IV categorizes psychopathy under antisocial personality disorder (ASPD), with ASPD serving as a fundamental dysfunction, and others including psychopathy simply falling

---

[6]Page 3. It should be noted that Theophrastus' characterization is consistent with Aristotle's own schema of virtue and vice, with the psychopath deviating from a mean through his exclusive focus on self satisfaction at the inevitable expense others – although clever, not wise, although practically intelligent, unable to fuse the horizons of self and other in the essential human project, according to Aristotle being politics. Indeed, as this chapter proceeds, we will confront examples of psychopathic social construction, and realize in a more fine-grained way that Aristotle's schema remains effective in underscoring the viciousness of the psychopathic political vision, and thus the deficiency of the psychopath in realizing humanity's highest potentials according to the Western philosophical tradition descended from the Greeks, including Aristotle.

[7]Page 22.

under its heading, as one of its many variants.According to the DSM-IV, ASPD is often referred to as "psychopathy," "sociopathy," and "dyssocial personality disorder," though properly these are all sub-variants of ASPD.[11]According to Robert Hare, this is the wrong approach.Though certainly "antisocial tendencies represent an empirically demonstrable feature of the psychopathy construct, in conjunction with features reflecting disturbances in interpersonal, affective, and impulsive behavioral functioning," according to Hare the psychopathic construct belongs in a different class altogether.[28][8]Speaking of the classification system in the DSM-IV:

> Most psychopaths (with the exception of those who somehow manage to plow their way through life without coming into formal or prolonged contact with the criminal justice system) meet the criteria for ASPD, but most individuals with ASPD are not psychopaths.[12]

Proving that the verdict of science is often the whim of convention, the (upcoming) DSM-V will see substantial revisions to IV's categorization which may go a long way to answering Hare's criticisms.In the DSM-V, "antisocial psychopathic disorder" consists in fifteen traits, de-emphasizing IV's (excessive) weight on rule-breaking behavior, including the insistence on a diagnosis of conduct disorder in youth.The nominal traits are:

> Narcissism, Exploitativeness, Sadism, Conduct problems, Hostile dominance, Sensation seeking, Impulsivity, Suspiciousness, Egocentrism, Act aggressively, Amoral, Little insight, Engage in unlawful behaviour, Unreliable and irresponsible, Anti-authoritarian.[6][9]

Table 1. Cleckley's 16 Traits

Superficial charm and good "intelligence"
Absence of delusions and other signs of irrational thinking
Absence of "nervousness" or psychoneurotic manifestations
Unreliability
Untruthfulness and insincerity
Lack of remorse or shame
Inadequately motivated antisocial behavior
Poor judgment and failure to learn by experience
Pathologic egocentricity and incapacity for love
General poverty in major affective reactions
Specific loss of insight
Unresponsiveness in general interpersonal relations
Fantastic and uninviting behavior with drink and sometimes without
Suicide rarely carried out
Sex life impersonal, trivial, and poorly integrate
Failure to follow any life plan.

Compare this list of traits with those iterated by Cleckley and by Hare, themselves.Perhaps the most thorough account of psychopathy is found in Hervey Cleckley's*The Mask of Sanity.*Therein, Cleckley portrays an array of psychopathic individuals, and from these accounts, along with a lifetime of amassed experience, distills

---

[8]Page 234. In other contexts, comparing the relationship to that of a common cold, and pneumonia. One is pesky, the other might kill you. In any event, deserving its own study, treatment, and prophylaxis.
[9]Taken from Table 1, page 126.

what has since become a very influential set of characteristics.These broad traits of psychopathy have set the standard from which the current clinical profile has emerged (Table 1: Cleckley's 16 Traits)[13]:

Here the fully fledged psychopath is described (more) in terms of their inner processes rather than solely on their outward behavior (suicide rarely carried out an exception, as well as often a point of criticism).However, from this emphasis on personality traits,it is easily apparent how such a profile might behave in a given situation.This profile is motivated by emotional deficits, not by conceptual or rational ones.

Cleckley's portrait is of a personality unable to place adequate significance on certain dimensions of results of actions, due a paucity of morally significant emotions.Lacking certain affective processes, the psychopath exhibits apathy towards moral mistakes, characterized in its most mundane form as "unresponsiveness" in relationships with others.[10]

Cleckley's description of the psychopath survives in use, today, serving as it does as the basis for the Robert Hare's Psychopathy Checklist - Revised (PCL-R).The PCL-R has undergone some revisions since its birth, yet retains much of Cleckley's original conception, and many of the original conception's shortcomings.[11]However, there are important differences.Most importantly, Hare and Neumann point to one critical difference between their model and that of Cleckley.In Cleckley's work, psychopathy is not strongly related with aggression:

> First, Cleckley's description of the psychopath as not particularly hostile or aggressive is at odds with empirical data that the PCL-R is strongly related to "the personality traits of aggression and antagonism" and is "reliably predictive of aggressive behavior and violent recidivism in criminal offenders"[14][12]

This emphasis on aggression will be important later in this chapter.

Another important difference between the PCL-R and Cleckley's work is that Cleckley's account is unwieldly, unquantified, whereas the PCL-R is widely employed, especially in criminal settings where claims of psychopathy must be evaluated to determine punishments and definite results are required.[13]As it stands, if rehabilitation is to be precluded because of psychopathy, imprisonment intent on rehabilitation might be similarly precluded, and Hare's checklist is most often employed in such determinations.In fact, from its ubiquity, coupled with the weight given its results in situations in which persons are permanently labeled, and perhaps even permanently imprisoned, a recent criticism has emerged.There is some question over whether or not the "construct," the very concept, of psychopathy has been overwritten by a single diagnostic test.[14][14]

On the face of it, this is only a problem if the model, the construct of psychopathy represented in the test, cannot adequately account for any given instance thereof.We will have

---

[10]And, generally, antisocial tendencies, as Cleckley held that antisocial personality formed a core of psychopathy.
[11]Easy criticisms of either include over-generality, openness to interpretation, and that they serve merely as vehicles for disguised moral judgment. However, the same can be said for any such psychological device.
[12]Page 222.
[13]It is perhaps due to this fact that there is an emphasis on malice towards others, as we shall see illustrated in the next section.
[14]Hare and Neumann take pains to assure us that this is not the case. However, in practice, amongst non-professional psychologists, and indeed in the popular mind, psychopathy may indeed be perceived as equivalent to a certain score on the PCL-R. We shall see this naive attitude reflected in the *This American Life* illustration later on in this chapter.

more to say on this count later on.More importantly, in the context of the PCL-R specifically, this is a disconcerting criticism because the results of the test depend on who administers the test, to whom, and in what context.What the "test" identifies as psychopathy shifts depending on who, what, when and why it is put to use.For example, in court contexts, psychologists for the defense consistently score the same subjects lower on the scale than do psychologists for the prosecution.But, at least in this context there is record, and oversight.Perhaps more worrisome is the potential for (life altering) error introduced when the test is administered by people who are inadequately trained, in environments in which the correction of dubious applications are even more difficult to effect.

As for the model itself, there are (at least) two ways of visualizing, and quantifying, the relationships between the 20 total traits – eighteen main and two supplementary – that make up the PCL-R.[14][15][15]In either case, there are four subgroups, "factors," and each of the eighteen main traits belong to one of these.The twenty total traits arranged according to the four-factor model are given in Table 2. (Table 2: Hare's 20 Traits)[14][16]

Table 2. Hare's 20 Traits

"Interpersonal"	**"Lifestyle"**
Glib/superficial charm	Stimulation seeking/proneness to boredom
Grandiose self-worth	Impulsivity
Pathological lying	Irresponsibility
Cunning/manipulative	Parasitic orientation
"Affective"	Lack of realistic goals
Lack of remorse or guilt	**"Antisocial"**
Shallow affect	Poor behavior controls
Callous/lack of empathy	Early behavior problems
Failure to accept responsibility	Juvenile delinquency
Traits not correlated with either factor	Revocation of conditional release
Promiscuous sexual behavior	Criminal versatility
Many short-term relationships	

When we compare the three preceding lists, some factors appear throughout.One, a specific lack of insight into the morally significant emotional realm of non-psychopaths, evidenced by "shallow affect," "lack of remorse," and "specific lack of insight."This describes a "callous lack of empathy."Couple this lack of empathy with aggression, "hostile dominance," "lack of guilt" and selfishness (egoism and narcissism), and we describe an agent uninhibited by morality, and without capacity to adequately weight directly felt cues

---

[15]A somewhat different set of traits, showing the evolution of the PCL, is described by Hare in [10].

[16]By way of Hare's PCL-R, in terms of the DSM-IV, psychopathy is best considered a construct of three DSM specific disorders: narcissistic personality disorder, histrionic personality disorder, and antisocial personality disorder. Though the PCL-R is often referred to in this chapter, it plays no direct role in the model developed herein. The fact is that the PCL-R appears in a great deal of literature, either employed in psychological research as a tool and method, or itself the subject of discourse. Indeed, an interesting and important distinction along the lines of the two main factors originally specified in the PCL-R has been made between a purely biologically predisposed and a biological potential coupled with social factors eventuating in psychopathy. This separation, of innate and learned components, is a promising approach. However, just as the PCL-R bears no direct influence on model developed in the chapter, this distinction shall not be further pursued in this chapter, as our interest is in modes of information processing, and whether these are genetically determined or acquired modes is a matter of no direct importance to the discussion at hand. For more information on the distinction, however, see [16].

regarding the emotional well-being of others.Finally, "superficial charm," "parasitic orientation" (taking for one's self at another's expense), "fantastic" behavior, "exploitativeness," "pathological lying," all of these add up to an agent prone to purely self interested schemes undertaken at the expense of others, without the capacity to understand just how *wrong* such actions truly are.[17]We may summarize these findings thusly.The psychopath does not feel as if others in morally relevant ways.Emotionally deficient,[18] being incapable of empathy, "narcissistic" and self-important, the psychopath treats his/her own situation as the only situation of significance.From this lack of empathy, the psychopath puts others into bad situations without reservation, manipulating, deceiving and bending others to serve his/her own ends.Finally, the psychopath seeks selfish ends at others' expense, and feels fully entitled to do so, treating others callously, coldly and as if 'less than human.'These may be further summarized as selfish or egotistical, opportunistic or even parasitic, and predatory.Together, they constitute the portrait of a "social predator."[19]And, as this chapter continues, we shall apply these three criteria in the evaluation of both individual and institutional examples.

4. GETTING OUR HEADS AROUND THE SCOPE OF PSYCHOPATHY

> A very old Aristotelian idea is that "form follows function" (e.g., knifes were designed to cut, eyes designed to see). If something is known about a phenomenon's structural form, then it is possible to glean an understanding of how it functions.
>
> Robert Hare and Craig Neumann[14][20]

With this portrait in mind, there are four easy reasons to focus on psychopathy aside from other types of ASPDs, and indeed to focus on psychopathy as a special case.For one thing, the causes of psychopathy differ from other dysfunctions, as do the likely mechanisms.In a phrase, it is all about the emotions – or rather, the lack thereof – having been grouped with select other dysfunctions as exhibiting "zero-negative empathy."[17]Current thinking, and the view taken in this chapter, is that its development is due to specific deficiencies in emotional learning, a dysfunction which "increases the probability that the individual will learn antisocial motor programs for the achievement of goals," especially the use of instrumental rather than reactive aggression.[18][21]

Neurologically, psychopathy is marked by an hemispheric specific impaired ability to feel, recognize, identify, and verbally process emotional expressions of negative emotions including disgust, sadness, and fear.[19][20][21][22]Psychopaths appear to offset this deficiency through increased reliance on left-hemisphere resources [23], resulting in impaired verbal response performance when presented emotionally loaded content due to not having learned to associate emotional content with verbal representations directly, but rather after the fact.[18]Through a related deficient integration of the amygdala with the medial prefrontal

---

[17]These three groups roughly match those identified by Patrick and reported by Duggan: Mean, Bold, and Disinhibited.[6] (Page 128).

[18]The "affective factor" per Hare [4].

[19]I hesitate to use the term "intraspecies predator" due to nonhuman applications forthcoming.

[20]Page 231.

[21]Pages 110-111.

cortex, also involving the orbitofrontal cortex [24][22], psychopaths show an impaired capacity in coding for stimulus-response pairings around personal action-others' distress cues [25][26][27], removing barriers to marked aggression [18][27][28], an especially worrisome combination of traits given that the only apparent remedy is the removal of the amygdala and anterior frontal lobe.[29]

Neurochemically, psychopathic traits have been found to be motivated by excessive neuro-chemical rewards upon goal achievement.[30]Such neuro-chemical modulation affects socialization, and motivates towards the exhibition of aggression for selfish ends, consistent with the view taken in this chapter, that psychopaths exhibit instrumental aggression due to an incapacity to empathize with expressions of distress (fear, disgust, for example), thereby short-circuiting a normal mechanism for the inhibition of the use of violence in goal-seeking,[18][27] with the satisfaction of said goals rendered more urgent through neuro-chemical modulation.This not a revolutionary position, being a continuation of a long history of theoretical development on psychopathy, wherein an emotional learning dysfunction leads to direct, personal impairment in socialization, as well as impairs the ability to learn socially acceptable boundaries through the fearful, pained, or disgusted expressions of others.[23]

In terms of developmental precursors to psychopathy, there is good indication that it is the emotional constitution that is most predictive of psychopathy in adulthood.Youth evidencing psychopathic traits, as well as adult psychopaths, show an impaired ability to distinguish between merely conventional and moral situations.[18]In addition to impaired fear processing (both one's own and others'), adolescents with conduct disorder evidencing marked aggression are understood to experience good feelings (reward) upon causing others pain.[32][24][25]Taken together, we see both a felt condition as well as a neuro-chemical motivation for the instrumentally aggressive expression of callous, unemotional traits.Psychopaths develop, grow, and learn to get what they want according to abnormal neural processes.

Furthermore, callous unemotional traits, central to the construct of adult psychopathy - lack of guilt, lack empathy, callous use of others for one's own gain – are an especially stable group of traits that identify an especially dangerous subgroup of youth, providing a subject-centered (rather than third person, having been caught breaking a law, for instance) characteristic mark for early identification of and possible intervention in the lives of budding psychopaths.[33]Providing for this unique dimension will be a central concern as we turn to the information processing model in the 6th section of this chapter.

---

[22]The orbitofrontal region is also implicated in psychopathy due impairment in some planning tasks. See [18], pages 84-87 and 134-136 for review.

[23]The earliest such accounts were fear-based accounts. "What happens is that you are born without fear, so when your parents try to socialize you, you don't really respond appropriately because you're not scared." [31] quoting Patrick Sylvers. Although, any strictly fear-based account faces serious difficulties. See [18], pages 73-76 for discussion. Especially given the emphasis in this chapter is the following: "... the developmental literature indicates that moral socialization is not achieved through the formation of conditioned fear responses but rather through the induction and fostering of empathy." (page 75) More accurately, it may pay to extend Sylvers' assertion to other relevant emotions, and couple this with an addictive attachment to the achievement of selfish ends, and from this recipe a broad view of the dysfunction emerges.

[24]Interestingly, demonstrated aggression (indirect and direct forms) and antisocial behavior follow gender trends indicated in adult psychopathy, with male aggression (direct, the form of violent, dominant, instrumental rather than reactive) greatly outweighing female, and female:male indirect aggression almost equivalent.[34]

[25]Corresponding with "sadism" as incorporated in the upcoming DSM-V, and in contrast to normally functioning children, and adults.[35] These mechanisms do not change, but are established in youth and maintained through adulthood.

Perhaps most interesting amongst the characteristic marks of psychopaths is that psychopathy is marked by an insatiable pursuit of dopaminergic rewards.This fact alone explains the "get it at all costs" mentality evinced by observed psychopaths, a trait with which we shall deal a bit more in later sections.For all of these 'faults,' however, it would be wrong to think that psychopathy is insanity.Psychopathy is not "irrationality" in the contemporary sense.Psychopaths are not "out of their minds."More accurately, given the current neurological understanding, they are merely expressions thereof.Indeed, it has been said that the simplest definition of psychopathy is "sane but amoral."That is, "amoral," not "immoral," as there is not an inversion of morality, but rather an absence of it, and not "insane," as in out of control, but rather without impaired executive function and simply in control toward different ends on different neurological bases.

On another count, due to the preceding, psychopaths are prone to exhibit more often a radically different form of aggression than do other ASPDs, making them much more dangerous.They are instrumentally aggressive, using aggression, violence and threats of violence, to further their own selfish ends at the expense of others.[9][18][36]This is immoral by definition – though, once again, given the focus on selfish ends, hardly "insane" - and key to the understanding of psychopathy developed in this chapter.Meanwhile, the broad category of ASPD includes dysfunctions rooted in executive deficiencies, thereby better matching typical definitions of "insanity."These are dysfunctions characterized by irrational and reckless behavior, "reactive" rather than "instrumental" aggression, and a diminished (rather than, as we shall see in the case of some high-functioning psychopaths, an enhanced) capacity to live well in the modern world.These sorts of dysfunction disqualify agents from grand, political scale influence, while the most dangerous types of psychopaths, for all their faults, are not so encumbered.It is this recognition, itself, that marks a sort of sea-change in the way that psychopathy must be conceived:

> Most mental health experts, for a very long time, have operated on the premise that psychopaths come from impoverished backgrounds and have experienced abuse of one sort or another in childhood, so it is easy to spot them, or at least, they certainly don't move in society except as interlopers. This idea seems to be coming under some serious revision lately. ... In other words, they can be doctors, lawyers, judges, policemen, congressmen, presidents of corporations that rob from the poor to give to the rich, and even presidents.[3][26]

The potential for large-scale destruction from positions of power and responsibility is a third important reason to give psychopathy attention over and above other ASPDs.Given current events, recent revelations of corruption, vote-rigging, abuses and excesses amongst high-level leadership, ongoing wars of aggression for plunder based on lies and media manipulation and outright misrepresentation of facts, increasing disparities in wealth, police brutality, state-sponsored terrorism leveraging corporate interested "regime change," and on and on – in other words, evidence of psychopathy in the actions of the most powerful persons in global society - there can remain no doubt that psychopathy must be afforded special attention, and special tools for remediation, should we wish for such crimes to cease.Consider Robert Hare's observations on this point, conveying a special warning about the threat that is the high-functioning psychopath in today's social climate:

---

[26]Page 15.

psychopaths have little difficulty infiltrating the domains of business, politics, law enforcement, government, academia and other social structures. It is the egocentric, cold-blooded and remorseless psychopaths who blend into all aspects of society and have such devastating impacts on people around them who send chills down the spines of law enforcement officers.[12]

Finally, the fourth reason to attend to psychopathy outside of the context of apparently related disorders is that, due to the influence of psychopathic actors on the shape of the world, today, psychopathy has garnered and is gaining increased popular attention.In some contexts, psychopathic traits are actually desirable! In fact, due to their success in such environments, psychopaths, and persons with psychopathic tendencies, are sometimes taken up as personal heroes, even revered for having somehow tapped into forbidden modes of life leading to untold freedom and personal success.[38] Similar observations cannot be so easily made of other ASPDs.About this last point, we shall inquire directly in the next section.Before we move on, however, it will pay to add a few words on the apparent opposite of ASPD, and especially psychopathy, that being the prosocial personality.The prosocial, as opposed to the antisocial, personality is evidenced by actions which benefit others.Such actions need not come by way of (much) personal sacrifice.The prosocial personality exhibits a willingness to cooperate, a concern for others' welfare, and a willingness to share.[38]It involves a capacity, and a willingness, to take up the perspective of others, "perspective-taking," so that one might best cooperate, help, and share the right things in the right ways.[39]Indeed, the neural structures responsible for this capacity are integral to learning not only how to do things, but also how it feels to do things, and not only what to do, but most importantly, *why* to do it.[40]"Perspective-taking" is an interesting aspect of moral psychology, deserving more thorough explanation.First of all, it must be noted that it is not that psychopaths lack an ability to take the perspective of another, it is only that, even in so doing, their deficit of morally important emotional information invites an incomplete picture thereof.[27]This function, taking another's perspective, standing in another's shoes so to speak, has been variously described and has a deep neurological basis.It has been described by Damasio and colleagues as the "as-if" loop, suggesting the full and direct self-embodiment of perceived and internalized emotions.[41][42]

As well, it has been described as a (very strong version of) simulation on the basis of research into the mirror neural system(s) by Keysers and colleagues, as such retaining Damasio et al's "as-if" terminology:

> The discovery of mirror neurons has lead to the idea that we understand, at least in part, the goal-directed actions of others such as grasping and manipulating objects by activating our own motor and somatosensory representations of similar actions as if we had performed similar actions. This 'as if' component is why this process is called simulation.[43]

In particular, Keysers and colleagues approach the issue through an understanding that the feelings of an agent performing some action, of which expressing emotion is a special sort, can be directly understood because a witnessing, empathizing agent shares bodily

---

[27]An interesting side effect of this process being psychopaths' commonly reported feelings, special and different from others, isolated. In reflection on internal states, differences between self and other arise – as if part of the world is hidden from them. Our current focus denies further attention to this aspect of the psychopath's reported experience, but discussion on the generic mechanism at the core of this process can be found in [44].

constitution, including those neural "circuits" employed in expressing such emotions and actions in the first place, " ... as a general and basic endowment of our brain that involves a linkage between the first and third person experiences of actions, sensations and emotions."[45][28]This model confirms the untutored understanding that empathy, feeling "as-if" another, or in these terms "simulating" the 'what it feels like to be another person,' is central to the process of taking another's perspective implicated in prosocial personality.[29]Implicated regions include the anterior cingulate and insula in the experience of self and other affect, confirming the involvement of somatosensory cortices in the "simulation" of others' tactile experiences.[46][30]But, the simulation of affect generally involves "a mosaic of affective, motor and somatosensory components."[45]Thus, "simulation," feeling "as-if," is both deeper and more complex than simply constructing an approximation of some evidenced action or expressed emotion.It involves the recreation of the entire embodied condition[31] from which such emerge:

> For example, hearing someone gurgle will evoke an inner ''sense'' of gurgling because the brain activates some of the same mirror neurons that are active when we gurgle ourselves. Given that both perceiving and executing an action is not linked to the activity of a single neuron but of a widespread population of neurons, simulation and common coding theories can be interpreted as stating that the pattern of activity while performing an action should resemble the pattern while observing or listening to a similar action. This resemblance allows the brain to interpret an activity pattern similarly whether executing or perceiving.[47][32]

The important point here is in the interpretation of the activity pattern.Different actions are performed at different times for different ends, and it is in light of these ends that said actions are then determined appropriate, or not.Mirroring is holistic.One mirrors not merely some gesture, action, or expression in isolation.Rather, one mirrors actions, expressions, and gestures within the implicitly understood context that is shared human embodiment.For instance, it is in this light that a psychopath's lack of a startle-response to photos of mutilated persons is immediately felt to be inappropriate[33].Taking the perspective of another involves taking up the situation of another for one's own, at least for a moment, and it is only from this basis of interpretation that individual instances are interpretable as significant, and indeed readily and appropriately interpretable at all.Indeed, it is in taking up the perspective of a mutilated corpse that one may feel startled, immediately, with the startle response serving as an alert, to avoid such embodied ends.From this understanding, it is possible, as have Etzel and colleagues, Amodio and Frith, to inquire into how mirror neural systems facilitate human understanding not only of what others are doing, or how, but why these things are done.[47][48]To achieve good situations, and avoid others.Interestingly – to be important as our discussion turns to non-human entities later on – this capacity to take up another's

---

[28]Page 2391. Though the quote above is taken from a part of the referenced paper in which the authors are laying out two different views on simulation, this quotation succinctly expresses their own position.

[29]A capacity that is effective also when consciously directed, as well, as "thinking about the inner-states of others" is "effective at triggering mPFC activity."[47] (Page 9.) This bears note as we turn to issues of treatment/correction in the final pages of this chapter.

[30]Pages 379-80.

[31]With special attention to recognizable salient aspects therein.

[32]Page 1.

[33]Acquired sociopaths share a similar insensitivity.[49][50][51]

perspective extends beyond human beings, employing the "shared circuitry" on which this empathic capacity is based in the empathic understanding of the situations of critters which simply do not share such circuitry:

> the brain appears to automatically transform the visual and auditory descriptions of the actions, sensations and emotions of others into neural representations normally associated with our own execution of similar actions, and our own experience of similar sensations and emotions.... In the light of our results, it thus appears as though the shared circuit for actions responds to complex meaningful actions regardless of whether they are performed by humans and robots. Half way along this human–robot continuum, the premotor cortex also responds to the sight of animals from another species performing actions that resemble ours, such as biting.[46][34]

Prosocial empathy is not the same as altruism, and a point of distinction may be appropriate here.Altruism, naming a motivation to "increase another person's welfare," may or may not be prosocial in consequence, and so should be regarded distinctly.For example, should one be motivated to make a white-collar-war-criminal's retirement easier, sheltering him from prosecution for past crimes out of a desire to "increase his welfare," or for example to "save the Nation from the pain of putting past leadership on trial," then one's altruistic motivations are indeed quite obviously not prosocial.One can empathize with the war-criminal, but in so doing the prosocial exercise of empathy demands similar treatment for his victims, a constraint that altruism does not share.

In the end, with prosocial and antisocial psychopathic personalities in view, we are presented with the concepts necessary to envision two extremes between which most persons generally fall.Contrast prosocial attributes with the psychopath's egoism, lack of empathy, and selfish pursuit of personal ends and what emerges is a sliding scale of social value, from constructive to destructive, with most persons, and most actions falling somewhere in the middle.They stand at opposite ends of a spectrum, a spectrum that confronts us all with the rather uncomfortable notion that psychopathy is not an all-or-nothing phenomena, and that we each may be closer to psychopathy than an all-or-nothing account would allow.[35]

Some evidence for this continuity exists in the similarities that either extreme share.Psychopathic and prosocial personalities do share two things in common.It is unclear how to treat either: in the case of psychopathic personality, to diminish it, and in the case of prosocial personality, to encourage it.And, both proceed on the basis of information interred from the social situation in which the moral agent in question is embedded.The crucial difference being, as shall come more clear as this chapter continues, the sort of information getting processed.And, as far as wider social influence goes, the sorts of actions that get

---

[34]Page 394. Keyser et al describe a form of simulation that, as mentioned above, is "strong" in that it is independent of higher level rational considerations of the form 'What is another thinking/feeling?' These sorts of considerations employ, by Keysers' account, so-called "theory-of-mind" (ToM) apparatus, where direct somatosensory simulation of the primary sort under their consideration exists prior to ToM recruitment. It is, as it were, a 'bottom-up' affect first approach to understanding "empathic" mental processes, in spirit with Damasio's "as-if" loop. These issues are important for the model of moral cognition to be described later in this chapter, as such a model, if adequate, must provide for both high and low-level processes in appropriate form and relationship. As far as a high-level, top-down root cause and mechanism for psychopathy, "It seems not. Psychopathic persons show no theory of mind impairment."[27](Page 731)

[35]This is the author's central concern in [7].

passed along as informative, and worth re-enacting, as well as the sorts of emotional responses that are appropriate in given contexts, and so worth emulating.[36]We shall have a bit more to say on these points as this chapter closes.

5. WHO, OR WHAT, IS A PSYCHOPATH?

Just as there isa "revolution" in the way that psychopathy is conceived, so there is a similar revolution in the way that psychopaths are considered.For one thing, as mentioned in the last section, psychopathy is increasingly under popular consideration.It is not limited to professional discourse.Practically speaking, just who, or what, qualifies for psychopathy is often determined by a test.It is determined by the PCL-R, itself at least partially derived from the work of Hervey Cleckley.We briefly reviewed Hare's and Cleckley's respective checklists in the previous section, and from those and the upcoming DSM-V criteria, distilled three aspects – selfish, opportunistic, and predatory - that we shall employ in comparison in the following illustration.

For illustration, consider a recent episode of the very popular NPR program, *This American Life*, dedicated to the issue of psychopathy.[37]During this program, the host, Ira Glass, and his staff all were administered the PCL-R by psychologist David Bernstein.They all thought that each would score at least some points on the test.However, in the end, Dr. Bernstein assessed them all with the same score – 0.And, the reason that Bernstein gave for this result was a blanket one, covering all of the tested subjects - they never "really did anything maliciously."

> You never set out to predate, to hurt anyone. And even those of you who've done things, when I asked how do you feel about it? Most of you thought back on it with regret, and remorse. You're empathic, is what you all are, which is the opposite of psychopathy.[52]

This diagnosis was surprising to the subjects involved, who all believed, having seen the checklist for themselves, that each would score some points due to past experience.For instance, one participant recalled stealing test answers from a teacher as a youth, and feeling badly about it.However, according to the expert, any such experience cannot contribute to a diagnosis of psychopathy when presented with empathy.[38]On the other hand, the model psychopath is a "predator" for whom such empathetic remorse is impossible.These radio people, according to Bernstein, were "far too neurotic" to be predators – that is, they cared about people and things far too much to be psychopaths.

Given that empathy is a core motivating prosocial virtue, part and parcel to being a 'good person,' why would anyone wish himself to be a psychopath?Psychopaths are not good

---

[36]A process in which the mirror neural systems are central. For discussion on the first point, see [53]. For discussion on the importance of expressed emotions in providing information on emotional states, begin with [54].

[37]Named after and ostensibly inspired by the popular text *The Psychopath Test*, by J. Ronson.[55].

[38]Underscoring the necessity that the PCL-R be administered only by a properly trained psychologist operating without a secondary agenda, i.e. Increase conviction rates for friendly prosecution, or get a murderer off for a generous defense attorney.

people.The psychopath "... is constitutionally void of empathy and incurably blind to reasons to treat others in morally acceptable ways."[56][39]Who wants to be THAT person?The question, for some people, however, may be closer to "Who *doesn't* want to be that person?"Consider the following charge issued by famed economist Milton Friedman in his landmark text, *Capitalism and Freedom*:

> Few trends could so thoroughly undermine the very foundations of our free society as the acceptance by corporate officials of a social responsibility other than to make as much money for their stockholders as possible.[57][40]

Friedman here suggests that there is no obligation for the successful business leader to treat anyone in "morally acceptable ways."For example, on this formula, there is no obligation to maintain a stable work environment so that people who loyally work the best years of their lives for a company can plan how to live out the last of them, at least no felt obligation.People who want to succeed in the cut-throat world of business must be prepared to be, well, cut-throat.They must be ready to change quickly, respond to rapid change not only in order to survive, but to maximize wealth, regardless of social ties.On the face of it, this sounds like an environment ideally suited to psychopathic personalities.According to Paul Babiak:

> The psychopath has no difficulty dealing with the consequences of rapid change; in fact, he or she thrives on it.Organizational chaos provides both the necessary stimulation for psychopathic thrill seeking and sufficient cover for psychopathic manipulation and abusive behavior.[58]

Further, quoting Robert Hare:

> I always said that if I wasn't studying psychopaths in prison, I'd do it at the stock exchange.There are certainly more people in the business world who would score high in the psychopathic dimension than in the general population. You'll find them in any organization where, by the nature of one's position, you have power and control over other people and the opportunity to get something.[58]

Selfish.Opportunistic.And, in a world where whatever one wants, another already claims, *predatory*.Failing to treat others in morally acceptable ways is not a barrier to success in the world of corporate business, at all.In fact, it is something which might even, following Friedman, be required.Add to this recent evidence that empathy diminishes as wealth increases, and Friedman's capitalist injunction becomes a recipe for acquired empathy deficiency.[59][41]And, there is nothing wrong with that.

---

[39]Page 350.

[40]Page 133. For support, he recruits Adam Smith from the *Wealth of Nations*. However, Friedman is misguided in doing so, as we shall see in some detail as this chapter continues.

[41]Predicted by Lobaczewski in [3]: "During "happy times" of peace dependent upon social injustice, children of the privileged classes learn to repress from their field of consciousness the uncomfortable ideas suggesting that they and their parents are benefitting from injustice against others. Such young people learn to disqualify disparage the moral and mental values of anyone whose work they are using to over-advantage. Young minds thus ingest habits of subconscious selection and substitution of data, which leads to a hysterical conversion economy of reasoning. They grow up to be somewhat hysterical adults who, by means of the ways adduced

Consider the case of Al Dunlap.Interviewed in his own home by journalist Jon Rohnson for his book *The Psychopath Test* (and replayed in the *This American Life* episode named after the book), Dunlap found nothing wrong with any so-called "psychopathic traits."When prompted with a list of them, he recast the characteristic marks of psychopathy in favorable light.By his estimation, "manipulative" is the same as "leadership."Grandiose sense of self-worth (narcissism by any other name) becomes a mantra, "You've got to believe in you."Impulsivity? Quick analysis.Lack of remorse?"... frees you up to move forward and achieve more great things."

Here, it should be noted that, in fact, Dunlap satisfies Friedman's injunction in both word and action.During his tenure at Sunbeam, stock prices rose 400%.During his first four months on the job, he fired nearly 6,000 people, some of whom having had worked for the company for 30 years.Clearly, Dunlap was not encumbered by any sense of obligation to treat other people in "morally acceptable ways."In fact, when prompted to answer how he felt about ending so many careers, tossing so many people into poverty, he proudly replied, "Looking back at my life is like going to a movie about a person who did all this stuff. My gosh, I did that.And through it all, I did it my way."[52]

However, the opinions of others in similar positions are quite different.Said Windmere's CEO David Friedson of Dunlap's character, "He is the logical extreme of an executive who has no values, no honor, no loyalty, and no ethics. And yet he was held up as a corporate god in our culture. It greatly bothered me."[60]In this opinion, Friedson gives us two things.First, he gives a peer-level description of the sort of personality who is elevated to "god" status in the current corporate culture, ostensibly as an exemplar of corporate virtue.Second, he gives us an answer to our question, "Why would anyone want to be a psychopath?"(Or, at least, express some psychopathic traits.)Why? To be a corporate god.

Some interesting facts about Dunlap emerged from this interview.One being Dunlap's personal admiration for predators.The interviewer was surprised by "the unusually large number of ferocious sculptures there were of predatory animals."A collection of which Dunlap himself was quite proud."I believe in predators.Their spirits will enable you to succeed."Predators use aggression, violence, instrumentally, to succeed, to dominate others, itself a mark of psychopathy, and is something that administrators of the PCL-R are advised to be on the watch for; yet, his emulation of them is not something that shows up on the checklist, explicitly.

Another interesting fact about Dunlap is that he, at the time of the interview, had been married to the same woman for 41 years.He had not many shallow, short-term sexual relationships – at least not to which he would confess during an interview in front of his wife!And, given his history, this sort of discipline may not be all that surprising.He was not a disorderly child, and had no problems with conduct.In fact, he testified to having no problems conducting himself, as an adult, trumpeting the need for sound executive functions in order to reach any station in life:

---

above, thereupon transmit their hysteria to the next generation, which then develops these characteristics to an even greater degree. The hysterical patterns for experience and behavior grow and spread downwards from the privileged classes until crossing the boundary of the first criterion of ponerology: the atrophy of natural critical faculties with respect to pathological individuals. (Page 176).

Listen, this psychopath thing is rubbish. You can't be successful unless you have certain," he pointed at his head, "controls. It won't happen. How do you get through school? How do you get through your first and second job, when you're formulating yourself?[52][42]

Two things are of interest, here.One is that the preceding dimensions are increasingly given less weight as the consensus on psychopathy evolves.Being married for a long time does not make a psychopath any less dangerous and destructive.In fact, one might easily argue the contrary.Another is that Dunlap's last statement strikes to the heart of the issue, distinguishing psychopathy from other "personality disorders." ASPD may involve diminished executive functioning.Psychopathy, however, does not.In fact, the prior assumption that psychopaths were of lower than average intelligence has been thrown out the window. The facts are quite opposite, leading to the descriptive phrase "snakes in suits." Cold.Cunning.Amoral.But, not stupid.Dangerously clever.All of this speaks to the need to conceive of psychopathy outside of other disorders.

In a way, Al Dunlap is correct: this psychopath thing IS rubbish.At least *part* of it is.Who, or what, is a psychopath?Given systemic pressures due to the neo-liberal capitalist environment, successful people, leaders, and in fact non-human entities designed to succeed in this field – corporations and other institutions – are prime candidates.

Indeed, it is easily observed that the contemporary economic and political environment is a haven for psychopaths, with the rapid change, the systemic capacity for selfish manipulation, and the seemingly unforeseeable, seemingly spontaneous presentation of opportunities for personal gain at others' expense providing the best of all possible hunting grounds for social predators."Most importantly, these opportunities are not limited to simple profit maximization.When increasing wealth at all costs is one's only felt obligation, this invites more egregious acts of aggression, and violence, in the pursuit of the predatory dominance that secures that wealth.Consider in this light current events, in Nigeria, Yemen, Iraq, in Libya, in Syria, in Afghanistan, and in Iran, alongside the following recent comments from noted political economist Edwin Veira:

Psychopaths - with whom modern governments have been staffed to superfluity throughout the Twentieth Century and even unto this very day - do not usually think in strict economic terms of "cost versus benefit."...I harbor no doubt that psychopaths in positions of power would not shrink from murdering anyone who stood in their way – whether particular individuals, economic classes, races, and so on. Have they ever shrunk from mass murder?[61]

Granted the accuracy in Veira's reflections – he seems to hold that most if not all major social conflict is due to the actions of psychopaths from especially politically powerful positions in society and the world - the full scale of influence of psychopathy on the contemporary world is difficult to address.Indeed, given that any psychopathic directive to

---

[42]In fact, this point can be taken to emphasize a distinction between the so-called "successful" and "unsuccessful" psychopath. It is the unsuccessful psychopath who is prone to impulsive behavior and physical aggression. This distinction can be attributed to Belinda Board and Katarina Fritzon, as reported in [58].

"mass murder" will not be carried out by the commanding psychopath, himself, in order to address the full influence of psychopathy on global society, we must focus on the structures of institutions that act on psychopathic schemes, themselves.

This scale of organization is beyond conventional psychological approaches to understanding psychopathy.[43] In today's pursuit of fine-grained neural-level models of moral-psychological phenomena, missing the immorality of psychopathic institutions is akin to a "forest for the trees" phenomena. It is easy to lose sight of the "moral" in the "moral psychology" of psychopathy, when the subject will not it into a portable MRI and "treatments" may not fit the easily patented and marketed single-vector pharmacological model. In the frenzy of research, largely deriving from the recent technological revolution in brain imaging, all of the talk of deficiently integrated amygdala, lack of excitement upon the presentation of pained facial expressions, deficient hippocampus, various higher-order speculations on gestational exposure to chemicals, zero-negative empathy, Stroop task performance, and so on, can easily cover over the most important aspect of psychopathy, and the motivating rationale behind understanding psychopathology in the first place – psychopaths hurt people, make the world a worse place in which to live, and, when vested with power in powerful positions, exercise this power in - especially poignantly given current affairs – extremely destructive ways.

Psychopaths are not limited to acting alone, in the mold of the well-worn profile of charming serial killers like Ted Bundy and John Wayne Gacy. They use tools, institutions, to extend their reach. The revolution in the conception of psychopathy, likewise, must not be limited to individual psychopaths should we wish to fully understand the impact of psychopathy on the social order. In order to understand the full impact of psychopaths on the contemporary social order, we must understand not only psychopathic personalities, but psychopathic institutions.

Some popular attention has been directed to this issue, already. Consider the popular film (and book) *The Corporation*.[62] This film develops the notion that the modern corporation – especially given its legal status as a 'person' with all corresponding rights, yet few of the corresponding responsibilities – is a psychopathic entity.[44] According to *The Corporation*, corporations pursue their own self-interest against and exclusive of the interests of any and all affected parties, corporate, individual, conventional/legal, or natural. This view accords with the fact that the executive functions of corporate entities are effectively those of their leadership, and their leadership is effectively driven to satisfy Friedman's above quoted injunction, to maximize profits as sole social obligation. However, even when the actual leadership is not constituted of psychopathic personalities, the mission statement of the corporation constitutes a psychopathic entity in the corporation, itself. Since the 19th century, and reaffirmed as recently as 2010 in *Citizens United versus the Federal Election Commission*, corporations are legally designated artificial persons, with (most) all of the rights afforded to natural person, yet none of the obligations to society, to self, and indeed to

---

[43] It is the focus of [3], however.
[44] A corporation is an artificial entity created to ideally embody and so permit action motivated according to Friedman's injunction, as quoted above. Thus, the notion that a corporation may 'treat people in morally acceptable ways' due anything but simple accident, that a corporation has a "conscience," is pure fabrication, contrary as it is to the very spirit of its creation. Indeed, pure public relations spectacle.

the natural world.[45]An expectedly unfriendly review of the film, from *The Economist,* summarizes the corporate profile as follows:

> Like all psychopaths, the firm is singularly self-interested: its purpose is to create wealth for its shareholders. And, like all psychopaths, the firm is irresponsible, because it puts others at risk to satisfy its profit-maximizing goal, harming employees and customers, and damaging the environment. The corporation manipulates everything. It is grandiose, always insisting that it is the best, or number one. It has no empathy, refuses to accept responsibility for its actions and feels no remorse. It relates to others only superficially, via make-believe versions of itself manufactured by public-relations consultants and marketing men.[63][46]

The message of *The Corporation* is that corporate entities, by design and regardless of constituent proclivities otherwise, instill an unhealthy environment within and create an unhealthy environment outside of their confines, destroying ecosystems, social networks and political systems in their single-minded pursuit of power and profit.Regardless of who runs them - just as regardless of who detonates a bomb – it is in their nature to be destructive.In the film, Noam Chomsky provides the following analysis:

> When you look at a corporation, just like when you look at a slave owner, you want to distinguish between the institution and the individual. So, slavery, for example or other forms of tyranny, are inherently monstrous, but the individuals participating in them may be the nicest guys you could imagine – benevolent, friendly, nice to their children, even nice to their slaves, caring about other people. I mean, as individuals they may be anything. In their institutional role they're monsters because the institution is monstrous. And then the same is true here.[62][47]

Free from human moral constraints, these psychopathic institutions, these "monsters," continue to exercise increasing influence over the shape of the world and civilization at large, as one would expect from an immortal predator for which growth and dominance at others' expense are the principle goods."Corporations are artificial creations. You might say they're monsters trying to devour as much profit as possible at anyone's expense."[62][48]Such is the world we live in, an economic order exactly the inverse of that envisioned by Adam Smith, populated by entities, human and otherwise, seemingly designed for its destruction:

---

[45]Though immortal, corporations do not depend on clean air and water for health, as they do not "live," even though presumed through legal convention to be entities of the for of persons under law. As for the recent cited Supreme Court ruling, "Citizen's United," especially poignant language supporting the point, that corporations are held to be persons under law, in this case regarding freedoms of speech to affect political elections, can be found in the court's opinion delivered by Justice Kennedy, on pages 25-26. Here, Kennedy speaks of (natural) persons – human beings - and of corporations in under the same general terms, "persons," in opposition to any Government intervention (law) that should "may impose restrictions on certain disfavored speakers," (page 25) concluding this point with the following declaration: "The Court has thus rejected the argument that political speech of corporations or other associations should be treated differently under the First Amendment simply because such associations are not "natural persons."(page 26) This judgement can be read at http://www.law.cornell.edu/supct/pdf/08-205P.ZO.

[46]A summary fully in concordant with the film's interview with Robert Hare, and likely based thereupon. Of course, the reviewer, given the medium and audience, deflects any criticisms away from corporate malfeasance, to State malfeasance, in a sort of "But THEY do it TOO!" display of tit-for-tat.

[47]Page 14. Text checked against transcript retrieved from http://hellocoolworld.com/files/TheCorporation/ Transcript_finalpt1%20copy.pdf.

[48]*Ibid.* Page 3, quoting Howard Zinn.

Society ... cannot subsist among those who are at all times ready to hurt and injure one another. The moment that injury begins, the moment that mutual resentment and animosity take place, all the bands of it are broke asunder, and the different members of which it consisted are, as it were, dissipated and scattered abroad by the violence and opposition of their discordant affections.[64][49]

6. THE ACTWITH MODEL

One of the major challenges in trying to elucidate the structure of psychopathy is that, as a latent construct, it is not directly observable.

Robert Hare and Craig Neumann[14][50]

Although not due to direct clinical observation, from the preceding discussion it becomes clear that a model of psychopathy applicable to both individual human and to institutional subjects is necessary in order to evaluate, identify, and perhaps rectify psychopathic agents in the current global economic and social environment.And, although natural persons differ from artificial legal constructs in their form of embodiment, incarnation, or "incorporation," these entities do share one important dynamic.All such entities process information, and due to the sorts of information that are processed, in which contexts, and how, different actions can result.We reviewed some of the differences in the sorts of information available to psychopaths in previous sections.Psychopaths have a diminished, specific capacity to realize fear, disgust, and so fail to appreciate emotional cues which serve otherwise to discourage actions harmful to other sentient entities.When this deficiency is integrated into the perspective taking consonant with prosocial personalities, through Damasio's "as-if" loop understood as a somatically rich manifestation of mirror neural system potential, the agent in question is not hindered in putting others into worse situations, as, effectively, the agent processes no information that might dispose him/her/it to the contrary.

Given this summary, any model of psychopathy must, as an adequate model of moral cognition, generally, be equally able to model the broad scale of moral action, from "monstrous" to "altruistic," from antisocial to prosocial, from individual to institutional.[51]The ACTWith model is designed to do this very thing, to provide the minimum necessary information processing representation of moral cognition in an implementation/neuro-biologically/organizationally non-specific format suitable for evaluation of moral agency.In essence, the ACTWith model was conceived in order to answer questions like the following, in a form consistent with contemporary neurology and moral psychology, while remaining popularly accessible through a simple and intuitive form representing deeply held popular moral convictions:

Not only do we feel that we need very little explicit thoughts to understand the actors, we actually share their emotions and motivations: our hands sweat and our heart beats faster while we see actors slip off the roof, we shiver if we see an actor cut himself, we grimace in disgust as the character has to eat disgusting food. This sharing experience begs two related

---

[49]Page 129. And, directly contrary to Friedman's interpretation of Smith's designs.
50Page 231.
[51]Likewise, "A theory of psychopathy needs to be a theory of healthy cognition together with an account of how the systems can become dysfunctional so that the disorder can emerge." [18] (Page 79)

questions: How do we manage to slip into the skin of other people so effortlessly? Why do we share the experiences we observe instead of simply understanding them?[46][52]

The ACTWith model is primarily an information processing model.Information processing models are central to cognitive science, likening the way that human beings think and feel to the way that a computer processes information.On this approach, both take in information, both organize and store information to be used in formulating responses, whether these be actions and decisions or simply ready retrieval of data.Both have processing systems, and both have subsystems dedicated to the processing of specific information.Computers have graphics cards, storing maps of screens and levels so that a young computer gamer can navigate that new first-person-shooter at 60 frames-per-second, human beings have a neocortex.The computer has a keyboard, mouse, trackpad, joystick, microphone, camera, and other forms of input.The human, an array of sensory organs together constituting the sensory register.

In this chapter, we have identified some areas of brain thought responsible for psychopathy, as well as for normal moral cognition.Psychopathy is largely confined to subsystems responsible for a specific form of information processing, emotional processing.As for the rest of it, theory of mind apparatus (something perhaps approximated in some computer game software agent level a.i.'s, but otherwise missing from modern computers so far as being a part of hardware goes), sensory register, and graphics processing, we can assume that in the general case of psychopathy, all is in relatively good order.[53]

The ACTWith model was originally conceived as a model of conscience.We have briefly reviewed the responsibilities of conscience in the second section of this chapter.The responsibilities of conscience map onto those now accounted for by other means, such that conscience can be understood as that complex of reason and emotion that guides conscientious agents to do the right things at the right times, becoming through their actions the best that they can be.Conscience by this understanding is not a faculty, a module, or an isolated "voice."The ACTWith model is conceived of as a dynamic systems model, and conscience effectively determines the values of dimensions guiding the activities natural to a dynamic system.[68][69]A dynamic system seeks a low-energy stable state, or equilibrium, in terms of its environment.Conscience effectively determines in which dimensions this situation is evaluated, and how these dimensions are weighed.

For illustration, consider "pathological lying."For many people, reporting untruths is the cause of great stress – a high-energy state.Being caught in an untruth is not a situation that most persons actively seek, and the surest way to avoid it is to not utter untruths in the first place.This proclivity may be accounted for in many ways - accounts in terms of evolutionary biology or social psychology are easily enough generated – but in terms of the ACTWith model, as in traditional moral terms, lying is the wrong thing to do because it puts one's self

---

[52]Page 379.
[53]Specifically, we can understand psychopathy as local to one thread of the mirror neural system, that dedicated to mirroring emotions rather than actions. In the psychopath, action-mirroring apparatus (mirror neural structures coupled with premotor and in some cases motor structures) are fully operational, while affect-mirroring apparatus (mirroring and emotively-expressive domain matching structures) are not. For more on the distinction, see [65]. For discussion on the activity of 'anti-mirror' neurons that keep motor neurons from mimicking every perceived action, see [66].

(and others) into bad situations.[54] Contrast the above with a psychopath who employs untruths to manipulate others in self-centered pursuit of his own selfish ends.Gone is the stress of being caught.Though still not a situation actively sought, here being caught in a lie is avoided for different reasons.Foremost, it may mean not securing his selfish end.This is not why most other people want to avoid being caught in a lie, however.In short, having bad information means entering into situations that are inaccurately understood – it means doing the wrong things at the wrong times to the wrong ends – and this is to be avoided because doing the wrong thing at the wrong time can be painful.Lying to others can cause suffering.[55]And, we have already seen that this is not a factor for the psychopathic mind.

The ACTWith model is a cycle of information processing, bottom-up, affect-first.[56]It was originally informed by Ron Sun's CLARION architecture, modeling human learning.[72][73] From human neural processing, the original model proceeds from two key insights into neural mechanisms of moral cognition, disgust and mirroring of expressed action and emotion.[74][75][76] From a dynamic systems approach, it models not isolated agents, but situated agents, and is thus essentially a model of situated cognition.Although not designed according to any given theory of situated cognition, the influence being a deep and philosophical one, it is consistent with situationist psychology [77][78], and represents a strong form of embodiment.[79].

ACTWith stands for "As-if Coming-to-Terms-With."It consists of four modes, which can be considered in isolation.Two belong to a top (rational) level and two to a bottom (affective) level.The "as-if" operations involve feeling a situation out (one's own or another's), while the "coming to terms with" operations involve defining the situation in terms of the things originally felt.[57]

This is straightforwardly bottom-up hybrid in conception, intended to represent the bare minimum architecture providing for the eventual emergence of morality. In all, routine information processing styles add up to cognitive styles, or habits, and in terms of the ACTWith model these can be rendered as characters, habitual modes of moral cognition. First, for the model itself, see Figure 1. (Figure 1: The basic ACTWith model)

The model consists in 4 modes, each representing a combination of closed and open affective and rational operations:

- As-if (closed) coming to terms with (closed)
- As-if (open) coming to terms with (closed)
- As-if (closed) coming to terms with (open)
- As-if (open) coming to terms with (open)

---

[54]This is effectively Kant's analysis, directed as well by conscience, as detailed in terms of the ACTWith model in [68][69] and [70]. Interestingly, Kant and Mill agree on the role of conscience, analysis in [68] and [70]. I will provide only a brief summary of these arguments in illustration, here. In the study of neurology, one point of interest is the complexity involved in planning for the interests of different, often disparate, others deep into a future temporal field. Some work into this area is undertaken by Grafman and colleagues, as reported in [71].

[55]And, interestingly, arguments for exceptions to the imperative "Do not lie" are typically sought under the headings "But, it won't hurt anyone" and " But, it will minimize suffering."

[56]This structure is consistent with results from experiments involving psychopaths and images of mutilation, for instance, where immediate affective reactions are missing (startle-response), and involving the verbal characterization of emotionally laden images, in which psychopaths give relatively delayed responses. As the ACTWith cycle is affect-first, there is a corresponding delay in rendering top-level determinations.

[57]It is at this top level that ToM reconstructions of another's situation come into play, for instance.

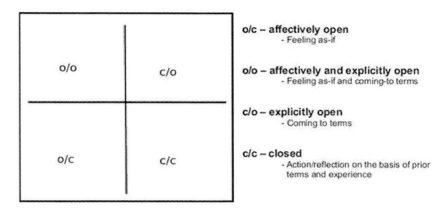

Figure 1. Basic ACTWith model consisting of four static modes.

The best way to illustrate these four modes of computation is through an actual description of their exercise.Consider the following passage from Adam Smith's *Theory of Moral Sentiments*:

> By the imagination we place ourselves in his situation, we conceive ourselves enduring all the same torments, we enter as it were into his body, and become in some measure the same person with him, and thence form some idea of his sensations, and even feel something which, though weaker in degree, is not altogether unlike them. His agonies, when they are thus brought home to ourselves, when we have thus adopted and made them our own, begin at last to affect us, and we then tremble and shudder at the thought of what he feels.[64][58]

In this passage, there are a number of processes that require representation, and all of these are related in a systematic way.There are affective and rational processes, and they are employed in an affect-first empathetic movement as an exercise in "perspective taking."This process doesn't describe mere pity.One does not merely feel badly for another person's suffering.Smith describes a completely immersive condition in which one takes another's situation for one's own, brings that situation home to one's self.In this way, one feels as-if one were in that situation, and from this stable perspective, is able to take time to reflect on the complex horizons that would be a life lived from that position forward.Only from this point of view do the threats and urgencies come clear, and due to shared bodily constitution one may realize threats to health and happiness, even risks of death and injury, that belong to another's situation.Thus, Smith describes a process far more complex than simple empathy, though it is rooted in empathy.Smith describes a holistic mirroring process, from bottom to top, much as we find described in recent literature today.

---

[58]Section 1.1.2. Smith is most famous for authoring his *Wealth of Nations,* but he was renowned before that for having authored *Sentiments.* There is some debate over the contiguity of these two works, with some suggesting that Smith broke from the motivation to virtue (effectively Aristotlean) that he suggested drives progress in *Sentiment,* to trumpet pure self-interest in *Wealth.* I am not one of those persons, however, as there is no evidence for any such shift in deep personal values in the rest of Smith's life to motivate such a dramatic loss of faith in human virtue. Others, such as Friedman as quoted earlier, focus on the rational self-interest apparent in *Wealth,* for two reasons in my opinion. One, ignorance of Smith's life, career, and early work. And, two, self-interest.

In Smith's description, each operation of the ACTWith model has its role.Consider the same passage, appended with ACTWith shorthand:

> By the imagination we place ourselves in his situation [O/C], we conceive ourselves enduring all the same torments [O/O], we enter as it were into his body[C/O], and become in some measure the same person with him [C/C], and thence form some idea of his sensations [O/C], and even feel something which, though weaker in degree, is not altogether unlike them[O/O]. His agonies, when they are thus brought home to ourselves [C/O], when we have thus adopted and made them our own [C/C], begin at last to affect us, and we then tremble and shudder at the thought of what he feels [O/C].

As we can see, the different operations within the ACTWith model work in a cycle to bridge the differences between situations until another's situation can be "adopted" and made one's own.But, in order to represent the movement through this cycle, the basic static model of conscience must be rendered dynamic.Traditionally, conscience has been equated with the human heart, the heart long ago being thought as the seat of compassion, and love.In deference to tradition, in order to retain deep-rooted folk-psychological moral concepts, this dynamic version of the ACTWith model is called the "Beating Heart of Conscience."See Figure 2. (Figure 2: The Beating Heart of Conscience)

In Figure 2, we see that the information processing cycle begins with affect, with the perceiving agent opening to the input of affective information.At this first stage, incoming affect, if interpreted, is interpreted in terms already belonging to the perceiver's experience and understanding.

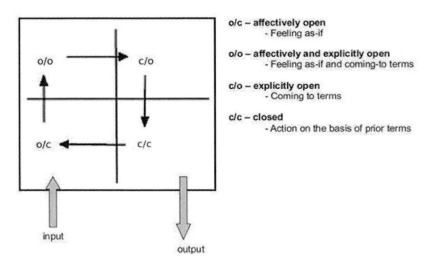

Figure 2.The Beating Heart of Conscience.

At the next stage, the perceiver opens rational faculties to understand the other's affect as-if that other's situation were his/her own. This means 'putting one's self into the shoes' of that other, completely, taking that other's interests for one's own, confronted as it were with all the anxieties that confront a living being in terms of that situation. In the third stage, the perceiver closes to further affective input, and turns top-level faculties to 'digest' the information gathered, weighing significances of objects, searching for options, evaluating apparent opportunities, and generally generating the resources necessary to answer questions in the form of "If I were you" or "If you were me...?" The final stage is an action stage, where information is no longer coming in, and one acts (or not) on the basis of information already gained and reflection already carried out.

Now, there are some points to highlight, here.First, action is not required at the final stage.There is no reason internal to the model keeping an agent from spinning around in this cycle, feeling out situations as deeply as time allows, empathizing 'till the cows come home.'And, in any case, more than one computational cycle is likely necessary in order to gather enough information in order to ground responsible actions.Second, all top-level interpretation is limited by personal experience.One cannot understand what one does not understand, simple as that.[59]In the end, it is this limitation by experience that is both the most inspiring, and the most intimidating, aspect of the the model.In terms of psychopathy, however, the implications are much easier to grasp.

7. INTERPRETING THE MODEL

Psychopaths are specifically right-hemisphere deficient in the recognition of specific vicarious emotions, especially disgust, pain, and other negative emotions, and so are effectively blind to emotional distress cues.These processes are represented by affective processes in the ACTWith model.Psychopaths are not deficient in left-hemisphere specific verbal proficiency – i.e. psychopaths are able to describe, account for, and thereby manipulate non-psychopaths into presuming that the psychopath feels similarly to non-psychopaths, almost as efficiently as non-psychopaths, when this is only a post-hoc remediation.These processes are represented by rational processes in the ACTWith model.

Altogether, the psychopath is easily modeled by the ACTWith model's dynamic.Failing to open affectively to specific emotional information in the form of facial expressions, for example, in the first and second modes of the model, the psychopath is able to bring high-level reasoning functions to bear in tracking the visual data against changes in others' behaviors.This delayed reasoning process, embodied in the model as a "skipped" first two modes of affective processing (being as it is a bottom-up affective- first model of cognition) squares with received data regarding a lack of startle response when confronted with visual representations of mutilated bodies (i.e. fear and disgust invoking images).[18]There is no startle response because the psychopath does not begin processing startling information at a stage that generates reflex actions, generically bottom-up, but rather only during stages of processing from which top-down actions originate.

What about institutions, corporations, States, and collective entities generally speaking?The advantage of the information processing approach modeled in the ACTWith model is that there is no specification of shared circuitry.Rather, the emergent property of properly functioning human neural circuitry, i.e. empathically motivated moral cognition, can be traced to any given functional group in which relevant and necessary processes are carried out.In the case of a human being, these may include the insula, anterior cingulate, amygdala, medial prefrontal cortex, and others.In the corporation, the analysis may focus on these same

---

[59]A point supported in recent research in mirroring actions and activities, to say nothing of the selective attention naturally given to that which one does understand.

regions within the minds of corporate leadership, or, if claims of corporate personhood are to be taken literally and at face value, then on offices within the corporate structure designated for the performance of such processes.In either case, actions can be evaluated on the basis of information processed, weighted, and implicit in motivation.And, in neither case, regardless of the fundamental capitalist injunction to maximize profits regardless of other social obligations, should immoral action go without sanction, externally imposed when internal sanctions fail.

A note about sanction may be useful, here.At the forefront of Western moral philosophy, John Stuart Mill placed conscience at the heart of his utilitarian theory.Conscience serves two purposes on his account.First, any proposed end or action to pass his utilitarian formula must first pass the muster of conscience.No action, regardless of payoff, is right if it doesn't feel right.Second, any action undertaken that does not pass this muster, yet is undertaken in any event, is subject to the sanction of conscience after the fact.Indeed, for Mill, the pangs of conscience are so acute as to motivate anyone with conscience away from its violation, and by this estimation conscience, for Mill, was enough to guarantee that his theory of utility would no be misinterpreted and misapplied.[60]

Sadly, Mill did not account for the modern corporate person, an entity by purpose and design without conscience.And as it has been said that corporations as essentially entities without conscience, then corporations are essentially without sanction for immoral actions on Mill's schema.Should we seek to reform such entities, it seems that sanctions common today, mostly monetary fines, are not the answer.After all, these monies are merely transferred from one institution to another, from corporation to State, and it is difficult to see how moving currency from one entity without conscience to another is going to deter future immorality.The offending entity merely performs a cost-benefit analysis, weighing risks against potential profits, and then acts on the basis of Friedman's injunction – this is all perfectly rational.Expected.

This observation demands some further considerations for the treatment of psychopathy in both individual agents as well as collective entities like corporations and States.On the one hand, there are issues internal to the entities in question that bear attention.On the other, as the previous passage implies, there are issues endemic to the system within which we all live, and along with corporate persons, act.In my mind, the way to stem the social damage caused by psychopathy at both levels of organization lies primarily in the direction of systemic reform.In any event, an information processing model like the ACTWith model should prove a useful tool.

The ACTWith model provides a map of information processing against which the processes of agents can be checked and measured.For example, the model makes clear that, should executive level intervention be desired, time and resources must be permitted for the reflection on morally relevant information.In the ACTWith model, this is represented by specific modes of information processing.In a corporate environment, this means specific modes of information processing.In the individual agent, the same.Consider in another instance the impaired capacity for psychopaths to distinguish between the moral and the conventional.Should reform be desired, entities in question must be made to "feel" the moral

---

[60]In the third chapter of Mill's *Utilitarianism*, "Of the Ultimate Sanction of the Principle of Utility," he writes that conscience is a "mass of feeling which must be broken through in order to do what violates our standard of right, and which, if we do nevertheless violate that standard, will probably have to be encountered afterwards in the form of remorse."[80] (Page 277.)

contents which form the distinction.In ACTWith terms, they must not "skip" the first two stages of information processing.And, regardless of constitutional incapacities to directly effect the processes within these stages, some surrogate must be provided for so that down-field processing weighs moral dimensions appropriately.[61]A similar approach may be envisioned in terms of psychopathic entities who harm others and, even when confronted with the damage done, continue to act in the same ways.Here, bear in mind the abusive cop who consistently applies excessive force in unwarranted situations, the callous sweat-shop owner who maintains a strict no-bathroom policy throughout long workdays even after some employees have committed suicide complaining about harsh conditions, and the global corporation which, say, destroys an ocean ecosystem cutting corners while trying to maximize profits causing a series of devastating oil leaks begun with a spectacular explosion causing the immediate deaths of perhaps a dozen people, the near-term deaths of countless sea-creatures, and the long-term deaths and sickness of millions more local human and animal residents, only to continue in the same practices in remote areas of the world.All of these cases show that morally relevant information is not being fed downstream, from the first stages to the action stage of the ACTWith model, so that offending acts continue to be executed.By the model, the situation of the other must be "brought home" to one's self, or the empathic cycle is not complete.Thus, the ACTWith model may be in these cases used as a template into which the offending entities are placed, perhaps in extreme cases physically removed from present positions and placed in positions alike those of their victims.The cop, perhaps put into general population, in prison.The sweat-shop owner, perhaps made to work in the same conditions that he imposes on others.These suggestions are not revolutionary.They reflect deeply-held moral convictions, that justice is fairness, and that an eye deserves and eye.The ACTWith model only provides a formal framework into which the offending entity can both enter, and from which he/she/it can leave once evidence of appropriate downstream processing is embodied.

Of these cases, the corporation poses a particular trouble, as the situations that are to be traded do not readily translate from natural to artificial persons.BP cannot take the place of a 5th generation Gulf fisherman and his family, ruined because BP executives felt only a single social obligation, to maximize the profits of shareholders who in no way suffer from the ruination of what had once been one of the most bountiful natural reserves on the planet.In such cases, it may be useful to consider some modification to existing corporate law, such as that put forward in [67], with an additional caveat, that any natural person serving in direct executive functions towards corporate actions which evidence psychopathic traits – selfish, opportunistic, predatory – must rather directly take the place of some offended party to be determined either by lottery or democratically, amongst the field of offended parties, while the victim gains trusteeship over those same executive functions without reservation and at the expense of the corporation and its shareholders, at least and until evidence of appropriate downstream processing is, by interred executives, embodied.

Now, as extreme and unlikely as this proposal may seem, it brings to attention two important points.One, such avenues to correction and prevention of social injustice caused by psychopaths at every station and level of organization depend on systemic changes.Presently, "lawful" corporate influence over the political process in the U.S., as reflected in the Citizens

---

[61]Some efforts have been made, for example, in exposing psychopaths to the victims of their crimes, in essence forcing an approximation of the o/c stage of the ACTWith model.

United case and decision, forbids any such mechanism.Until laws that permit the corruption of the system through which such laws emanate are overwritten, no such mechanism is possible, and the corporate monsters reign freely.This dysfunction is itself a dynamic that can be modeled according to the ACTWithmodel, with the State apparatus taking the role of the corporate entity, but this analysis must wait for another time.

Second, moral reform differs from individual to collective entity.As for psychopathy induced by deficient or defective neural integration of the amygdala with relevant regions, or defects in the amygdala and/or the insula and perhaps other relevant regions, directed moral self-education may not prove useful, and indeed may prove impossible.Hardwired deficiencies may not be overcome, regardless of constant exercise intended to heighten top-level awareness to morally relevant dimensions.But, such remains to be seen.

In some ways, there is promise of structural correction beyond the removal of dysfunctional regions.As is well known, deficiencies in neural processing, when regions are damaged during traumatic injury, especially, can be offset by recruitment of other brain regions to the processing of necessary task information.This process may hold promise in the correction of psychopathy of purely physical origins, given the right sort of therapy and enough time.The ACTWith model could provide an easily accessible model for the patient of the sort of processing that *should* be going on in his/her brain, give him/her something to envision, and aim toward during therapy exercises, as well as illustrate the sort of processing that actually is going on, and that stands in need of correction.In such an approach, thus, the ACTWith model may prove an indispensable tool, as would any similar model so long as it were conceptually accessible and morally significant to the patient.

However, it is not clear how the brain can be brought to recruit unrelated regions to processing tasks that it had, globally, never undertaken, as would be the process involved for psychopaths born with amygdala and/or insula dysfunctions, for example.Christian Keysers, speculating on the question whether new mirror neurons can be grown, suggests that they might.[81][62]

If Keysers' speculation extends throughout the neural system, not limited to mirroring neurons alone, perhaps aided with chemical/medicinal stimulus,[63] then there may be some hope for the reformation of psychopathic neural systems through directed moral training.As far as treatment of artificial entities goes – corporations, institutions, States, and other forms of "collective entity" - the trick here is to "grow" the mirroring apparatus, and provide necessary resources for the mirrored affects to be matched within said entities.Moreover, such matching must be permitted to be motivational, both in one-off actions and in matters of policy (moral habit formation).Surprisingly, given the fact that the pieces of a corporate entity are more easily interchanged, or "grown," the reformation of corporations may prove easier than that of individuals.[64]It may be that corporations *can* have a conscience, after all.This is a promising note, and a promising note is a good place to end.

---

[62]"Can we develop new mirror neurons? Hebbian learning suggests that performing an action while seeing and hearing oneself perform it should be enough for neurons involved in performance to start responding to the sight and sound of the same action. The fact that five hours of piano lessons suffice for the premotor cortex to start responding to piano music supports this view." (Page 972).

[63]For instance, marijuana has been shown to encourage the growth of new neurons in the hippocampus, a rather encouraging fact.[82]

[64]On this count, given accessible and actionable information, Lobaczewski is upbeat: "If societies are furnished an understanding of the pathological nature of evil, they will be able to effect concerted action based on moral and naturalistic criteria."[3] (Page 302)

REFERENCES

[1]   Kouri, J. (2009, June 12) Serial Killers and Politicians Share Traits.*Law Enforcement Examiner.* Retrieved from http://www.examiner.com/law-enforcement-in-national/serial-killers-and-politicians-share-traits.

[2]   Dodge, K.A., Coie, J.D., and Lynam, D. (2008) Aggression and Antisocial Behavior in Youth.In W. Damon and R.M. Lerner (Eds.), *Child and Adolescent Development An Advanced Course.* Hoboken: John Wiley and Sons, Inc.

[3]   Lobaczewski, A., Knight-Jadczyk, L., and See, H. (2006). *Political Ponerology: A science on the nature of evil adjusted for political purposes.* Grande Prairie, AB, Canada: Red Pill Press.

[4]   Hare, R. D. (1999). *Without conscience: The disturbing world of the psychopaths among us.* New York: Guilford Press.

[5]   Verplaetse, J., Braeckman, J., and DeSchrijver, J. (2009). Introduction. In Verplaetse, J., *The moral brain: Essays on the evolutionary and neuroscientific aspects of morality.* Dordrecht: Springer.

[6]   Duggan, C. (2011). National Institute for Health and Clinical Excellence antisocial personality disorder guidance in the context of DSM-5: Another example of a disconnection syndrome? *Personality and Mental Health.* 5, 122-131.

[7]   Carveth, D. (2007). Degrees *of Psychopathy vs. "The Psychopath."* Retrieved from http://www.yorku.ca/dcarveth/psychopathyFA.pdf.

[8]   Millon, T. and Davis, R.D. (1996). *Disorders of Personality: DSM-IV and Beyond.* New York: John Wiley and Sons, Inc.

[9]   Kiel, K.A. (2010). The Making of a Psychopath. *Scientific American Mind.* September/October 2010. 22-29.

[10]   Hare, R.D. (1994) The Charming Psychopath.*PsychologyToday.* Retrieved from http://www.psychologytoday.com/articles/199401/charming-psychopath.

[11]   American Psychological Association. (1994). *Diagnostic and statistical manual of mental disorders* (4th ed.). Washington, D.C.

[12]   Hare, R.D. (1996) Psychopathy and Antisocial Personality Disorder: A Case of Diagnostic Confusion. *Psychiatric Times.* 13(2).

[13]   Cleckley, H. (1941). *The mask of sanity (1st ed.).* St Louis, MO: Mosby.

[14]   Hare, D.R., Neumann C.S. (2008). Psychopathy as a clinical and empirical construct. *The Annual Review of Clinical Psychology.* 4, 217-246.

[15]   Hare, R. D. (2003). *Manual for the Revised Psychopathy Checklist (2nd edition).* Toronto, ON, Canada: Multi-Health Systems.

[16]   Mealey, L. (1995). The sociobiology of sociopathy: an integrated evolutionary model. *Behavioral and Brain Sciences.* 18, 523–559.

[17]   Baron-Cohen, S. (2011). *Zero degrees of empathy: A new theory of human cruelty.* London: Allen Lane.

[18]   Blair, J., Mitchell, D.R., and Blair, K. (2005). *The psychopath: Emotion and the brain.* Malden, MA: Blackwell.

[19]   Kosson, D.S., Suchy, Y., and Libby, J. (2002) Facial Affect Recognition in Criminal Psychopaths. *Emotion.* 2(4), 398-411.

[20] Nauert, R. (2011, May 20). Difficulty Processing Fear Tied to Risk of Psychopathy. *PsychCentral.com*.Retrieved from http://psychcentral.com/news/2011/05/20/difficulty-processing-fear-tied-to-risk-of-psychopathy/26.

[21] Menon, D. (2011, May 18). Is Fear Deficit a Harbinger of Future Psychopaths? (press release). *Association for Psychological Science*. Retrieved from http://www.psychologicalscience.org/index.php/news/releases/is-fear-deficit-a-harbinger-of-future-psychopaths.html.

[22] Dolan, M., and Fullam, R. (2006). Face affect recognition deficits in personality-disordered offenders: Association with psychopathy. *Psychological Medicine*. 36, 1563–1569.

[23] Gordon, H.L., Baird, A.A., and End, A. (2004). Functional differences among those high and low on a trait measure of psychopathy. *Biological Psychiatry*. 56, 516-521.

[24] Blair, R.J.R., Colledge, E., and Mitchell, D.G.V. (2001). Somatic Markers and Response Reversal: Is There Orbitofrontal Cortex Dysfunction in Boys with Psychopathic Tendencies? *Journal of Abnormal Child Psychology*. 29(6), 499-511.

[25] Blair, R.J.R. (2007). The amygdala and ventromedial prefrontal cortex in morality and psychopathy. *Trends in Cognitive Sciences*. 11(9), 387-392.

[26] Mitchell, D. G., Fine, C., Richell, R. A., Newman, C., Lumsden, J., Blair, K. S., and Blair, R. J. (2006). Instrumental learning and relearning in individuals with psychopathy and in patients with lesions involving the amygdala or orbitofrontal cortex. *Neuropsychology*. 20, 280–289.

[27] Blair, R.J.R. (2001) Neuro-cognitive models of aggression, the antisocial personality disorders and psychopathy. *Journal of Neurology, Neurosurgery and Psychiatry*. 71, 727 – 731.

[28] Weber, S., Habel, U., Amunts, K., and Schneider, F. (2008). Structural brain abnormalities in psychopaths - A review. *Behavioral Sciences and the Law* 26(1), 7-28.

[29] Kiehl, K. A. (2006). A cognitive neuroscience perspective on psychopathy: Evidence for paralimbic system dysfunction. *Psychiatry Research*. 142, 107-128.

[30] Buckholtz, J.W., Treadway, M.T., Cowan, R.L., Woodward, N.D., Benning, S.D., Li, R., Ansari, M.S., Baldwin, R.M., Schwartzman, A.N., Shelby, E.S., Smith, C.E., Cole, D., Robert M Kessler, R.M. and Zald, D.H. (2010) Mesolimbic dopamine reward system hypersensitivity in individuals with psychopathic traits. *Nature Neuroscience* 13, 419–421.

[31] Nauert, R. (2011, May 20). Difficulty Processing Fear Tied to Risk of Psychopathy. *Psych. Central*.Retrieved from http://psychcentral.com/news/2011/05/20/difficulty-processing-fear-tied-to-risk-of-psychopathy/26350.html.

[32] Decety, J., Michalska, K.J., Akitsuki, Y., Lahey, B.B. (2009). Atypical empathic responses in adolescents with aggressive conduct disorder: a functional MRI investigation. *Biological Psychology*. 80(2), 203-11.

[33] Frick, P. J., and White, S. F. (2008). Research Review: The importance of callous-unemotional traits for developmental models of aggressive and antisocial behavior. *Journal of Child Psychology and Psychiatry*. 49(4) 359-375.

[34] Card, N. A., Stucky, B. D., Sawalani, G. M., and Little, T. D. (2008). Direct and Indirect Aggression During Childhood and Adolescence: A Meta-Analytic Review of Gender Differences, Intercorrelations, and Relations to Maladjustment. *Child Development*. 79(5) 1185-1229.

[35] Decety, J., Michalskaa K.J., and Akitsuki, Y. (2008). Who caused the pain? An fMRI investigation of empathy and intentionality in children. *Neuropsychologia.* 46(11), 2607-2614.

[36] Blair, R. J. R. (2010). Psychopathy, frustration, and reactive aggression: The role of ventromedial prefrontal cortex. *British Journal of Psychology.* 101(3), 383-399.

[37] Hyatt, C. S., and Willis, J. (2003). *The psychopath's bible: For the extreme individual.* Tempe, Ariz: New Falcon Pub.

[38] Batson, C. D. and Powell, A. A. (2003). Altruism and Prosocial Behavior. In Damon., W. (ed), *Handbook of Psychology.* New York: J. Wiley. 463–484.

[39] Eisenberg, N., Fabes, R.A., and Spinrad, T.L. (2006). Prosocial Development. In Damon, W., Lerner, R.M., and Eiseberg, N. (eds.) *Handbook of Child Psychology: Social, emotional, and personality development (6th edition, Vol. 3).* Hoboken: John Wiley and Sons.

[40] Thioux, M., Gazzola, V., and Keysers, C. (2008). Action Understanding: How, What and Why. *Current Biology.* 18(10) 431-434.

[41] Damasio, A. R. (1994). *Descartes' error: Emotion, reason, and the human brain.* New York: Putnam.

[42] Adolphs, R., Damasio, H., Tranel, D., Cooper, G., and Damasio, A.R. (2000). A Role for Somatosensory Cortices in the Visual Recognition of Emotion as Revealed by Three-Dimensional Lesion Mapping. *The Journal of Neuroscience.* 20(7), 2683-2690.

[43] Schippers, M. B., Gazzola, V., Goebel, R., and Keysers, C. (2009). Playing charades in the fMRI: are mirror and/or mentalizing areas involved in gestural communication? *Plos One*, 4(8).

[44] Keysers, C., and Gazzola, V. (2007). Integrating simulation and theory of mind: from self to social cognition. *Trends in Cognitive Sciences.* 11(5), 194-6.

[45] Bastiaansen, J. A. C. J., Thioux, M., and Keysers, C. (2009). Evidence for mirror systems in emotions. *Philosophical Transactions of the Royal Society B: Biological Sciences.* 36491528), 2391-2404.

[46] Keysers, C., and Gazzola, V. (2006). Towards a unifying neural theory of social cognition. *Progress in Brain Research.* 156, 379-401.

[47] Etzel, J. A., Gazzola, V., and Keysers, C. (2008). Testing simulation theory with cross-modal multivariate classification of fMRI data. *Plos One,* 3(11).

[48] Amodio, D.M., Frith C.D., (2006) Meeting of minds: the medial frontal cortex and social cognition. *Nature Reviews of Neuroscience.* 7, 268–277.

[49] Blair, R.J.R. (2003). Neurobiological basis of psychopathy. *British Journal of Psychiatry.* 182, 5–7.

[50] Damasio, A.R., Tranel, D., and Damasio, H. (1990) Individuals with sociopathic behaviour caused by frontal damage fail to respond autonomically to social stimuli. *Behavioral Brain Research.* 41, 81-94.

[51] Broomhall, L.G.J. (2005). Acquired sociopathy: A neuropsychological study of executive dysfunction in violent offenders. *Psychiatry, Psychology and Law.* 12, 367–387.

[52] Ira Glass (host). (2011, May 27). The Psychopath Test [radio episode].In J. Snyder (producer)*This American Life.* Chicago: Public Radio International.

[53] Schippers, M. B., Roebroeck, A., Renken, R., Nanetti, L., and Keysers, C. (2010). Mapping the information flow from one brain to another during gestural communication. *Proceedings of the National Academy of Sciences.* 107(20), 9388-9393.

[54] Jabbi, M., and Keysers, C. (2008). Inferior Frontal Gyrus Activity Triggers Anterior Insula Response to Emotional Facial Expressions. *Emotion.* 8(6), 775-780.

[55] Ronson, J. (2011). *The psychopath test: A journey through the madness industry.* New York: Riverhead Books.

[56] Litton, P. (2008). Responsibility Status of the Psychopath: On Moral Reasoning and Rational Self- Governance.*Rutgers Law Journal.* 39(351), 349-392.

[57] Friedman, M. (1982). *Capitalism and Freedom.* Chicago: The University of Chicago Press.

[58] Deutschman, A. (2005, July 1).Is Your Boss a Psychopath?*Fast Company.* Retrieved from http://www.fastcompany.com/magazine/96/open_boss.html?page=0%2C1.

[59] Kraus, M. W., Piff, P. K., and Keltner, D. (2011). Social class as culture: The convergence of resources and rank in the social realm. *Current Directions in Psychological Science.* 20(4) 246-250.

[60] Byrne, J.A. (1998) How Al Dunlap Self-Destructed.*BusinessWeek.* Retrieved from http://www.businessweek.com/1998/27/b3585090.htm.

[61] Vieira Jr., E. and Wile, A. (2011, July 24) On the Power Elite, the Police State and Opposing the Authoritarian Trend.*The Daily Bell.* Retrieved from http://www. thedailybell.com/2720/Anthony-Wile-Edwin-Vieira-Jr-on-the-Power-Elite-the-Police-State-and-Opposing-the-Authoritarian-Trend.

[62] Achbar, M., Simpson, B., Crooks, H., Abbott, J., Mikael, M. J., Moore, M., Chomsky, N., ... Zeitgeist Films. (2005). *The corporation.* United States: Zeitgeist Films.

[63] Face Value (2004, May 6). The lunatic you work for: If the corporation were a person, would that person be a psychopath? *The Economist.* Retrieved from http:// www.economist.com/node/2647328?story_id=2647328.

[64] Smith, A. (1982). *The Theory of Moral Sentiments.* In Raphael, D.D., and Macfie, A.L. (eds.), *Volume I of the Glasgow Edition of the Works and Correspondence of Adam Smith (1759).*Indianapolis: Liberty Fund.

[65] Van der Gaag, C., Minderaa, R. B., and Keysers, C. (2007). Facial expressions: what the mirror neuron system can and cannot tell us. *Social Neuroscience.* 2, 3-4.

[66] Keysers, C., and Gazzola, V. (2010). Social Neuroscience: Mirror Neurons Recorded in Humans. *Current Biology.* 20(8), 353-354.

[67] Greenwood, D.J.H. (2010, March 16). *Restoring Democracy After Citizens United. Huffington Post Politics.*Retrieved from http://www.huffingtonpost.com/daniel-j-h-greenwood/restoring-democracy-after_b_500807.html.

[68] White, J. (forthcoming) Manufacturing Morality: A general theory of moral agency grounding computational implementations: the ACTWith model. *Computational Intelligence.* New York: Nova Publications.

[69] White, J. (2010) Understanding and Augmenting Human Morality, the ACTWITH model. In Magnani, L., Pizzi, C., and Carnielli, W. (eds.) *Studies in Computational Intelligence #314: Model-Based Reasoning in Science and Technology.* Springer. 607-620.

[70] White, J. (forthcoming). *Conscience: the mechanism of morality*. (monograph, 190,000 words).

[71] Stimson, D. (2007, April 4). Inner Workings of the Magnanimous Mind. *National Institute of Neurologic Disorders and Stroke*. Retrieved from http://www.ninds.nih.gov/ news_and_events/news_articles/brain_activity_during_altruism.htm.

[72] Sun, R. (2002). *The Duality of Mind: A Bottom-Up Approach to Cognition*. New Jersey:L. Erlbaum and Associates.

[73] Sun, R. (2009). Motivational Representations within a Computational Cognitive Architecture. *Cognitive Computing*. 1, 91-103.

[74] Umilta, M.A., Kohler, E., Gallese, V., Forgassi, L. Fadiga, L., Keysers, C. and Rizzolatti, G. (2001). I Know What You Are Doing: A Neurophysiological Approach. *Neuron*. 31, 155-165.

[75] Wicker, B., Keysers, C., Plailly, J. Royet, J., Gallese V., and Rizzolatti, G. (2003). Both of Us Disgusted in My Insula: The Common Neural Basis of Seeing and Feeling Disgust. *Neuron*. 40, 655-664.

[76] Singer, T. and Frith, C. (2005). The Painful Side Of Empathy. *Nature Neuroscience*. 8, 845-846.

[77] Barsalou, L.W. (1999). Perceptual symbol systems. *Behavioral and Brain Sciences*. 22, 577–660.

[78] Vargas, M. (2010). Situationism and Moral Responsibility: Free Will in Fragments. In Vierkant, T., Kiverstein, J., and Clark, A. (eds.) *Decomposing the Will*. New York: Oxford University Press. Retrieved from http://usf.usfca.edu/fac_staff/mrvargas/ Papers/Situationism.pdf.

[79] Clark, A. (1998). Embodiment and the Philosophy of Mind. *Current Issues in Philosophy of Mind: Royal Institute of Philosophy Supplement*. Cambridge:Cambridge University Press. 43, 35-52.

[80] Mill, J. S. (1985). Utilitarianism. In Robson, J.M. (ed.) *The Collected Works of John Stuart Mill, Volume X – Essays on Ethics, Religion, and Society*. University of Toronto Press, Toronto. Retrieved from http://oll.libertyfund.org/title/241.

[81] Keysers, C. (2009). Mirror neurons. *Current Biology*. 19(21), 971-973.

[82] Jiang, W., Zhang, Y., Xiao, L., Van, C. J., Ji, S. P., Bai, G., and Zhang, X. (2005). Cannabinoids promote embryonic and adult hippocampus neurogenesis and produce anxiolytic- and antidepressant-like effects. *The Journal of Clinical Investigation*, 115(11), 3104-16.

In: Psychology of Morality
Editors: A. S. Fruili and L. D. Veneto

ISBN: 978-1-62100-910-8
© 2012 Nova Science Publishers, Inc.

Chapter 2

COPING WITH OFFLINE PROHIBITED ACTIONS IN GAMESPACE: A PSYCHOLOGICAL APPROACH TO MORAL WELL-BEING IN GAMERS

Garry Young[*1] *and Monica Whitty*[2]
[1]Nottingham Trent University, UK
[2]The University of Leicester, UK

ABSTRACT

Video games provide virtual spaces for the representation and enactment of prohibited offline behaviour, be it in the form of more conventional violence (e.g., assault, killings, murder) or other forms of taboo violation (e.g., torture, rape, even cannibalism). This chapter considers the ways in which gamers cope with the moral freedoms afforded by gamespace and the strategies adopted by gamers to morally manage and otherwise cope with virtual behaviours that are severely prohibited offline. We argue that virtual acts of violence and taboo (as noted above) should not be judged by a moral system constitutive of our offline world. Instead, the permissibility of virtual representation and interaction should be informed by psychology rather than morality. This chapter therefore provides an overview of psychological research investigating factors which have been shown to impact on gamers' moral-well being, as well as strategies for managing virtual violence and taboos. It also proffers a new direction for research into gamers and game content, in the hope that it will provide further insight into who is more susceptible to the potential negative impact of video game violence on moral well-being.

1. INTRODUCTION

Within the virtual spaces of video games it is possible to murder, rape, torture, or even eat another virtual character. To say that such virtual actions *should* be judged wrong, because

---

[*] E-mail: garry.young@ntu.ac.uk

they are wrong offline, is to import a system of morality from our offline world into a given virtual space; but such heterogeneous spaces are by definition constituted from different contingency relations (i.e., involving virtual interaction set in futuristic or ancient, apocalyptic, fantasy, or alien worlds, and with characters from these worlds). As such, the types of interactions and representations that occur in these spaces are governed (potentially, at least) by different moral codes. It would therefore be inappropriate, we contend, for moral systems built on different contingency relations to transcend these spaces. In effect, when it comes to the *virtual act* itself, it is arguably the case that there is no moral issue to consider; no rightness or wrongness to debate (see Young and Whitty, 2012, for a detailed discussion on this point). Klimmt, Schmid, Nosper, Hartmann and Vorderer (2006) appear to share this view:

> Obviously, in violent video games no living creatures are harmed and no real objects are damaged. Dead bodies, blood, and injuries are nothing more than pixels. The non-reality status of video games can therefore be used to explain why moral concerns are not 'necessary', applicable, or rational in their context; there simply seems nothing to be 'real' in a game that moral concerns could arise from. Consequently, players are not required to cope with moral ruminations. (p.313)

Sicart (2009) seems to concur, but adds an important caveat when he states: "There is nothing essentially wrong in games with unethical content... But this does not mean that computer games can use unethical content and expect their users not to be affected" (p.199). In keeping with Sicart's warning, it seems fair to say that those who *do* wish to question the morality of such (violent) games do not limit their moralizing to the virtual act itself. By far the most extensive research on the effects of video game content has focused on the behavioural consequences of playing these games. In particular, researchers have studied the extent to which gamer behaviour offline has become more aggressive or otherwise anti-social (see Sections 2 and 3) or in other ways problematic (see Section 7).

Research of this nature, which focuses on the *psychological* effects of playing violent video games (including any affective and cognitive changes within the gamer), has clear moral implications if/when these effects transcend the virtual realm – that is, if/when how a gamer thinks, feels and/or behaves changes as a result of the representations and interactions available within gamespace.

This chapter considers the means by which gamers cope with the possibility for change afforded by gamespace; particularly when this change permits the virtual enactment of activities which are violent or otherwise taboo offline – what we have elsewhere referred to as *symbolic taboo activities* (STAs) (see Whitty, Young and Goodings, 2011).

Does the moral freedom afforded by gamespace have a detrimental impact on the gamer's moral well-being? And how might an individual manage this freedom so as to counter this potential impact? For the purposes of this chapter, we define moral well-being in rather broad and perhaps superficial terms as that which enables the individual to function offline in a manner decreed acceptable within his/her society.

In Sections 2 and 3, we present an overview of key research into the effects of playing violent video games in both single- and multiplayer formats, and critically examine one of the main models devised to explain more general aggressive behaviour – the General Aggression Model – which has been applied to video game violence. In Section 4 we discuss recent research which has begun to look at the ways in which gamers manage their virtual interactions, including, in Sections 5 and 6, the role of interpretation and the significance of identification with the character when managing (or not) virtual violence and other STAs. In Section 7 we consider the potential negative impact of gamespace beyond increased offline aggression when discussing the more general issue of 'problematic Internet use'.

Finally, in Section 8, we introduce the concept of psychological parity as a means of better understanding who is more likely to cope with the moral freedoms afforded within gamespace, or indeed any alteration between the virtual and offline realms, and who is more susceptible to the potential negative impact of these freedoms on their moral well-being.

2. THE GENERAL AGGRESSION MODEL AND RELATED GAMING RESEARCH

There have been a number of theoretical models proposed to account for the psychological effects of playing violent video games. The more popular of these models is the General Aggression model (GAM). The GAM is based on a theoretical framework which integrates a conglomeration of mini-theories, predominantly social learning and social-cognitive in nature (see Anderson, 1997, 2004; Anderson and Bushman, 2002; Anderson and Dill, 2000; Bushman and Anderson, 2001), and draws from research which examines the development and use of knowledge structures that guide perception, interpretation, decision making and action. According to the model, both situational and person variables interact to affect a person's internal state. The internal state contains cognitions, affects and arousals, which all influence each other and effect the individual's appraisal of an aggressive act. Once appraised, the individual then decides how to act next.

According to the GAM, violent video games have both short- and long-term effects. Anderson et al. (2003) found that many studies reported a number of short-term negative effects of playing video games. Sherry's (2001) meta-analysis likewise found that games have some kind of effect on aggression; *however*, the effect is smaller than that produced by watching television. Moreover, in the studies Sherry considered, the treatment time varied from 5 to 75 minutes, making it difficult to determine precisely how long the effect actually lasts. In addition, Giumetti and Markey (2007) found that *only* those with higher levels of anger prior to playing the game were adversely affected, whereas, in Markey and Scherer's (2009) study, a negative effect occurred only in those with elevated levels of psychoticism.

Unsworth and Devilly (2007) also reported that levels of aggression were mediated by the player's feelings immediately prior to playing the game, along with their temperament (disposition toward aggression). Polman, Orobio de Castro and van Aken (2008), for their part, found that actively engaging in a violent video game produced higher levels of aggression than passively watching the same game (in boys but not girls).

Similarly, Ivory, and Kalyanaraman (2007) found that the more immersed an individual was in a game the greater their physiological and self-reported levels of arousal, and aggression. Related to this, Konijn and Bushman (2007) found that boys who felt more immersed in the game, and identified more with the protagonist, exhibited more aggressive behaviour.

There is currently very little literature available on long-term effects of playing violent video games. Möller and Krahé (2009), however, recently conducted a 30 month longitudinal study in which they found links to aggressive behaviour. Likewise, few studies have focused on *online* games (compared to more traditional single-player video games). Having said that, Williams and Skoric's (2005) longitudinal study of MMORPGs (massively multiplayer online role-playing games) found no evidence for the claim that online violent games cause substantial increases in real-world aggression; neither did playing online violent games result in more accepting beliefs about violent behaviours. Nevertheless, any firm conclusions remain speculative (for a more detailed discussion, see Young and Whitty, 2012).

Some writers have suggested that violent video games, such as shooter games, might explain previous school shootings, given that these games lead to strong desensitization effects (Grossman and DeGaetano, 1999). Currently, however, there is no hard evidence to support this claim. Nonetheless, there is research to support the view that playing violent video games can lead to desensitization. As Carnagey, Anderson, and Bushman (2007) point out:

> [T]he term 'desensitization' has been used by scholars, public policy analysts, politicians, and the lay public to mean effects as varied as: (a) an increase in aggressive behavior; (b) a reduction in physiological arousal to real-life violence; (c) a flattening of affective reactions to violence; (d) a reduction in likelihood of helping a violence victim; (e) a reduction in sympathy for a violence victim; (f) a reduction in the sentence for a convicted violent offender, (g) a reduction in the perceived guilt of a violence perpetrator; and (h) a reduction in judged severity of a violence victim's injuries. (p.490)

They propose that a clearer definition of desensitization to violence is "a reduction in emotion-related physiological reactivity to real violence" (p.490). They argue that their definition fits well with cognitive behavioural treatment of phobias, where the point of therapy is to reduce unwanted negative emotional reactions to stimuli. Others too have used this definition when studying desensitization to violence (e.g., Bartholow, Bushman and Sestir, 2006)

It has been found that media violence initially produces emotions such as fear and disgust (Cantor, 2000). With increased play, these emotions have been found to decrease and eventually there is an increase in aggressive approach-related motivational states (Bartholow et al. 2006). In fact, Bartholow et al. argue that the reason why studies find that playing violent video games leads to increased aggressive behaviour and a decrease in helping behaviour is because players become desensitized to violence (see, for example, Anderson, 2004; Anderson and Bushman, 2001; Silvern and Williamson, 1987) In their research, Bartholow et al. found that, compared with gamers who do not play violent video games, gamers who did play showed reduced P300 amplitude and increased P300 latency to non-violent images but not to other equally negative non-violent images.[1]

Others, too, have argued that repeated exposure makes individuals less physiologically responsive to the pain and suffering experienced by victims of violence (Carnagey et al., 2007; Funk, Bechtoldt-Baldacci, Pasold and Baumgartner, 2004). Carnagey et al. (2007) found that participants who played a violent video game for 20 minutes compared with those

---

[1] P300s are event related potential that are understood to be a measure of an individual's reaction to a (perceived to be) meaningful/significant stimulus.

who played non-violent games were less likely to be physiologically aroused by watching real violence. Moreover, participants playing violent video games were more likely than those who played non-violent games to have lower heart rates and galvanic skin responses while watching actual footage of people being beaten, stabbed and shot. It is important to note, however, that while the study found evidence for physiological desensitization it did not then go on to test whether participants were more likely to be aggressive or less likely to engage in helping behaviours. Related to this point, one might conjecture that police officers (and such like) who are regularly exposed to violence are likely to exhibit signs of desensitization without suggesting that they are more likely to be aggressive or less likely to help those in need. Indeed, Hinte (1971) asks us to consider whether techniques for desensitization ought to be part of police recruitment training.

3. CRITIQUING RESEARCH ON THE EFFECTS
OF VIOLENT VIDEO GAMES

Cumberbatch (2004, 2010) has strongly criticized researchers who claim that watching violent media or playing violent video games leads to aggressive acts. He states:

> The real puzzle is that anyone looking at the research evidence in this field could draw any conclusions about the pattern, let alone argue with such confidence and even passion that it demonstrates the harm of violence on television, in film and in video games. While tests of statistical significance are a vital tool of the social sciences, they seem to have been used more often in this field as instruments of torture on the data until it confesses something to justify a publication in a scientific journal. If one conclusion is possible, it is that *the jury is not still out. It's never been in.* Media violence has been subjected to lynch mob mentality with almost any evidence used to prove guilt. (2004, p.34)

To date, meta-analysis conducted on studies drawing from the GAM have found only weak effects (Ferguson, 2007a, 2007b; Sherry, 2001). (Recall how Sherry found that the effects of violent video games were weaker than for television.) Ferguson and Kilburn (2009), for their part, found that the better validated measures of aggression produced the weakest results. Moreover, they found no evidence for the claim that video games produce stronger effects owing to their interactive nature (unlike Polman et al., 2008, noted above). In fact, Ferguson and Rueda (2009) claim the opposite: that playing violent video games can *decrease* hostile feelings and depression. To understand why such contradictory conclusions might be drawn, consider the work of Schmierbach (2010) who found that game characteristics had an important mediating effect of violent content. Schmierbach studied the extent to which game mode – cooperative, competitive, or solo – shaped aggressive cognition. He found that solo players exhibited the most frustration and anger (aggressive affect) when playing against computer-generated opponents, or when having to navigate through difficult parts of the gameplay. In contrast, in competitive gameplay, when combat was against a fellow gamer, task difficulty varied depending on the skill of the opponent, and so frustration diminished and was replaced by aggressive cognition. In contrast, those engaged in cooperative strategies exhibited less aggressive cognition (as perhaps one might expect), although they did show an increase in frustration and aggressive affect. Schmierbach attributed the increase in aggressive cognition shown by those employing competitive strategies to social learning, suggesting that players (particularly men) "feel more rewarded for aggressive play in competitive situations, and that these rewards – rather than frustration – account for increases in violent cognition" (p.270).

Ferguson (2007a) likewise critiqued advocates of the GAM, suggesting that a close reading of these researchers' papers revealed questionable and inconsistent evidence, and that some of the measures of aggression used in previous studies, such as the Taylor Competitive Reaction Time Test, lacked external validity (e.g., Anderson and Dill, 2000). He also claimed that there is a publication bias towards positive results in this area. In his analysis of the 'third' era of video games, he contends that there is no compelling evidence to support the existence of either a correlational or causal relationship between violent gameplay and actual aggressive behaviour. In fact, as intimated earlier, Ferguson (2010) goes so far as to state that estimates for the size of the effect of violent video game content on aggressive behaviour "range from (using r^2 x 100) effectively zero through 2.5%" (p. 74). However, he does maintain that research on aggressive thoughts provides the strongest evidence for a link, although the question still remains as to whether these aggressive thoughts transfer to aggressive behaviours.

In a similar vein, Olson (2004) concluded that, overall, there is little evidence for any link between exposure to violent interactive games and serious real-life violence or crime. Instead, she argues that the strongest childhood predictors of youth violence are involvement in crime, male gender, illegal substance use, physical aggressiveness, family poverty, and antisocial parents. Olson also points out that, for adolescents, peer relationships become more important predictors. What is perhaps more interesting is her argument that most aggressive children do not grow up to be violent adolescents or adults. Conversely, most violent adolescents were not aggressive children. In fact, arguably the most important point made by Olson, which seems to have been ignored within the literature, is her suggestion that violent gameplay may disproportionately affect more vulnerable children – that is, those who lack protective factors such as a nurturing relationship.

As a final point, some scholars warn that concerns about the effects of playing violent video games might move beyond objective scientific examination into the realm of moral panic (e.g., Ferguson, 2010). For Ferguson, this potential moral panic, as well as stemming from the aforementioned publication bias (i.e., the tendency in psychology to publish papers with a positive statistical result over a null result), could also be fuelled by the media (where it is often implied that the concern is *fact*). Politicians, he suggests, draw from these media reports, which yet again perpetuate the moral panic. Instead of focusing on the potential vices of video games, Ferguson encourages researchers to consider what individuals might learn from playing them. He argues that it is plausible to maintain that individuals can learn visuospatial cognitions, information about maths, science and medical diseases from such games. This is because this type of learning does not require internal shifts in personality characteristics. He further states that "video games may be effective in communicating raw data or information, but they aren't effective in transmitting moral beliefs, personality traits, and so forth. Information transfers but personality traits such as aggressiveness do not" (p.76).

In sum, if the conclusions of Ferguson are to be adopted, in conjunction with the lack of clear evidence for a link between violent video game content and actual aggressive behaviour or otherwise detrimental effects, then it would seem that there are no grounds for condemning violent video game content beyond the offense it causes some, or general issues to do with taste.

If this is the case, then reasons for distinguishing between permitted content involving killings, mutilations, torture and murder and other STAs such as rape and paedophilia appear, on the face of it, to be arbitrary because they are equally related to offense caused and questions of taste. Or is there something different about rape and paedophilia, along with other STAs such as necrophilia, incest, bestiality and cannibalism that would cause, even within a virtual context, increased moral concern? In the next section, we consider the findings of psychologists and other researchers studying the ways in which gamers manage offline prohibited behaviours within gamespace.

4. MANAGING VIRTUAL VIOLENCE AND TABOOS

As noted above, research findings on the effects of video game violence on offline behaviour are far from unambiguous; and, to date, any attempt to posit a direct causal link between game content and violent offline behaviour should be regarded as somewhat simplistic, largely uncorroborated, and ultimately contentious.

More recently, the way gamers cope with violent gameplay – referred to by Klimmt, Schmid, Nosper, Hartmann and Vorderer (2008) as *moral management* – has become the focus of research interest. Moral management involves cognitively managing the conflict that potentially arises within the gamer between enjoying the gameplay and any aversion they may have towards the violent acts represented and even virtually engaged in. According to Klimmt et al. (2006):

> [F]indings support the proposition that dealing with moral issues is a cognitive task that players of violent video games have to resolve in order to maintain or enhance their entertainment experience. Therefore, the players' ways to deal with game violence display some similarities to individuals who perform aggressive behavior in real life. (p.325)

Klimmt et al. argue that the same mechanisms of *moral disengagement* (Bandura, 2002) found within perpetrators of real-life violence are often found at work within many individuals who play violent video games. To support this view, Klimmt et al. interviewed ten players of violent video games, asking them to discuss their thoughts and feelings about playing their favourite games, particularly with a mind to the types of strategies used to cope with the violent behaviour and any moral concerns they may have with this. Klimmt et al. identified a number of themes that link to the mechanisms of moral disengagement (e.g., the dehumanization of game characters and the use of euphemistic labelling). Of particular interest, here, is their identification of the themes *Game violence as self-defence* (in which gamers justify their actions in terms of 'kill or be killed') and *Fighting evil: Narrative-normative justification of game violence* (whereby the game narrative positions them as fighting evil, for example). Each of these themes, we contend, is compatible with what Young and Whitty (in press) refer to as the principle of *sanctioned equivalence*.

Sanctioned equivalence holds that certain violent acts – killing, for example – can occur in legitimate or illegitimate ways. A sanctioned equivalent of killing is state authorized execution, or the death of combatants during a war. Torture, has been justified in the past by legitimate authorities (Costanzo, Gerrity and Brinton Lykes, 2007; Soldz, 2008), and in some cases still is; or at least its legitimate use is debated (in the 'ticking bomb' scenario, for example – see Brecher, 2007; Opotow, 2007). The unofficial law of the sea maintains that cannibalism is acceptable, or is at least tolerated, when one's life depends on it and the victim is already dead, or was selected through the mutually agreed drawing of lots. (A similar scenario was famously debated by Fuller in his 1949 paper *The Case of the Speluncean Explorers*.) In real life, passengers of Uruguayan Air Force Flight 571 (which crashed in the Andes Mountains on October 13th, 1972) survived by resorting to cannibalism. All were Catholic and all received absolution from the Catholic Church. However, it is difficult to think of a sanctioned equivalent in the case of rape or necrophilia, or of cases in which one's life depended on an act of incest or bestiality. Sanctioned equivalence differentiates between equivalent outcomes that are either legitimate or illegitimate. All legitimate outcomes are judged to be essentially *instrumental* – a means to an end. On the other hand, actions that do not have sanctioned equivalence appear *pathological* – an end in themselves.

Alternatively, moral management may involve other ways of coping which, by not adhering to the principle of sanctioned equivalence, allow for more 'moral flexibility'. Klimmt et al. identified further themes that give some insight into what these other coping strategies may be – namely, *Game-reality distinction* (it's just a game and therefore not real) and *Game violence as necessary part of (sports-like) performance* (the nature of the game is such that aggressive action is necessary to win). Gamers who justified their actions within the game with reference to these strategies report thinking of game violence as morally irrelevant or, because it is just a game, as not having any *real* consequences. Within the game, however, such violence was often thought of as a necessary part of winning. Whang and Chang (2004) categorized gamers who adopted this type of approach as an *off-real world player*. These players are said to "use every possible means to achieve personal success inside the game world" (p.595), including harming other players – even though they would not do this offline. Related to this point, Shibuya, Sakamoto, Ihori and Yukawa (2008) state: "Players in video games may have few chances to be sympathetic toward victims because players need to win the battle and continue the game" (p.536).

In a similar vein, Glock and Kneer (2009), when commenting on the findings of a study by Ladas (2003), note how gamers seemed "to focus on competition, success, thrill, and the virtual simulation of power and control rather than damaging other persons" (p.153). Glock and Kneer consider this way of thinking about the game (notably, *not* in saliently aggressive terms) to be suggestive of the existence of *differentiated knowledge structures* in those with prolonged violent game exposure when compared to novice gamers. In may be, they surmise, that novice players associate violent video games with aggression because of media coverage to that effect; however, through "repeated exposure to violent digital games, links to game-specific concepts are strengthened, thereby overrunning [media-related] associations to aggression" (p.153). For De Vane and Squire (2008), the idea that prolonged engagement with video game violence may actually lead to less aggression (see Sherry, 2001) suggests that experienced players "develop metacognitive understandings of how violence is represented" within the game (p.267) – namely, as instrumental to the success of the game, or even as immersed within a narrative that extols the principle of sanctioned equivalence (for example). De Vane and Squire go on to note that the meaning players derived from interaction with various media (such as violent video games) must be contextualized. In other words, for researchers to understand the meaning of seemingly or symbolically violent interaction, they must understand what these interactions are taken to mean by those engaged in them within the context in which they occur.

In the next section, we consider the significance of interpretation when managing one's moral stance and, equally, the role of gamer-avatar identity when faced with video game violence and other STAs.

5. THE ROLE OF INTERPRETATION AND IDENTITY IN MANAGING VIRTUAL VIOLENCE AND TABOOS

According to Potter and Tomasello (2003) research into the effects of viewing more traditional media violence (television/films) has tended to concentrate on exposure factors such as whether the perpetrator of the violence was rewarded or punished (Bryant, Carveth and Brown, 1981), or whether the violent act was depicted realistically (Cantor, 1994), or graphically (Ogles and Hoffner, 1987), or even in a humorous way (Gunter, 1985). In addition, mediating factors have concerned gender or age differences (Eron, Huesmann, Lefkowitz and Walder, 1972) or other demographics such as social class (Huesmann, Lagerspetz and Eron, 1984) or ethnicity (Greenberg, 1988), or traits such as aggression (Lagerspetz and Engblom, 1979) or states of arousal (Zillmann, 1971) or frustration (Geen, 1975). Such research, Potter and Tomasello assert, typically adheres to the following model (see Figure 1):

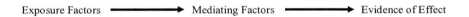

Exposure Factors ⟶ Mediating Factors ⟶ Evidence of Effect

Figure 1. A simple model indicating the role of exposure and mediating factors in accounting for the effects of media violence. Taken from Potter and Tomasello (2003), p.315.

Absent from Figure 1, they point out, is how the viewer *interprets* the violence, which may account for the variation found within the same experimental condition – that is, differences found between participants with similar mediating factors who are assigned to the same task and therefore exposed to the same act of violence presented in the same way. Williams, Yee and Caplan (2008) similarly criticize the General Aggression Model (GAM) and GAM-based research (see Section 2) because, in their view, it does not distinguish between those who seek to be competitive within a game, for example, and achieve personal success, and those who might be playing in order to socialize with a friend. Similarly, Shibuya et al. (2008), after conducting a longitudinal study (involving 10-11 year old children in Japan) concluded that "quality and context of video game violence can be more important than the presence and quantity of violence in the long term" (p.537). They also recognized that how these children interpreted the violent content had not been fully investigated in their study. In fact, the switch in emphasis from the effects of video content on the individual to how the individual extracts meaning from it within a given context is, according to Williams (2005), symptomatic of differences between more traditional social scientists who adopt a quantitative approach and humanists who endorse a more qualitative methodology.

To be clear, Potter and Tomasello are not claiming that exposure/mediating factors have no part to play in the effect viewing violence has on the individual; rather, they argue that it is our interpretation of the act, which may be shaped by the aforementioned factors in terms of meaning and personal significance, that ultimately determines how we react to what we are witnessing. As they explain:

> Whereas demographics, traits, and states all potentially influence how a person interprets the *meaning* of elements in a media portrayal, it is the set of receiver interpretations that most likely influences the probability of an *effect*. Therefore, if we want to explain better the differences in effects, we need to improve our understanding about the interpretive elements that influence participants' reactions to the treatment materials. (2003, p.316; italics added)

Potter and Tomasello discuss the explanatory significance of *receiver interpretations* within the context of film and television; yet we see no reason why this additional factor cannot be incorporated within theories and models looking at the effects of video game violence, including STAs.

In the previous section we discussed the work of Klimmt and colleagues on moral management. Klimmt (and colleagues) identified a number of strategies used by gamers to manage the freedom they have within games to engage in activities that are morally proscribed offline. A gamer, adopting a strategy of moral management, might therefore *interpret* the violence as instrumental to their success at the game, and no more than that, or as having no real-world consequences. Alternatively, the personal meaning the STA is imbued with may be such as to prevent one from either taking part in the specific activity (e.g., torture or rape), or continuing with the gameplay.

How one interprets and interacts with such content has led Juul (2005) to think of video games as '*half-real*': for the way we interact with the game provides some indication of our relation to the game 'in reality'. In such cases, the separation of spaces and, with it, the fiction-reality divide may be blurred. As we have already noted, some players may consider the video game to be just that – a game – and separate more or less completely the online action and representation from offline reality, even in cases of extreme violence and other STAs. However, for some, the half-reality noted by Juul's may mean that the space does provide a means of exploring one's self – how one thinks, feels and wishes to behaviour, including one's moral stance, in various contexts.

Of course, a difference between traditional media violence and video game violence is the level of interaction available to the gamer compared to the viewer of television or film. Hamlen (2011), for example, found that a large (unspecified) percentage of children in her study were motivated to play certain video games because they get to "punch and kill people" (p.537). Hamlen asks us to consider why this is so appealing for some children (a large percentage, apparently), and, based on sales figures, adults as well (it would seem). Of course, it would be a bold claim to say that it is because such gamers (young or old) actually wish to punch and kill people offline. Nevertheless, it is an important question because the personal meaning integral to the interpretation of the violence, as noted by Potter and Tomasello, is likely to be the personal meaning given to a violent act, or other STA, that *I* am engaged in through my avatar.

Thus the interpretation of the act will be influenced by the identity of my character within the game – this is what a soldier, or a dragonslayer, or a serial killer is supposed to do in this situation or even this game (or not, as the case may be). Or this is what even an ordinary citizen can be driven to do when protecting their family.

Krcmar, Farrar and McGloin (2011) found that strength of identification with the character correlated with level of aggression shown whilst playing the video game *Doom 3*. Similarly, Eastin (2006) found that aggression in females increased when identifying with a female character in the first-person shooter game, *Unreal Tournament: Game of the Year Edition*. Hefner, Klimmt and Vorderer (2007), for their part, argued that identification with the character is "an essential element of game enjoyment" (p.40): describing identification "as 'feeling like' or as creating the illusion to 'become' a key person within a computer game's universe" (pp.39-40).

According to Pohl (2008), although emotional involvement is a characteristic of video games, we must differentiate between two types. On the one hand, we tend to play a game in order (to try) to win the game, and this produces the sort of emotional involvement that is automatic and spontaneous. But there is another level of emotional involvement that is more akin to gamer-avatar identification; for we are also:

> ...concerned about the avatar's fate, not only because the avatar is our representative in the fictional world and the instrument we need in order to actually play and win the game, but because we feel for him, we identify with his concerns and want to know how the story turns out for him and for us. (pp.100-101)

Depending on the game mechanics, one's avatar may be more developed and so more entrenched within the pre-determined narrative of the game than in others. The degree to which one is free to express oneself within the gamespace will therefore always be, to a greater or lesser extent, constrained by the game mechanics: this is no more evident than in terms of how much one can 'customize' one's avatar, or the choices and types of engagement available. Arguably, the most restrictive game mechanics are to be found in single-player games, although such games may still offer considerable scope (e.g., *Heavy Rain*), and so are likely to include 'events' that may impact on one's identity with the avatar, particularly when played in their most extreme and violent form.

With more traditional media, the relationship between audience and characters/events has been understood to be largely passive and *dyadic* – in so far as "viewers or media users perceive a social distinction between themselves (the observers) and the media characters" (Klimmt, Hefner and Vorderer, 2009, p.352). However, according to Liebes and Katz (1990), dyadic identification operates on three levels, each, we argue, increasingly blurring the distinction between self and other. One may simply *like* the fictional character, finding certain characteristics appealing, or one may see oneself as *being like* (similar to) the character, or one may desire *to be like* (to model oneself on) the person from fiction. According to Cohen (2001), these varying levels of identification manifest perhaps the extent to which one is willing to replace one's own perspective with another's, and in the process forget, however temporarily, oneself: for "[t]hrough identification with characters in books, films, and television, we extend our emotional horizons and social perspectives" (p.249). Moreover, for Oatley (1994), an important antecedent for identification is that the individual understands the intentions of the character – their goals within the context of the unfolding drama – and can experience something of what the character feels when these goals/intentions succeed or are quashed.

Thus, with *monadic* identification, when we feel for the character/avatar, we feel for ourselves. Hefner et al. (2007) further state that part of the enjoyment experienced through identification is when one finds certain attributes or characteristics of the fictional character appealing – perhaps because they match attributes and characteristics one wishes to possess or at least try out. In the former case, by identifying with the object of fiction, even temporarily, one reduces the discrepancy between how one typically perceives oneself and how one wishes to be perceived; and according to Hefner and colleagues, this discrepancy-reduction creates an enjoyable experience.

6. THE SIGNIFICANCE OF IDENTITY TO HOW ONE INTERPRETS VIOLENCE AND TABOOS

In order to foster monadic identification, the fictional character must possess a degree of attractiveness and personal desirability, including what it (the character) does or what the game mechanics afford it (afford oneself, in effect). We are reminded of Turkle's (1995) comment: when one plays, one may play who one wants to be or even who one does not want to be. She argued that playing out different characters online provides individuals with the opportunity to explore and examine their own identity. It may be, then, that by way of exploration, I am attracted to the character and narrative of a particular game, even in cases of STAs, or precisely because the game involves STAs. Conversely, identity-based interpretation may cause me to question whether it is what any of these characters *should* do (and therefore what *I* should do in this context). Depending, then, on the situation I find myself in, the narrative, and whether the principle of sanctioned equivalence is being adhered to (for example), normative consideration may increase my enjoyment of the game – this is precisely how a highly skilled special operative would engage the 'enemy' and even interrogate them – or it may *decrease* it: after all, I may not like the idea of having to torture, even 'in character'. This last point illustrates the heightened complexity of identification with a video game character – namely, the extent to which I not only identify with the character but with the *activity* I (*qua* my character) am undertaking or being asked to undertake.

To illustrate the significance of this, consider a study by Bösche (2009) who recruited participants inexperienced at playing violent video games to test two "paradigmatically opposite perspective" (p.145) on the effects of such games on performance (habitual players were not selected, nor anyone who had played within a week of the study). Bösche was interested in whether playing a violent video game would, because of one's normal aversive reaction to even virtual violence, inhibit task performance compared to an equivalent task in a non-violent game (one perspective), or whether the virtual violence would be perceived as harmless, fun and exciting, thereby enhancing performance compared to the non-virtual equivalent (alternative perspective). What he found was that performance was enhanced in the 'extremely violent' condition (compared to non-violent or moderately violent conditions). From this, he tentatively concluded that violent video games "are perceived as an essentially harmless acting-out of playful fighting behaviour" (p.149).

The idea that virtual violence is essentially mock violence, what Bösche refers to as a kind of digitized *rough-and-tumble play*, seems to accord well with reports on the attitude of a number of players of such games. We have seen how Klimmt (and colleagues) identified the view held by some gamers that violence is "just part of the game" or "necessary for successful performance" as a strategy of moral management. It maybe, then, that, in certain violent games, the violence *is* typically perceived to be a kind of digitized rough-and-tumble play, easily distinguished from real violence. However, the 'extreme violence' depicted by Bösche in his study was of a cartoon rabbit being hit over the head with a hammer. Contact with the head produced sounds of pain and the head was dismembered. Such an act, or similar, could easily feature in violent video games; but it also seems quite simplistic compared to the sorts of violence depicted in many modern video games. Compare the fate of Bösche's rabbit to victims in *Manhunt* (for example) who may be 'dispatched' by being bludgeoned to death with a baton, baseball bat or hammer, or stabbed through the neck with a crowbar or more conventionally with a hunting knife. Missing from Bösche's example, we contend, is both narrative and a virtual agent to carry out the violence.

In Bösche's study, the participant simply activated the virtual hammer; there was no avatar in place to wield it. These differences are important, we maintain, because they increase (potentially facilitate) the possibility for gamer identification with the character. To illustrate, consider the description by Crick (2011):

> [W]hen playing in first-person mode..., the player might notice a shadow that follows the avatar's movements, and they will also see the avatar's reflection when looking through a mirror. Such details... reinforce the player's sense of being inside the game world and not merely acting on it. (p.250)

For some gamers, identification may be minimal; its purpose to function purely as a point of agency within the space – what Newman (2002) refers to as *vehicular embodiment*. Similarly, Fuller and Jenkins (1995) describe avatars as offering "traits that are largely capacities for action, fighting skills, modes of transportation, preestablished goals...[In effect,] little more than a cursor which mediates the player's relationship to the story" (p. 61, cited in Crick, 2011). On the other hand, and as Crick points out, "the stylized designs of iconic avatars, such as Lara Croft in the third-person game Tomb Raider or player-customized designs... may play an important role in helping the player to identify with the avatar, heightening their affective response to the game" (p.250).

Wissmath, Weibel and Groner (2009), by drawing on the work of Green and Brock (2000; see also Gerrig, 1993), refer to this transition as *transportation theory,* which they use to describe how the media user is drawn away from their own physical location into the narrative of the fictional (or virtual) world. Transportation theory, they inform us, promotes the idea that the gamer "plunges in the world of a narrative by suspending real-world facts" (p.117). Moreover, an important antecedent to experiencing transportation is identification with characters immersed within the narrative. Cohen (2001), however, offers a caveat to this heightened enjoyment through identification – namely, that it may reduce one's ability to adopt a critical stance towards (in this context) what is being represented and what one is doing within the gamespace. However, in response, we would argue that whatever critical stance (or lack thereof) is adopted, one must understand it not only within the context of the game, but in relation to how the gamer interprets the representation and action.

Returning to the Bösche study, it is interesting to note that habitual players were not included. This could be for a number of methodological reasons, of course. However, it worth considering the fact that as the participants were not regular gamers they would not have had the opportunity to identify (even potentially) with characters (had there been any), or become accustomed to the association. In addition, Bösche focused on what might be described as more conventional video game violence. Might he consider STAs such as rape (as it is possible to carry out in the Japanese video game, *RapeLay*), paedophilia, necrophilia (etc.) to be examples of digitized rough-and-tumble play?

With the advent of video game technology, not only has the relationship between audience (or gamer) and media become more (inter)active but also the distinction between gamer and character (protagonist) reduced, perhaps even eliminated. Consequently, comprehending the characters goals should be easier to manage when the character's goals are the gamer's goals. In the words of Klimmt et al.:

> Instead of providing opportunities to follow autonomous characters' actions, playing video games simulates the circumstances of *being* a media character (or holding a social role), for instance, of being a war hero or a police officer. Video games thus seem to facilitate a nondyadic or *monadic* user-character relationship in the sense that players do not perceive the game (main) character as a social entity distinct from themselves, but experience a merging of their own self and the game protagonist. This understanding of a monadic user-character relationship converges with the concept of *identification*. (2009, p.354)

Identification is expressed by Klimmt et al. as a set of increased associations between the gamer's self-concept and certain selective concepts which contingently characterize the online protagonist (e.g., courage, agility, honour, charisma, social status and physical and sexual prowess). In addition, identification is typically defined as a *temporary* state of emotional and cognitive connection with the character (Oatley, 1999). As Klimmt et al. (2009) explain:

> For most people, their image of themselves under the condition of identification with James Bond [for example] would differ substantially from their usual self-image. After game exposure, internal processes (e.g., cognitions about the working day) and external cues (e.g., friends addressing the media user by his/her real name instead of saying ''007'') will quickly realter the situational self-concept toward the original configuration. (p.356)

Typically one's self-concept differs substantially from the protagonist featured in video games, especially violent ones; and, typically, on exiting the game, one's original self-concept is restored and is no longer aligned with, say, '007'. Nevertheless, it is our view that for those whose identity merges strongly with their gameworld character – perhaps because the character embodies characteristics that match those sought by the gamer – the restoration of their original self-concept makes salient to them the very discrepancies that mark out the protagonist from themselves (see Section 7 for further discussion on this point). Discrepancies that exist between one's self offline and one's self *qua* online character, especially in relation to those characteristics that may be valued – strength, honour, courage etc. – are made salient as a *loss*: one experiences a loss of strength, a loss of honour, a loss of courage, etc.

If this discrepancy is salient when leaving the gaming environment of single-player games, where often one is the sole gamer, and therefore socially isolated, then how much more, we contend, is there scope for discrepancy between one's online and offline self when engaged in social games constitutive of MMORPGs.

7. PROBLEMATIC INTERNET USE

The potential for disparity between those aspects of oneself presented online compared to offline is implicated within a more general cognitive-behavioural model of *problematic Internet use* (PIU) proposed by Davis (2001).[2] According to Davis, psychosocial problems (such as depression or loneliness) may make an individual vulnerable to certain maladaptive thoughts about the self – such as "I am only good on the Internet" or "I am worthless offline, but online I am someone" or even "I am a failure when I am offline" (p.191) (see also Montag, Jurkiewicz and Reuter, 2010, for a discussion on 'self-directedness' as a predictor of PIU). The resulting need for the kind of "social contact and reinforcement obtained online results in an increased desire to remain in a virtual social life" (Davies, 2001, p.188). Such maladaptive, Internet-biased, thoughts and behaviours are deemed by Davis to be a necessary, proximate cause of PIU.

By way of an amendment to Davis' model, Caplan (2003, 2005) proposed that the likelihood of PIU was further mediated by *a preference for online socializing*. As Caplan (2003) explains:

> [P]reference for online social interaction is a cognitive individual-difference construct characterized by beliefs that one is safer, more efficacious, more confident, and more comfortable with online interpersonal interactions and relationships than with traditional FtF [face-to-face] social activities. (p. 629)

For Caplan, then, it is not just that those vulnerable to PIU hold more positive views of themselves when interacting in an online environment, or that they enjoy being in that environment because of its perceived personal and social benefits; more than this, they *prefer* interacting online. In other words, the individual's desire to be online, as noted by Davis, quickly turns into a preference to be online, which comes at a cost of relegating their offline social engagements to a lower level of personal importance – in some cases, perhaps even discarding them altogether.

Caplan, Williams and Yee (2009) note how relatively little attention has been given to MMORPGs in relation to PIU (some exceptions being Meerkerk, Van Den Eijnden, and Garretsen, 2006; Morahan-Martin and Schumacher, 2000; and Ng and Wiemer-Hastings, 2005). Yet these games are of relevance to the study of PIU not only because they are an increasingly popular form of Internet activity but, equally (perhaps even because of this), they

---

[2] Davis (2001) uses the term pathological Internet use; however, in more recent years, the word 'problematic' has typically replaced 'pathological' within the literature discussing his original model and suggested amendments to it (see Caplan, 2002). This convention will be adhered to here. In addition, Davis distinguishes between specific problematic Internet use and generalised problematic Internet use. Most discussion on PIU has tended to focus on generalised problematic Internet use; only occasionally is this referred to as GPIU (see, for example, Caplan, 2010). Here, PIU refers to what Davis understood to be generalised problematic Internet use.

promote interpersonal engagement and potentially complex forms of social interaction which are an established and even sought after feature of the gaming experience. According to Liu and Peng (2009), PIU produces *negative life consequences*. Based on prior research on MMORPGs (see Charlton and Danforth, 2007; Chen, Weng, Su, Wu, and Yang, 2003; Suhail and Bargees, 2006; Young, 2004), these negative life consequences have been categorized into the following three types: (i) *physical problems* (such as fatigue, physical pain, reduced sleep, missing meals), (ii) *personal life problems* (such as conflicts with friends or family, or generally low social engagement, or decreased time management skills), and *professional/academic problems* (such as missing work or school, or a deterioration in one's performance) (adapted from Liu and Peng, 2009, p.1306). Liu and Peng also integrated Davis' 'maladaptive cognitions' and Caplan's 'preference for online socializing' within their own hypothesized construct, which they call *preference for virtual life* (PVL), defined as: "one's cognitions or beliefs that one will perform better, feel better about oneself, and perceive [oneself] to be better treated by others in the online virtual game world than in offline or real life" (2009, p.1307).

Liu and Peng found that those scoring high(er) on PVL were more likely to experience psychological dependency on MMORPG playing. Caplan et al. (2009) likewise found strong predictive associations between PIU and online social behaviour. This, Caplan anticipated, was owed to MMORPGs high degree of social engagement. Interestingly, Jansz, Avis and Vosmeer (2010) found that males (including boys) scored higher on social motivation to play the online game, *Sims 2*, than females (including girls). Jansz et al. surmised that this was because males use the game as a means of socialising whereas females perhaps prefer to use other means. Across different types of online games, Stetina, Kothgassner, Lehenbauer and Kryspin-Exner (2011) found that MMORPG users showed more problematic gaming behaviour, symptoms of depression, and lower levels of self-esteem than gamers who played online shooter games or real-time strategy games.[3] In fact, Ng and Wiemer-Hastings (2005) argued that it is the increased social element associated with *online* multiplayer games that attracts the more 'hard core' player, such that players of these games are more likely to develop symptoms characteristic of the negative life consequences (noted above) than offline players.

In a longitudinal study, Lemmens, Valkenburg, and Peter (2011) found that social competence, self-esteem and loneliness were significant predictors of pathological gaming (even six months after the initial trial began), but that loneliness was also a *consequence* of the pathology. They surmised that "[a]lthough playing online games may temporarily reduce negative feelings associated with social deficiencies, pathological gaming does little to facilitate the development or maintenance of real-life contacts" (p.150). Thus, even if pathological gaming requires an antecedent detriment in one's psychosocial competence, an unfortunate consequence of the pathology is likely to be the further deterioration, if not complete abandonment, of one's offline relationships; what Putnam (2000) referred to as *social capital*.

In addition, more specific game-related variables, such as high immersion motivation and use of voice technology (as opposed to text-based communication), have been positively associated with PIU. Immersion motivation was seen to support the view that individuals

---

[3] Smahel, Blinka & Ledabyl (2008) report that gamers spend more time playing MMORPGs than other games (see also Peters & Malesky, 2008).

were engaging in unhealthy escapism (see Yee, 2006a, 2006b, 2007), thereby using MMORPGs to avoid more (perceived to be) stressful face-to-face encounters, and so further reinforcing their acquired preference for online socialising, or even Liu and Peng's broader PVL (see also Calleja, 2010). The use of voice technology to communicate within the MMORPG was seen to facilitate further the player's interpersonal engagement, and so strengthen their sense of online community. Williams, Caplan and Xiong (2007) reported higher levels of trust and an increased strength of relationship amongst groups using voice technology compared to text. Higher levels of happiness and lower levels of loneliness were also reported when engaging in online activities, leading the authors to suggest a displacement of the aforementioned social capital away from more traditional offline relationships and social interactions towards online engagements. However, Wadley, Gibbs and Benda (2010) found voice technology was beneficial only in cases of small groups who already knew each other. In larger groups consisting of more unfamiliar co-players, they found that difficulties could arise in knowing who was communicating; with too many people talking, there occurred the increased likelihood of confusion and congestion. Group cohesion is also lost if some players choose not to use voice technology – as this may arouse suspicion. Alternatively, it may be that some prefer text if they do not know who they are playing with.

The scope for differing forms of social interaction is evident in MMORPG; but how is this related to the individual's sense of self? Liu and Peng offer further commentary:

> [B]y identifying with game characters who can achieve various unusual goals in MMOGs [massively multiplayer online games], gamers may regard themselves as more valuable and successful people in the game world than in the offline real world, and this may lead to unpleasant feelings or withdrawal symptoms when MMOG playing is suddenly unavailable. (2009, p.1307)

Hsu, Wen and Wu (2009) reported that MMORPG addiction is associated with the player's motivation to develop their character (in order to progress within the game). If I identify strongly with my avatar then the avatar's progression and increased status become my progression and increased status (unless my aim is *solely* to win the game; in which case, avatar progression and status may be viewed as instrumental to that goal and nothing more). Hsu et al. also found MMORPG addiction to be associated with emotional attachment to one's avatar, and, on a more communal level, to a strong sense of belonging and obligation to the virtual group.

The gamer, in identifying with the gaming avatar, recognizes or accepts aspects of the avatar's features as representative of their own self-concept, or even as the virtual embodiment of an ideal *possible self* (Markus and Nurius, 1986)[4]. This is particularly so when game mechanics allow for the extensive *customization* of one's default avatar: for, as Boellstorff (2008) notes (in the context of *Second Life*), very little is left to chance or randomization; instead, one can assume "near-total intentionality with regard to virtual embodiment" (p.129). Boellstorff further states that such intentional (sometimes time

---

[4] According to Markus and Nurius, possible selves are significant, personalized, yet ultimately social representations of ourselves that we either aspire to be like or fear becoming. They are intimately connected to our now selves (our current self-concept), and represent our "hopes, fears and fantasies" (1986, p.954), derived from what we know of ourselves and the society in which we live. Possible selves are also understood to regulate – qua motivate or deter – future behaviour and constitute a means of evaluating and interpreting the status of our now selves.

consuming) customization makes one's self-concept/possible self transparent to others; for as a participant in his research commented: "I've come to observe that the outward appearance really does communicate a lot about who you are, because it is made up of conscious choices about how you want to present yourself" (p.130). By way of a caveat, however, it may also be the case that the avatar is understood simply as an object one controls within the particular space – instrumental to one's being there, as it were. So, whilst there may exist valid cases of, for example, online gender swapping occurring so that players can explore different genders (Hussain and Griffiths, 2008), we must also accept that, for some, this may not be the case.[5] As Huh and Williams (2010) note: "many male players have quipped that they play a female avatar because it is a pleasing visual object, not a source of identification" (p.170).

Nevertheless, the manner and extent of the identification with the virtual character is an important factor that should be considered within any explanation of gamer interaction, both on- and offline – because it has important implications for the gamer's psychological and, by way of a corollary, moral well-being also. To understand how, in the next section we discuss the notion of *psychological parity* – that is, how gamers cope with changes to the way they are represented or represent themselves in these divergent spaces and, as a consequence, how they act. As ever, of particular interest are those spaces that afford actions that are prohibited offline.

8. PSYCHOLOGICAL PARITY: A NEW RESEARH TOPIC

A critical aspect of engaging in video game violence, including all manner of ills (STAs), or in fact any prolonged engagement within a virtual world in which one's virtual personal – *qua* self-concept – is somehow altered (likely enhanced, perhaps in the guise of one's ideal possible self), is not whether such acts violate one's offline moral values *per se*, but whether they impact negatively on how one conceives of and experiences oneself *across* these potentially diverse spaces; what Young and Whitty (2010, 2011, in press) refer to as *psychological parity*. Psychological parity amounts to a continuity of self across spaces that is both conceptual and experiential (Young & Whitty, 2011). In seeking to maintain psychological parity, there is a risk that some gamers will seek continuity of self across virtual/non-virtual domains and, importantly, between what are incommensurable psychological identities (serial killer – university lecturer, for example). Ultimately, this may lead the gamer to favour and even fixate on their virtual persona, resulting in the psychological dominance of the virtual over the non-virtual – a persona, that if constructed around violence and STAs is certainly incommensurate with our offline world. If the virtual identity transfers across domains into a world where violence and other taboo violation is morally and perhaps legally proscribed, then this has potential dire consequences for the individual.

To clarify, we are not advocating that the university lecturer would become an offline serial killer simply because he/she identified with that character in a video game. What we are saying, is that the gamer may identify with certain characteristics of the virtual character and/or the moral freedoms afforded within that space. On leaving this space, the gamer

---

[5] For further research on gender-related issues, see Greenberg, Sherry, Lachlan, Lucas and Holmstrom (2010); Jenson and de Castell (2010); and Williams, Consalvo, Caplan and Yee (2009).

experiences a change in themselves: the characteristics of the virtual persona and the freedoms once available are now absent. This absence is made salient as a loss. How the individual copes with this sense of loss has important implications for their psychological and, potentially, moral well-being. Conversely, and in its own way unfortunate, if the allure of these virtual characteristics (etc.) leads one away from the offline world towards the virtual world of gamespace, then the motivation will be to spend more and more time in that space – where one's identity and what one is permitted to do are congruent. Of course, divergent 'spaces' continue to exist, and indeed existed long before cyberspace; and in these non-virtual spaces one can be a different self (Gergen, 1991). As such, the parity issue is not unique to the era of cyberspace. Nevertheless, what cyberspace affords – namely, the potential for changes to oneself and how one interacts – can be far more extreme and immediate than has typically been available prior to the existence of this technology: something Young and Whitty (2010, 2011, in press) call *virtual immediacy*.

To date, there is limited research that specifically targets the issue of psychological parity when engaged in STAs (see Whitty et al., 2011, for a rare example of such research). However, according to newspaper reports, the psychological effects of the disparity between virtual and non-virtual space are beginning to emerge. The 'allure of the virtual' and the psychological impact this can have on the individual was felt shortly after the release of James Cameron's *Avatar* (Piazza, 2010; Sandler, 2010). Apparently, movie-goers began experiencing depression and suicidal thoughts after disengaging with the film's immersive environment. To be emotionally moved by fiction, of course, is nothing new (Young, 2010), although to feel (allegedly) depressed and suicidal may seem like an extreme reaction. Even more extreme is a rare condition discussed by Ballon and Leszcz (2007) that has some relevance here: *cinematic neurosis*, which amounts to "the development of anxiety, somatic responses, dissociation, and even psychotic symptoms after watching a film" (p.211). Ballon and Leszcz note how persons vulnerable to the condition "include those who have issues with their identity" (p.212) which can be influenced by the symbolic, often horror-based, nature of the film narrative. Perhaps, cinematic neurosis is an extreme clinical manifestation of the much more ubiquitous issue of divergent spaces and psychological parity alluded to above. By 'ubiquitous issue' we mean simply that the need for parity is not elicited solely by horror symbolism or taboo violation, but by any space in which the discrepancy between the possibilities for action within that space and the space one typically occupies is more extreme.

The degree of immersion that is becoming possible with advances in virtual technology is also of concern: for if such effects as those described above (in the *Avatar* example) are being felt by someone in the relatively passive position of 'movie-goer', then how much more might they be felt when one is actively engaged as a character in virtual space? How much greater would the psychological effects of *Avatar* be, for example, if one could be a character immersed in the filmspace and so interact with others in that space and develop the narrative?

The need to maintain psychological parity is particularly acute, we suggest, in MMORPGs (compared to single-player games), because of the social element integral to these gameplays. Here, one has a greater opportunity to develop aspects of one's self-concept and engage in real social interactions.

The loss of these developing aspects of self, when one re-enters what may be for some a socially impoverished offline world, is therefore all the more salient and the motivation to return to the virtual world, and for longer, even greater.

Alternatively, as alluded to earlier, one may be motivated to enact these characteristics offline which, in the case of STAs, is extremely problematic.

CONCLUSION

In this chapter we have discussed the question of violent video game content and other STAs, as well as those factors which we consider important to how an individual manages the moral freedoms afforded by gamespace. In essence, what we have argued is that there is nothing morally problematic with virtual acts of violence in and of themselves. Importantly, however, the potential moral ramifications of this type of content are better informed by a greater understanding of the psychological mechanisms involved in coping with virtual engagement characteristic of STAs then any moral arguments for the permissibility *per se* (or not) of this content. By understanding the strategies used by gamers to cope with virtual representations and interactions that are typically contrary to that which is permissible offline, we can build a picture of moral management and psychological coping that will provide clearer, testable hypotheses to aid the further develop of our understanding of those factors which impact on the moral well-being of gamers, or anyone who regularly transcend the divide between the virtual and non-virtual.

REFERENCES

Anderson, C. A. (1997). Effects of violent movies and trait irritability on hostile feelings and aggressive throughts. *Journal of Personality and Social Psychology, 45,* 293-305.

Anderson, C. A. (2004). An update on the effects of violent video games. *Journal of Adolescence, 27,* 113-122.

Anderson, C. A., Berkowitz, L., Donnerstein, E., Huesmann, L. R., Johnson, J. D., Linz, D., Malamuth, N. M., and Wartella, E. (2003). The influence of media violence on youth. *Psychological Science in the Public Interest, 4*(3), 81-110.

Anderson, C. A., and Bushman, B. J. (2002). Human Aggression. *Annual Review of Psychology, 53,* 27-51.

Anderson, C. A., and Dill, K. E. (2000). Video games and aggressive thoughts, feelings, and behavior in the laboratory and in life. *Journal of Personality and Social Psychology, 78,* 772-790.

Ballon, B., and Leszcz, M. (2007). Horror Films: Tales to Master Terror or Shapers of Trauma? *American Journal of Psychotheraphy, 61*(2), 211-230.

Bandura, A. (2002). Selective moral disengagement in the exercise of moral agency. *Journal of Moral Education, 31*(2), 101-119.

Bartholow, B. D., Bushman, B. J., and Sestir, M. A. (2006). Chronic violent video game exposure and desensitization to violence: Behavioural and event-related brain potential data. *Journal of Experimental Social Psychology, 42,* 532-539.

Boellstorff, T. (2008). *Coming of Age in Second Life: An Anthropologist Explores the Virtually Human.* Princeton: Princeton University Press.

Bösche, W. (2009).Violent Content Enhances Video Game Performance. *Journal of Media Psychology, 21*(4), 145-150.

Brecher, B. (2007). *Torture and the ticking bomb*. Malden, MA.: Blackwell.

Bryant, J., Carveth, R.A., and Brown, D. (1981). Television viewing and anxiety: An experimental examination. *Journal of Communication, 31*(1), 106-119.

Bushman, B.J., and Anderson, C.A. (2001). Is it time to pull the plug on the hostile versus instrumental aggression dichotomy? *Psychological Review, 108,* 273-279.

Calleja, G. (2010). Digital Games and Escapism. *Games and Culture, 5*(4) 335-353.

Cantor, J. (1994). Fright reactions to mass media. In J. Bryant and D. Zillman (Eds.), *Media effects: Advances in theory and research* (pp.213-245). Hillsdale, NJ: Erlbaum.

Cantor, J. (2000). Media violence. *Journal of Adolescent Health, 27*(2), 30-34.

Caplan, S. E. (2002). Problematic Internet use and psychosocial well-being: Development of a theory-based cognitive-behavioral measure. *Computers in Human Behavior, 18,* 533-575.

Caplan, S. E. (2003). Preference for online social interaction: A theory of problematic Internet use and psychosocial well-being. *Communication Research, 30,* 625-648.

Caplan, S. E. (2005). A social skill account of problematic internet use. *Journal of Communication, 55,* 721-736.

Caplan, S.E. (2010). Theory and measurement of generalized problematic Internet use: A two-step Approach. *Computers in Human Behavior, 26* (2010) 1089-1097.

Caplan, S., Williams, D., and Yee, N. (2009). Problematic Internet use and psychosocial well-being among MMO players. *Computers in Human Behavior, 25,* 1312-1319.

Carnagey, N.L., Anderson, C.A., and Bushman, B.J. (2007). The effects of video game violence on physiological desensitization to real-life violence. *Journal of Experimental Social Psychology, 43,* 489-496.

Charlton, J. P., and Danforth, I. D. W. (2007). Distinguishing addiction and high engagement in the context of online game playing. *Computers in Human Behavior, 23,* 1531-1548.

Chen, S. H., Weng, L. Z., Su, Y. R., Wu, H. M., and Yang, P. F. (2003). Development of a Chinese Internet addiction scale and its psychometric study. *Chinese Journal of Psychology, 45,* 279-294.

Cohen, J. (2001). Defining Identification: A Theoretical Look at the Identification of Audiences With Media Characters. *Mass Communication and Society, 4*(3), 245-264.

Costanzo, M., Gerrity, E., and Brinton Lykes, M. (2007). Psychologists and the Use of Torture in Interrogations. *Analysis of Social Issues and Public Policy, 7*(1), 7-20.

Crick, T (2011). The Game Body: Toward a Phenomenology of Contemporary Video Gaming. *Games and Culture, 6*(3), 245-258.

Cumberbatch, G. (2004). Video Violence: Villain or victim? A review of the research evidence concerning media violence and its effects in the real world with additional reference to video games. *A report prepared for the Video Standards Council* (pp.1-44). Retrieved September 14, 2010 from: http://www.xlq50.dial.pipex.com/sections/downloads/pdfs/Video%20Violence%202004.pdf.

Cumberbatch, G. (2010). Effects. In The Media and introduction. (third edition) (pp.354-368). Harlow, England: Pearson.

Davis, R. A. (2001). A cognitive-behavioral model of pathological Internet use. *Computers in Human Behavior, 17,* 187-195.

De Vane, B., and Squire, K.D. (2008). The Meaning of Race and Violence in Grand Theft Auto: San Andreas. *Games and Culture*, *3*(3-4), 264-285.

Eastin, M. (2006). Video game violence and the female game player: Self- and opponent-gender effects on presence and aggressive thoughts. *Human Communication Research*, *32*(3), 351-372.

Eron, L. D., Huesmann, L. R., Lefkowitz, M. M., and Walder, L. D. (1972). Does television violence cause aggression? *American Psychologist*, *27*, 253-63.

Ferguson, C. J. (2007a). Evidence for publication bias in video game violence effects literature: A meta-analytic review. *Aggression and Violent Behavior, 12,* 470-482.

Ferguson, C.J. (2007b). The good, the bad and the ugly: A meta-analytic review of positive and negative effects of violent video games. *Psychiatric Quarterly*, *78*(4), 309-316.

Ferguson, C. J. (2010). Blazing angels or resident evil? Can violent video games be a force for good? *Review of General Psychology, 14*(2), 68-81.

Ferguson, C.J., and Kilburn, J. (2009). The public health risks of media violence: A meta-analytic review. *Journal of Pediatrics, 154,* 759-763.

Ferguson, C.J., and Rueda, S. M. (2009). The Hitman Study: Violent video game exposure effects on aggressive behavior, hostile feelings and depression. *European Psychologist, 15*(2), 99-108.

Fuller, L. (1949). The Case of the Speluncean Explorers. *Harvard Law Review*, *62*(4), 616-645.

Fuller, M., and Jenkins, H. (1995). Nintendo and New World Travel Writing: A Dialogue. In S. G. Jones (Ed.), *Cybersociety: Computer-mediated communication and community* (pp. 57-72). London: Sage Publishers.

Funk, J. B., Bechtoldt-Baldacci, H., Pasold, T., and baumgartner, J. (2004). Violence exposure in real-life, video games, television, movies, and the internet: Is there desensitisation? *Journal of Adolescence, 27*, 23-39.

Geen, R.G. (1975). The meaning of observed violence: Real vs fictional violence and consequent effects on aggression and emotional arousal. *Journal of Research in Personality*, *9*, 270-281.

Gergen, K. J. (1991) *The Saturated Self.* New York: Basic Books.

Gerrig, R. J. (1993). *Experiencing narrative worlds.* New Haven: Yale University Press.

Giumetti, G. W., and Markey, P. M. (2007). Violent video games and anger as predictors of aggression. *Journal of Research in Personality, 41*(6), 1234-1243.

Glock, S., and Kneer, J. (2009). Game Over? The Impact of Knowledge about Violent Digital Games on the Activation of Aggression-Related Concepts. *Journal of Media Psychology, 21*(4), 151-160.

Green, M. C., & Brock, T. C. (2000). The role of transportation in the persuasiveness of public narratives. *Journal of Personality and Social Psychology, 79*(5), 701-721.

Greenberg, B.S. (1988). Some uncommon television images and the drenched hypothesis. In S. Oskamp (Ed.), Applied *Social Psychology Annual, vol. 8: Television as a social issue* (pp.88-102). Beverly Hills, CA.: Sage Publications.

Greenberg, B. S., Sherry, J., Lachlan, K., Lucas, K., and Holmstrom, A. (2010). Orientations to video games among gender and age groups. *Simulation and Gaming, 41*(2), 238-259.

Grossman, D., and DeGaetano, G. (1999). *Stop teaching our kids to kill: A call to action against TV, movie and video game violence.* New York: Crown.

Gunter, B. (1985). *Dimensions of television violence*. Aldershot, UK: Gower.

Hamlen, K.R. (2011). Children's choices and strategies in video games. *Computers in Human Behavior, 27*(1), 532-539.

Hefner, D., Klimmt, C., and Vorderer, P. (2007). Identification with the player character as determinant of video game enjoyment. In L. Ma, R. Nakatsu, and M. Rauterberg (Eds.), *Proceedings of ICEC 2007, 6th International Conference on Entertainment Computing*, 39-48.

Hinte, F. (1971). Should desensitization techniques be part of police recruit training? *Group Psychotherapy and Psychodrama, 24*(3-4), 107-110.

Hsu, S. H., Wen, M. H., and Wu, M. C. (2009). Exploring user experiences as predictors of MMORPG addiction. *Computers and Education, 53*, 990-998.

Huesmann, L. R., Lagerspetz, K., and Eron, L. D. (1984). Intervening variables in the TV violence-aggression relation: Evidence from two countries. *Developmental Psychology, 20*(5), 746-777.

Huh, S., and Williams, D. (2010). Dude Looks Like a Lady: Gender Swapping in an Online Game. In W.S. Bainbridge (Ed.). *Online worlds: Convergence of the real and the virtual* (pp.161-174). London: Springer.

Hussain, Z., and Griffiths, M.D. (2008). Gender Swapping and Socializing in Cyberspace: An Exploratory Study. *CyberPsychology and Behavior, 11*, 47-53.

Ivory, J.D., and Kalyanaraman, S. (2007). The Effects of Technological Advancement and Violent Content in Video Games on Players' Feelings of Presence, Involvement, Physiological Arousal, and Aggression. *Journal of Communication, 57*, 532-555.

Jansz, J., Avis, C., and Vosmeer, M. (2010). Playing The Sims 2: An exploration of gender differences in players' motivations and patterns of play. *New Media and Society, 12*(2), 235-251.

Jenson, J., and de Castell, S. (2010). Gender, Simulation, and Gaming: Research Review and Redirections. *Simulation and Gaming, 41*(1) 51-71.

Juul, J. (2005). *Half-Real: Video Games between Real Rules and Fictional Worlds*. Cambridge, Mass.: MIT Press.

Klimmt, C., Hefner, D., and Vorderer, P. (2009). The Video Game Experience as "True" Identification: A Theory of Enjoyable Alterations of Players' Self-Perception. *Communication Theory, 19*, 351-373.

Klimmt, C., Schmid, H. Nosper, A., Hartmann, T., and Vorderer, P. (2006). How players manage moral concerns to make video game violence enjoyable. *Communications, 31*, 309-328.

Klimmt, C., Schmid, H., Nosper, A., Hartmann, T., and Vorderer, P. (2008). "Moral management": Dealing with moral concerns to maintain enjoyment of violent video games. In A. Sudmann-Jahn, and R. Stockmann (Eds.), *Computer games as a sociocultural phenomenon: Games without frontiers – wars without tears* (pp. 108–118). Hampshire, UK: Palgrave.

Konijn, E.A., and Bushman, B.J. (2007). I wish I were a warrior: The role of wishful identification on the effects of violent video games on aggression in adolescent boys. *Developmental Psychology, 43*(4), 1038-1044.

Krcmar, M., Farrar, K., and McGloin, R. (2011). The effects of video game realism on attention, retention and aggressive outcomes. *Computers in Human Behavior 27*(1), 432-439.

Lagerspetz, K.M.J., and P. Engblom (1979). Immediate reactions to Tv-violence by Finnish pre-school children of different personality types. *Scandinavian Journal of Psychology 20*, 43-53.

Lemmens, J.S., Valkenburg, P.M., and Peter, J. (2011). Psychosocial causes and consequences of pathological gaming. *Computers in Human Behavior, 27*(1), 144-152.

Liebes, T., and Katz, E. (1990). *The export of meaning: Cross-cultural readings of "Dallas."* New York: Oxford University Press.

Liu, M., and Peng, W. (2009). Cognitive and psychological predictors of the negative outcomes associated with playing MMOGs (Massively Multiplayer Online Games). *Computers in Human Behavior, 25,* 1306-1311.

Markey, P.M., and Scherer, K. (2009). An examination of psychoticism and motion capture controls as moderators of the effect of violent video games. *Computers in Human Behavior, 25*(2), 407-411.

Markus, H., and Nurius, P (1986). Possible selves. *American Psychologist, 41,* 954-969.

Meerkerk, G. J., Van Den Eijnden, R. J., and Garretsen, H. F. (2006). Predicting compulsive Internet use: It's all about sex! *CyberPsychology and Behavior, 9*, 95-103.

Möller, I., and Krahé, B. (2009). Exposure to violent video games and aggression in German adolescents: A longitudinal analysis. *Aggressive Behavior, 35*(1), 75-89.

Montag, C. Jurkiewicz, M., and Reuter, M. (2010). Low-self-directedness is a better predictor for problematic internet use than high neuroticism. *Computers in Human Behavior, 26*, 1531-1535.

Morahan-Martin, J., and Schumacher, P. (2000). Incidence and correlated of pathological Internet use among college students. *Computers in Human Behavior, 16*, 13-29.

Newman, J. (2002). The myth of the ergodic videogame: Some thoughts on player-character relationships in videogames. *Game Studies* [online], *2*, 1-8.

Ng, B. D., and Wiemer-Hastings, P. (2005). Addiction to the Internet and online gaming. *CyberPsychology and Behavior, 8*, 110-113.

Oatley, K. (1994). A taxonomy of the emotions of literary response and a theory of identification in fictional narrative. *Poetics, 23,* 53-74.

Oatley, K. (1999). Meeting of minds: Dialogue, sympathy, and identification in reading fiction. *Poetics, 26,* 439-454.

Ogles, R.M., and Hoffner, C. (1987). Film violence and perception of crime: The cultivation effect. In M.L. McLaughlin (Ed.). *Communication Yearbook 10* (pp.384-394). Thousand Oaks, CA: Sage Publication.

Olson, C. K. (2004). Media violence research and youth violence data: why do they conflict? *Academic Psychiatry, 28*(2), 144-150.

Opotow, S. (2007). Moral exclusion and torture: The ticking bomb scenario and the slippery ethical slope. *Peace and Conflict: Journal of Peace Psychology*, *13*(4), 457-461.

Peters, C.S., and Malesky, jr., L.A. (2008). Problematic usage among highly-engaged players of massively multiplayer online role playing games. *CyberPsychology and Behavior, 11*(4), 481-484.

Piazza, J. (2010). Audiences experience 'Avatar' blues. *CNN Entertainment*, 11 January, 2010. Retrieved January 28, 2010, from: http://www.cnn.com/2010/SHOWBIZ/Movies/01/11/avatar.movie.blues/index.html

Pohl, K. (2008). Ethical Reflection and Involvement in Computer Games. In S. Günzel, M. Liebe, and D. Mersch (Eds.), *Conference Proceedings of the Philosophy of Computer Games,* 2008 (pp.92-107): Potsdam University Press.

Polman, H., Orobio de Castro, B., and van Aken, M.A.G. (2008). Experimental study of the differential effects of playing versus watching violent video games on children's aggressive behaviour. *Aggressive Behavior, 34*(3), 256-264.

Putnam, R. D. (2000). *Bowling alone: The collapse and revival of American community.* New York: Simon and Schuster.

Sandler, E.P. (2010). Avatar blues? *Psychology Today,* 13 January, 2010. Retrieved January 28, 2010, from: http://www.psychologytoday.com/blog/promoting-hope-preventing-suicide/201001/avatar-blues.

Schmierbach, M. (2010). "Killing Spree": Exploring the Connection Between Competitive Game Play and Aggressive Cognition. *Communication Research, 37*(2), 256-274.

Sherry, J.L. (2001). The effects of violent video games on aggression: A meta-analysis. *Human Communication Research, 27*(3), 409-431.

Shibuya, A., Sakamoto, A., Ihori, N., and Yukawa, S. (2008). The effects of the presence and contexts of video game violence on children: A longitudinal study in Japan. *Simulation and Gaming, 39*(4), 528-539.

Sicart, M. (2009). *The Ethics of Computer Games.* Cambridge, Mass.: MIT Press.

Silvern, S. B., and Williamson, P. A. (1987). The effects of video game play on young children's aggression, fantasy, and prosocial behavior. *Journal of Applied Developmental Psychology, 8,* 453-462.

Smahel, D. Blinka, L., and Ledabyl, M.A. (2008), Playing MMORPGs: Connection between addiction and identifying with a character, *CyberPsychology and Behavior, 11*(6), 715-718.

Soldz, S. (2008). Healers and Interrogators: Psychology and the United States Torture Regime. *Psychoanalytic Dialogues, 18,* 592-613.

Stetina, B.U., Kothgassner, O.D., Lehenbauer, M., and Kryspin-Exner, I. (2011). Beyond the fascination of online-games: Probing addictive behavior and depression in the world of online-gaming. *Computers in Human Behavior, 27*(1), 473-479.

Suhail, K., and Bargees, Z. (2006). Effects of excessive Internet use on undergraduate students in Pakistan. *CyberPsychology and Behavior, 9,* 297-307.

Turkle, S. (1995). *Life on the Screen: Identity in the Age of the Internet.* Cambridge, Mass.: MIT Press.

Unsworth, G., and Devilly, G.J. (2007). The effect of playing violent video games on adolescents: Should parents be quaking in their boots? *Psychology, Crime and Law, 13*(4), 383-394.

Wadley, G., Gibbs, M.R., and Benda, P. (2010). Speaking in Character: Voice Communication in Virtual Worlds. In W.S. Bainbridge (Ed.). *Online worlds: Convergence of the real and the virtual* (pp.187-200). London: Springer.

Whang, L. S., and Chang, G. (2004). Lifestyles of virtual world residents: Living in the on-line game "lineage". *CyberPsychology and Behavior, 7*(5), 592-600.

Whitty, M.T., Young, G., and Goodings, L. (2011). What I won't do in pixels: Examining the limits of taboo violation in MMORPGs. *Computers in Human Behavior, 27*(1), 268-275.

Williams, D. (2005). Bridging the methodological divide in game research. *Simulation and Gaming, 36*(4), 447-463.

Williams, D., Caplan, S., and Xiong, L. (2007). Can You Hear Me Now? The Impact of Voice in an Online Gaming Community. *Human Communication Research, 33*, 427-449.

Williams, D., Consalvo, M., Caplan, S., and Yee, N. (2009). Looking for Gender: Gender Roles and Behaviors Among Online Gamers. *Journal of Communication, 59*, 700-725.

Williams, D., and Skoric, M. (2005). Internet Fantasy Violence: A Test of Aggression in an Online Game. *Communication Monographs, 22*(2), 217-233.

Williams, D., Yee, N., and Caplan, S.E. (2008). Who plays, how much, and why? Debunking the stereotypical gamer profile. *Journal of Computer-Mediated Communication 13*, 993-1018.

Wissmath, B., Weibel, D., and Groner, R. (2009). Dubbing or Subtitling? Effects on Spatial Presence, Transportation, Flow, and Enjoyment *Journal of Media Psychology, 21*(3), 114-125.

Yee, N. (2006a). Motivations for play in online games. *CyberPsychology and Behaviour, 9*(6), 772-775.

Yee, N. (2006b). The demographics, motivations and derived experiences of users of massively-multiuser online graphical environments. *PRESENCE: Teleoperators and Virtual Environments, 15*, 309-329.

Yee, N. (2007). Motivations of play in online games. *CyberPsychology and Behavior, 9*, 772-775.

Young, G. (2010). Virtually Real Emotions and the Paradox of Fiction: Implications for the use of virtual environments in psychological research. *Philosophical Psychology, 23*(1), 1-21.

Young, G., and Whitty, M.T. (2010) Games without frontiers: On the moral and psychological implications of violating taboos within multi-player virtual spaces. *Computers in Human Behavior, 26*(6), 1228-1236.

Young, G., and Whitty, M.T. (2011). Progressive embodiment within cyberspace: Considering the psychological impact of the supermorphic persona. *Philosophical Psychology, 24*(4), 537-560.

Young, G. and Whitty, M.T. (2012). *Transcending Taboos: A moral and psychological examination of cyberspace.* London: Routledge.

Young, G., and Whitty, M.T. (in press) Should gamespace be a taboo-free zone? Moral and psychological implications for single-player video games. *Theory and Psychology, 21*(6).

Young, K. S. (2004). Internet addiction: A new clinical phenomenon and its consequences. *American Behavioral Scientist, 48*, 402–415.

Zillmann, D. (1971). Excitation transfer in communication-mediated aggressive behavior. *Journal of Experimental Social Psychology, 7*, 419-434.

In: Psychology of Morality
Editors: A. S. Fruili and L. D. Veneto

ISBN: 978-1-62100-910-8
© 2012 Nova Science Publishers, Inc.

Chapter 3

MORAL THINKING VS. MORAL ACTING OR MORAL THINKING AND MORAL ACTING

Mladen Pecujlija

Faculty of Technical Sciences, Novi Sad

ABSTRACT

We conducted a survey about moral thinking at the abstract level of students of the Faculty of Technical Sciences in Novi Sad, Serbia. Our comprised sample 1.057 students who finished a secondary school and begin their studies. Seven questions which describe their moral thinking indicate to their moral thinking at the abstract level. When we performed the exploratory factor on the randomly selected sample half, analysis showed us the existence of two independent patterns which best describe their moral thinking at the abstract level. The first pattern is called AUTHENTIC PATTERN and the second pattern is called EGOISTIC PATTERN. Also, our results showed us that female respondents have significantly higher second pattern activation level. Performed confirmatory factor analysis on second half of our sample confirmed this factor structure.

This research shows that during the process of moral thinking at the abstract level both patterns are activated simultaneously (analogy with the computer dual core processor) and that difference in their activation level determinate direction of someone`s moral behavior. Putting in this way this model overcomes gap between moral thinking and moral acting.

Research has shown that EGOISTIC PATTERN activation level during the process of moral thinking at the abstract level is more dominant among women of the same age, which means that women`s process of moral thinking at the abstract level is prone to the influences of the environment, so they more develop moral thinking that is a product of environmental influences. On the other hand, AUTHENTIC PATTERN activation level during the process of moral thinking at the abstract level is higher among male respondents, whereas their EGOISTIC PATTERN activation level is quite below the average. These findings coincide with the findings obtained so far related to the gender difference in the process of ethical decision-making. These findings also shed a new light on the nature of the difference since women are more ethical with respect to a cultural model or a philosophical construct.

We have unsolved problem of thinking-acting gap problem. One fresh theory (Belimp theory) created by Petrides (2011) provides us fruitful approach to this problem.

Also We conducted an on-line survey to investigate the professor`s idea of "morality" and then to compare their moral thinking at the abstract level with their moral thinking in the real life situations by sampling 257 professors from the University of Novi Sad. . Our results show (after we performed exploratory factor analysis) that the professor`s idea of "morality" consists of the three moral thinking patterns which are simultaneously activated during the process of their abstract moral thinking. We have identified these patterns in the following manner: deontological, formal and subjective pattern. In addition, our results show that of the three, the subjective pattern is more activated than the other two during their process of the moral thinking at the abstract level. We also discovered that there is a statistically significant difference (Bandura, 1987) between professor`s moral thinking patterns activation level at the abstract level and their moral thinking patterns activation level in the real life situation. The results, thus, confirmed general hypothesis of this research and showed that the investigation of moral thinking, without inclusion of dimension of activation and deactivation of the mechanism of moral control (Bandura, 1986), does not shed adequate light on this aspect of human behavior.

INTRODUCTION: *HOMO HOMINI LUPUS*

According the Stone (2010) individuals and organizations are facing numerous challenges in today's world. The recent financial crisis (it has fundamentaly ethichal origin) is resulted in large job losses, and increased poverty levels among people in many nations. Some estimates indicate that the economic downturn coupled with the increased cost of food and fuel have pushed more than 100 million people into extreme poverty (United Nations, 2009). Similarly, the worldwide recession has created a crisis of confidence in corporate leaders, and prompted concerns about corporate ethics and social responsibility. So understanding and predicting moral thinking and moral acting today is of essential importance.

VERITAS AMARA EST

Normative ethics largely falls in the domain of moral philosophy and it attempts to inform what someone should do in a particular situation. Conversely, descriptive ethics is concerned with explaining and predicting individual moral behavior. James Rest provides a good theoretical model to better understand descriptive ethics (Rest, 1986), the four components of which are: identifying the moral nature of an issue, making a moral judgment, establishing moral intent and engaging in moral action (Jones, 1991., Rest, 1986., Trevino 1986.)

A review of existing research that deals with individual moral thinking and the engagement of moral action (O`Fallon and Butterfield, 2005.) shows a dearth of research in this area. Most of the results, stemming from this review are only consistent when individual moral thinking are discussed in light of the idealism and relativism dichotomy (establishing moral intent and engaging in moral action are highly positive when correlated with idealism). However, these researches do not show an individual's moral conduct over time. What is more, research of this type poorly measures an individual's personal moral thinking framework because it is impossible to quantify such a framework if their individual ethical experienced is not measured. Put a different way, it is difficult, if not impossible to access an individual's process of moral thinking at the abstract level from this theoretical approach.

There are also significant methodological problems related to the investigation of morality with relevance to the respondent sample and material distributed to respondents during the course of the research. More than 40% of empirical research projects were conducted among students or designed to combine data obtained from students and other respondents (Weber, 1992). Many hold the view that it is adequate to use student samples, whereas there are also those who think those samples are an obstacle in generalizing obtained data. On the other hand, the material often distributed to respondents for examining moral thinking at the abstract level is the so called 'scenario' since it is a standardized social stimulus and a moral situation, real for respondents (Marshall and Dewe, 1997). This raises the question of the optimal number of situations to present respondents with so as not to err in deciding or overload them with situations they need to analyze. The same applies to questionnaires; in fact, there is a small number of simulations and laboratory research. It is hard to assess ethical and unethical behavior (Trevino, 1992).

REST`S FOUR STEP MODEL

The cognitive-developmental stage theory, initiated by Lawrence Kohlberg in late 1950s, dominated the research of moral psychology over two decades. The insufficiency of the cognitive developmental approach to explain moral behavior was critized for instance by Hoffman (1984) who claimed that in the cognitive approach the role of conflict, motivation and affect is minimized. Likewise, Blasi (1980) in the conclusions of his review of moral thinking at the abstract level and moral action considered the reasons for the existence of the gap between moral thinking at the abstract level and actual moral behavior. For instance, he asked, are there differences in people's readiness to interpret situations in moral terms? Do some people consider only a few situations as moral whereas other sees many? Moreover, what motivates individuals to behave according their judgments? Why some high-scoring respondents were able to resist temptation and some were not? Finally, it could be asked what kinds of defensive or coping strategies people use to avoid an unpleasant decision that follows from one's moral moral thinking at the abstract level, or what kinds of strategies they use to act consistently with their moral thinking at the abstract level? The dissatisfaction induced James Rest, a student of Lawrence Kohlberg's, to develop a four component model of moral behavior. Rest (1986) considered the psychological processes that are involved when people behave morally and ended up with four major psychological processes that must have occurred in order for moral behavior to take place (sequential model). The model was originally formulated when Rest did a literature review of morality and used it to classify the various studies carried out in the domain of moral development with different starting points (Rest, 1983). Firstly, in moral behavior, there must be some sort of interpretation of the particular situation. The first component, later called moral sensitivity, includes consideration of which actions are possible in the situation, which are the parties concerned, and how they would be affected by the consequences of each action. Secondly, one must be able to make a judgment about which course of action is morally right or fair, thus choosing one possible line of action as what one ought to do in that situation. Thirdly, one ought to give priority to moral values above other personal values such that an intention to do what is morally right is formed. The third component is called moral motivation in the sense that values motivate individuals to achieve goals and guide their behavior. Finally, the fourth component - moral character - involves having courage and implementing skills to carry out a line of action even under pressure. Rest (1986) stressed that the order of the components in the model is logical rather than chronological. Although it logically makes sense that for instance component 1 (sensitivity to the moral issues of the situation) precedes component 3 (motivation to behave morally), one's value priorities might affect the interpretation of situations as morally relevant and which aspects of the situation are considered important. The basic assumption is that the underlying psychological processes of moral behavior are distinct from each other, although they might interact and influence none another. For instance, a person might be capable of making adequate moral judgments but be insensitive to different moral aspects of the situation, or vice versa. Rest did not divide morality into cognitive, affective and behavioral components as had traditionally been done which each have their separate developmental paths. Instead he claimed that these three components are always interconnected, and that cognition, affect and behavior are incorporated in his model's components. Cognition and affect could be linked by several ways; there is not just one connection. Moreover, Rest (1986) emphasized the fact that the four components represent processes involved in the production of a moral act, not general traits of people. For instance, a person highly sensitive in one situation might be relatively insensitive in another. Thus, the model is situation-specific in a way that different situations promote different kinds of interpretations and moral judgments, heighten the importance of some values compared to others, and encourage an individual to implement a moral act or discourage her or him from doing so. One of the goals Rest and his associates had in developing the four component model was to have a theory and methodology for studying morality of everyday life, not only reasoning on hypothetical dilemmas. Rest and his colleagues at the University of Minnesota have conducted research on the components of morality mostly in the context of professional decision-making. According to Rest (1986) the target groups have been professionals partly because the professionals' experience to justify their decisions makes them easier to study, and partly because in professional decision-making situations the professionals' self interest and justice are not so often in conflict with each other as might be the case in other real-life dilemmas. Although Kohlberg's theory has not lost its importance in understanding people's constructions of moral issues, the four component model broadened the scope of moral psychology by taking into account the other processes of moral behavior as well or emphasizing that the components influence each other in complicated ways.

GENDER AND MORAL THINKING

Carol Gilligan was the first to consider gender differences in moral thinking in her research with the mental processes of males and females in their moral development. In general, Gilligan noted differences between girls and boys in their feelings towards caring, relationships, and connections with other people. More specifically Gilligan noted that girls are more concerned with care, relationships, and connections with other people than boys

(Lefton, 2000). Thus, Gilligan hypothesized that as younger children girls are more inclined towards caring, and boys are more inclined towards justice (Lefton, 2000). Gilligan suggests this difference is due to gender and the child's relationship with the mother (Lefton, 2000).

Child development literature often provides a heated comparison of Gilligan's theory with that of Lawrence Kohlberg's. Lawrence Kohlberg's theory entails the famous man "Heinz" who is portrayed to have a wife that is terminally ill. Kohlberg devised his theory by asking college aged students whether or not they would break into a drug store to steal the medicine to save his wife and why or why not (Wark & Krebs, 1996). Kohlberg's theory is comprised of three levels of moral development becoming more complex. Kohlberg's moral development theory did not take into account gender, and from Kohlberg's theory Gilligan found that girls do in fact develop moral thinking at the abstract level differently than boys. Gilligan's theory has had both positive and negative implications in the field of psychology. One positive implication is that her work has influenced other psychologists in their evaluations of morality. Also, Gilligan's work highlights that people think about other people in a humanly caring way. Gilligan also emphasized that both men and women think about caring when faced with relationship dilemmas, similarly both are likely to focus on justice when faced with dilemmas involving others rights. On the other hand, the most criticized element to her theory is that it follows the stereotype of women as nurturing, men as logical. The participants of Gilligan's research are limited to mostly white, middle class children and adults (Woods, 1996). In general, literature reviews have provided that Gilligan's work needs a broader more multicultural basis. In summary, Carol Gilligan has provided a framework for the moral orientations and development of women. Current research on explicit schemas as to how women come to real-life decisions when faced with real-life dilemmas is limited. Gilligan's theory is comprised of three stages: self-interest, self-sacrifice, and post-conventional thinking where each level is more complex. Overall, Gilligan found that girls do develop morality, differently than others. Gilligan's theory holds particular implications for adolescent girls specifically as this is typically when they enter the transition from level two to level three. However, as do all theories Gilligan's has advantages and disadvantages that should be considered when looking at moral orientations.

THE FIRST RESEARCH: *NON PROGREDI EST REGREDI*

This research is primarily explorative in character and its main purpose is to show that regardless of the Rest's model of moral thinking at the abstract level (Rest, 1986), which includes four basic components (sequential psychological processes), it is important to look at the process of moral thinking at the abstract level as a unique (paralell) process not as chain of different sequential processes and overcome the dichotomy between normative and descriptive ethics by trying to identify the structure of one's moral thinking at the abstract level – the patterns by which we can first describe it and then discuss the process of moral thinking at the abstract level and moral behavior itself. On the other hand, identifying patterns can help single out developmental aspects of each identified pattern. The dominant method used to collect data involves a hypothetical situation and it is usually unclear whether the researchers measured moral thinking at the abstract level or some other construct (intention for example). In the following paper we want to think past this dichotomy approach to moral thinking (descriptive ethics vs. normative ethics) by showing more clearly an individual's moral thinking at the abstract level. Also, we will try to show that individual notion of the morality is more complicated than once thought. Moral orientation is multifaceted, which is further complicated by its particular setting or circumstance. A subject's ethical framework cannot be quantified outside of the particular. For us dichotomies are not a satisfactory explanation of someone's notion of the morality (e.g. the *idealism vs. relativism* dichotomy). We base this claim on the idea that different moral orientations simultaneously underlie moral thinking (Pecujlija et al 2011). Also, we presumed that moral thinking have to be put in the term "patterns" rather than in the term "dichotomies" (a pattern, from the French patron, is a type of theme of recurring events or objects, sometimes referred to as elements of a set. These elements repeat in a predictable manner. It can be a template or model which can be used to generate things or parts of a thing, especially if the things that are created have enough in common for the underlying pattern to be inferred, in which case the things are said to exhibit the unique pattern. Pattern matching is the act of checking for the presence of the constituents of a pattern, whereas the detecting for underlying patterns is referred to as pattern recognition. The question of how a pattern emerges is accomplished through the work of the scientific field of pattern formation. The most basic patterns are based on repetition and periodicity. A single template, or cell, is combined with duplicates without change or modification. For example, simple harmonic oscillators produce repeated patterns of movement). Hence, I propose:

H1: The process of the future manager`s moral thinking at the abstract level is paralell, not sequential process, it consists of patterns

According to Gilligan, the central moral thinking at the abstract level problem for women is the conflict between self and other. Within Gilligan's theoretical framework for moral thinking development in females, she provides a sequence of three levels (Belknap, 2000). At level one of Gilligan's theoretical frameworks a woman's thinking orientation is towards individual survival (Belknap, 2000); the self is the sole object of concern. The first transition that takes place is from being selfish to being responsible. At level two of the moral thinking the main concern is that goodness is equated with self-sacrifice (Belknap, 2000). This level is where a woman adopts societal values and social membership. Gilligan refers to the second transition from level two to level three as the transition from goodness to truth (Belknap, 2000). Here, the needs of the self must be deliberately uncovered; as they are uncovered the woman begins to consider the consequences of the self and other (Belknap, 2000). One study by Gilligan & Attanucci, (1988) looked at the distinction between care and justice perspectives with men and women, primarily adolescence and adults when faced with real-life dilemmas. An example of one of the real-life dilemma subjects were asked to consider was a situation with a pregnant women considering an abortion (Gilligan & Attanucci, 1988). The study showed that: a) concerns about justice and care are represented in people's thinking about real-life moral dilemmas, but that people tend to focus on one or the other depending on gender, and b) there is an association between moral orientation and gender such that women focus on care dilemmas and men focus on justice dilemmas (Gilligan & Attanucci, 1988). Based on the research conducted so far that rested on the Rest's model of moral thinking at the abstract level, it is evident that independent variables related to respondents' gender provide relatively consistent results. According the O`Fallon and Butterfield (2005) there is no evidence for difference between the moral thinking at the abstract level of men and women. If we find that kind of differences we can say that there qualitative differences in moral thinking at the abstract level between man and women based on significant differences of patterns activation levels. Therefore, I propose:

H2: There is a gender difference regarding the patterns activation levels

Sample

The research included 1.034 freshmen enrolled at the Faculty of Technical Sciences, University of Novi Sad, Serbia. At the time of the research (2010), the students had just commenced their studies. They are future managers. The respondents are the same age, but regarding their gender, the situation is the following: (see Table 1) more male (71.2%) than female respondents participated in the research, which is normal due to the fact that more men than women decide for studying engineering.

Table 1. Respondents by gender

	Frequency	Percent	Valid percent	Cumulative percent
male	753	71.2	71.2	71.2
female	304	28.8	28.8	100.0
total	1,057	100.0	100.0	

Procedure

When enrolling in the first year of their studies at the Faculty of Technical Sciences, the respondents were asked to fill in a short questionnaire created for that occasion. It consisted of six items related to their ideas about morality. The respondents were informed that it was their free will to participate in the research and that they were not obliged to fill in the questionnaire.

Research Instrument

The Rest's model of ethical decision-making served as a theoretical foundation for creating the questionnaire as it includes items that relate to the very awareness of ethics, moral judgment, intention for moral behavior and moral behavior itself. On the other hand, the questionnaire encompasses those items that relate to the ethical attitude of respondents: deontological, subjective and utilitarian. On a five-level Likert-like scale the respondents needed to mark the extent to which they agreed or disagreed with the claims offered. The results given in the Table 2 indicate that the reliability of the questionnaire is quite high – Cronbach's Alpha is .82.

Table 2. Reliability of the questionnaire

Cronbach's Alpha	Cronbach's Alpha based on standardized items	No. of items
.81	.82	6

Results

Table 3. Item descriptive statistics

	Mean	Standard deviation
Ethics is very important to me.	4.11	1.02
The Faculty is a place for students' ethical improvement.	4.03	1.03
	4.00	1.02
I think about ethical consequences of my decisions.	2.96	1.18
During making decisions I also think about consequencies of my decisions.	2.83	1.21
	2.82	1.21
I am more a practical than an ethical person.		
I am on the firsth place when I make decisions about what to do.		

The findings presented in the Table 3 show that the most prominent respondents' idea is that they find ethics to be very important (M = 4.11, SD = 1.02), that the Faculty is a place for their ethical improvement (M = 4.03, SD = 1.03), as well that they are aware of ethical consequences of their actions (M = 4.00, SD = 1.02). On the other hand, the lowest-scoring items were those related to the practicality being more important than ethics (M = 2.83, SD = 1.02) and self-centeredness (M = 2.82, SD = 1.21).

KMO and Bartlett's Test as Conditions for Performing Exploratory Factor Analysis

Table 4 shows the KMO coefficient and Bartlett's test – the parameters whose values clearly indicate that it is justifiable to conduct the explorative factor analysis for the research findings with respect to KMO = 0.77 and the significance of Bartlett's test (Chi-Square = 1757.64, df = 0.00).

We divided our sample in two equal groups. ANOVA results show us that both group belong to same population (see Table 5). On first half we performed EFA and on second half we performed CFA.

After the exploratory factor analysis, it is obvious from Table 5 that the extraction criterion is a eigenvalue greater than 1, and that there are two factors that explain the 54.84% variance of the examined occurrence. The first factor exemplifies the greatest percentage of the variance of the examined occurrence – 35.47%. Table 6 shows extracted factors and it is obvious that among them not even a single item has negative factor saturation. Moreover, there is no evidence of approximate projection of an item on two extracted factors. Factor saturation of items ranges between 0.64 and 0.83.

Table 4. ANOVA: Questionnaire items by group (EFA and CFA)

		Sum of Squares	Mean Square	F	Sig.
Ethics is very important for me	Between Groups	1.25	1.25	1.18	.27
	Within Groups	1093.04	1.05		
	Total	1094.29			
I am more practical then ethical person	Between Groups	.01	.01	.022	.85
	Within Groups	1071.65	1.02		
	Total	1071.68			
I think about ethical consequences of my decisions	Between Groups	1.16	1.16	1.09	.31
	Within Groups	1102.46	1.07		
	Total	1103.62			
During making decisions I also think about ethical consequences of my decisions	Between Groups	.02	.02	.023	.87
	Within Groups	1072.75	1.03		
	Total	1072.78			
I am on the first place when I make decisions about what to do	Between Groups	2.16	2.16	2.16	.15
	Within Groups	1053.83	.99		
	Total	1056.00			
The faculty is a place for students ethical improvement	Between Groups	1.18	1.18	1.11	.29

Table 5. KMO and Bartlett's Test

Kaiser-Meyer-Olkin Measure of Sampling Adequacy		.77
Bartlett' test of Sphericity	Approx. Chi-Square	1757.64
df		28.00
Sig.		.00

Table 6. Total variance explained

Pattern	Initial Eigen Values			Rotation Sums of Squared Loadings		
	Total	% of variance	Cumulative %	Total	% of variance	Cumulative %
1	2.84	35.47	35.47	2.59	32.44	32.44
2	1.55	19.37	54.84	1.79	22.40	54.84
3	.74	9.25	64.10			
4	.71	8.91	73.01			
5	.63	7.95	80.97			
6	.59	7.44	88.41			

The Patterns of Moral Thinking at the Abstract Level

The first extracted pattern explains 35.47% of the total variance of the process of moral thinking at the abstract level (Table 6) and projects on it 4 questionnaire items with factor saturation ranging from 0.64 to 0.83 (Table 7). Furthermore, there is obviously no negative factor saturation regarding this pattern. The first item of this pattern is *Ethics is very important to me* with factor saturation of 0.72. The second item, *I think about ethical consequences of my decisions*, has the saturation of 0.83, whereas the third item, *During making decisions I also think about consequences of my decisions,* has the saturation of 0.64. The fourth item is *The Faculty is a place for students' ethical improvement* and its saturation is 0.74. Owing to the fact that in their essence items that project on the first extracted pattern generally relate to moral thinking, this extracted pattern explains the greatest part of the variance of the examined occurrence that could be named Authentic pattern.

The second extracted pattern explains 19.37% of the total variance of the process of moral thinking at the abstract level (Table 6). There are two questionnaire items projecting on it with factor saturation ranging from 0.74 to 0.75 without negative factor saturation (Table 7). This pattern encompasses the following questionnaire items: *I am more Egoistic then ethical person* 0.75 and *I am on the first place when I make decisions about what to do* 0.74. This pattern can be called Egoistic pattern as its component parts relate to ethical norms acquired during life.

Table 7. Rotated component matrix

	Component	
	1	2
Ethics is very important for me	.72	-.12
I am more practical then ethical person	-.22	.75
I think about ethical consequencies of my decisions	.83	.04
During making decisions I also think about consequences of my decisions	.64	.02
I am on the first place when I make decisions about what to do	.00	.74
The faculty is a place for student's ethical improvement	.74	.08

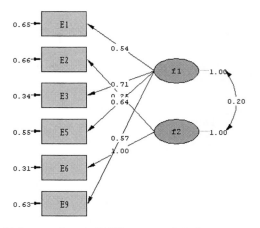

Chi-Square=16.70, df=8, P-value=0.03342, RMSEA=0.045

Figure 1. Confirmatory factor analysis.

The explorative factor analysis (EFA) indicates that our respondents' process of moral thinking at the abstract level is a complex two-pattern structure containing an inherited and a learned dimension. These patterns are simultaneously engaged during this process and their activation level is different. Confirmatory factor analysis confirmed our model (see Figure 1).

Gender Differences

Figure 2 represents factor scores our respondents' activation level of patterns of moral thinking at the abstract level in accordance with the independent variable 'Gender'. Factor scores were identified by the Anderson-Rubin method, a slight modification of the Bartlett's method. This method allows for orthogonality of a selected factor. Due to such factor scores that represent relative values compared to average values, it can be noted that among female respondents Egoistic pattern activation level is prevailing, whereas Authentic pattern activation level is below the average value. With male respondents the situation is totally opposite: Egoistic pattern activation level is below average, whereas Authentic pattern activation level is a bit above average. Based on those factor scores of extracted patterns activation level and with relevance to the respondents' gender it can be concluded that female respondents pertain to acquired moral norms whereas male respondents adhere more to inherent, inherited morality. In order to find out whether this difference among the participants is statistically significant, a one way analysis of variance (ANOVA) was performed. It is obvious from the Table 8 that there is statistically significant influence of the independent variable of 'Gender' on the relative relation among factor scores of Egoistic pattern in that among female respondents activation level is prevailing during the process of moral thinking at the abstract level as opposed to male respondents ($F = 13.16$, $p = 0.00$).

Table 8. ANOVA pattern by gender

		Sum of squares	Mean square	F	Sig.
Authentic pattern	Between groups	2.16	2.16	2.16	.14
Within groups		1053.83	.99		
Total		1056.00			
Egoistic pattern	Between groups	13.01	13.01	13.16	**.00**
Within groups		1042.98	.98		
Total		1056.00			

Degrees of Freedom = 8
Minimum Fit Function Chi-Square = 16.78 (P = 0.032)
Normal Theory Weighted Least Squares Chi-Square = 16.70 (P = 0.033)
Population Discrepancy Function Value (F0) = 0.016
90 Percent Confidence Interval for F0 = (0.0012 ; 0.046)
Root Mean Square Error of Approximation (RMSEA) = 0.045
90 Percent Confidence Interval for RMSEA = (0.012 ; 0.076)

Figure 2. Pattern's activation level presented by the gender.

As for Authentic pattern activation level during the process of moral thinking at the abstract level, there is no statistically significant difference among male and female respondents. Therefore, the research results have proved the first hypothesis regarding the complex structure of people's moral thinking as there were two independent patterns extracted. Moreover, the second hypothesis was proved too as gender affects the patterns activation level.

Discussion: *Natura Habet Sua Iura*

Research findings show that moral thinking at the abstract level is a unique dimension of one's behavior, as well as that it is very complex. Indentifying the structure of moral thinking (considered as a parallel process) will help understand better what moral thinking at the abstract level and moral behavior are since the findings suggest that moral thinking at the abstract level consists of some kind of an inherent part, as well as of a part that results from complex environmental factors that affect an individual. It seems that the Rest's model is insufficient in explaining the complexity of one's ethical behavior and thinking in the process of ethical decision-making. Moreover, realistic identification of the morality structure leads to formulating a new theoretical concept of the process of moral thinking at the abstract level analogous with Cathel's model of fluid and crystal intelligences whereupon fluid intelligence gradually deteriorates, and crystal intelligence improves. Therefore, it may be that Authentic pattern activation level during the process of moral thinking at the abstract level deteriorates over years, whereas Egoistic pattern activation level improves. The Authentic pattern dimension would not represent sheer morality that develops on its own. Egoistic pattern would represent morality acquired over years and through experience. Forsyth (1992) argued that two basic dimensions of personal moral philosophies (i.e., relativism and idealism) can impact moral thinking at the abstract level. Idealism refers to the individual's concern for the welfare of others. Strong idealism, according to Karande et al. (2002), indicates a belief that "harming others is always avoidable" and a preference to "not choose the lesser of two evils that will lead to negative consequences for others". On the other hand, relativism refers to a belief in how moral principles apply to a particular situation. Forsyth (1980) states that relativism "rejects the possibility of formulating or relying on universal moral rules when drawing conclusions about moral questions." Strong relativism indicates a person places more emphasis on the situation and the moral principle to determine if it is good, while weak relativism indicates a belief that moral principles should be followed regardless of the circumstances. According to Hunt and Vitell (1986), one's moral thinking at the abstract level is dependent on the existence of a perceived ethical issue(s). The perception of an ethical problem provides the "catalyst" for the process of moral thinking at the abstract level. Singhapakdi et al. (2000) identify that the "perception of an ethical issue or problem is considered to be an important prerequisite for moral thinking at the abstract level". Studies have been conducted to empirically validate this proposition. There has been a general assumption that intention will lead to action.

This research shows that during the process of moral thinking at the abstract level both patterns are activated simultaneously (analogy with the computer dual core processor) and that difference in their activation level determinate direction of someone's moral behavior. Putting in this way this model **overcomes gap** between moral thinking and moral acting. On the other hand CFA (see Figure 1) confirmed our findings so this new view on process of moral thinking at the abstract level should be accepted but still we have unsolved problem of thinking-acting gap problem. One fresh theory (Belimp theory) created by Petrides (2011) provides us fruitful approach to this problem (see Figure 3).

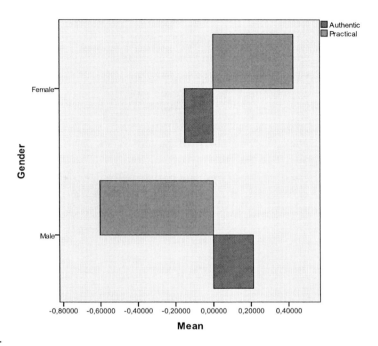

Petrides, 2011.

Figure 3. Belimp Theory.

By linking traits to processes within a model wherein personality consistency and flow can coexist (as the master and conditional belimp planes, respectively), belimp theory can relieve the uneasy cohabitation of the trait and social–cognitive approaches to personality. From the point of view of trait theory, we have a mechanism that, unlike traits, which are identified at an aggregate (population) level, is identified and can be applied at the level of the individual. Such mechanisms can help substantiate the reality of personality traits by bestowing explanatory power on them.Belimp theory should yield significant efficiencies and perhaps also improvements in our ability to predict action (behavior) over existing personality inventories. We expect this, first, because the belimp mechanism is a more proximal determinant of behavior than personality and, second, because position in a concordant belimp plane will reflect both one's personality traits as well as their attitudes towards a context (life domain, in our case patterns of moral thinking at the abstract level), thus carrying more information than either personality or context alone. The predictive power of belimp theory in relation to a particular criterion will be progressively enhanced as life domains become more concordant, and maximized when the life domain matches the criterion. Personality is a distal determinant of behavior and the mechanisms through which it affects it are largely unknown. If such mechanisms were to be successfully isolated, they should prove significant mediators or moderators (Baron & Kenny, 1986) of personality traits. In fact, because concordant belimp planes are hypothesized as more proximal and partially contextualized determinants of behavior, there may be cases where they emerge as full mediators and perhaps even as incremental predictors.

In general, according the our results, we have 2x3 matrix situation when we discussed someone's moral thinking (pattern type and it's activation level). Now we can create types of moral thinking (life domains according Belimp theory):

1) High Authentic pattern and high Egoistic pattern
2) High Authentic pattern and medium Egoistic pattern
3) High Authentic pattern and low Egoistic pattern
4) Medium Authentic pattern and high Egoistic pattern
5) Medium Authentic pattern and medium Egoistic pattern
6) Medium Authentic pattern and low Egoistic pattern
7) Low Authentic pattern and high Egoistic pattern
8) Low Authentic pattern and medium Egoistic pattern
9) Low Authentic pattern and low Egoistic pattern

It is obvious that successful and responsible managers and leaders belong to first, second and third category. Moral thinking is full mediator and incremental predictor of someone's behavior.

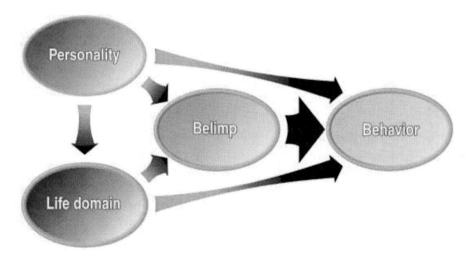

Figure 4. Matrix: pattern type x activation level.

Research has shown that Egoistic pattern activation level during the process of moral thinking at the abstract level is more dominant among women of the same age, which means that women's process of moral thinking at the abstract level is prone to the influences of the environment, so they more develop moral thinking that is a product of environmental influences. But we can not underestimate development factor (on this age according Gilligan). On the other hand, Authentic pattern activation level during the process of moral thinking at the abstract level is higher among male respondents, whereas their Egoistic pattern activation level is quite below the average. These findings coincide with the findings obtained so far related to the gender difference in the process of ethical decision-making. These findings also shed a new light on the nature of the difference since women are more ethical with respect to a cultural model or a philosophical construct.

There is a serious question regarding the nature of the philosophical construct that Authentic pattern is grounded on. It is evident that there are different philosophical concepts that Egoistic pattern is based on, but what about Authentic pattern? There is, however, no single, broadly accepted model of moral intuition. In fact Dane and Pratt (2007) list 17 different offerings in the literature, and these exclude definitions specific to ethical decision making. The contending theories of moral intuition vary primarily in the temporal sequence of the non-conscious processing of morally relevant information. There is also the question of whether the improvement of Egoistic pattern supports one's morality or interferes with the dimension of Authentic pattern. According Universal Moral Grammar model (UMG), affect is not the triggering component for the process, it is an outcome of intuitive cognitions that are innate and have had functional importance to human survival throughout the millennia. In part, this occurred because human interaction requires cooperation and altruism in order to survive (L. Cosmides & Tooby, 2005; L Cosmides & Tooby, 2008; Harman, 2000; Wright, 1994). An additional common theme among these models is that intuitive cognitions are **deontological** in nature. That is, a person perceives a stimulus and automatically applies a behavioral rule to it, rapidly and spontaneously, without the deliberative calculations necessary for moral rationality. This deontological characteristic is an important aspect of moral intuition recognized by both social psychologists working in the areas of moral psychology (Hauser, Cushman, Young, Jin & Mikhail, 2007; Mikhail, 2007, 2008) as well as those researching "**protected values**" (Baron & Spranca, 1997; Ritov & Baron, 1999). The implication of this deontological, innate nature, is that these rules are hard-wired and naturally occurring, universal components of the moral mind.

Conclusions, Restrictions, Directions for Future Research: *Coruptio Optimi Cuisque Pessima*

It goes without saying that this research has serious limitations that do not allow for the generalization of the research findings. One of the restrictions is age since the respondents are all peers. On the other hand, the questionnaire items pose a restriction as the questionnaire was designed for that occasion only and it can be remarked that if the items had been different, the questionnaire would have yielded different results too (questionnaire reliability from 0.81; contributes to a better impression of the research instrument). Moreover, a serious remark can be that the acquired results are a generalization of the Rest's model in a way. It would be important to conduct this research among different age groups so as to find out whether its structure is subject to change in accordance with the respondents' age. Future research goals should aim toward evaluating the interplay between conscious moral reasoning (Egoistic pattern) and intuitive responses (Authentic pattern), especially as they relate to each other and to behavioral outcomes, and further specifying the nature of intuition (Authentic pattern).

This research offers few primary contributions. First, that the process of Serbian future manager's moral thinking at the abstract level underlie of the different moral orientations of different intensity under the simultaneous consideration (not of the unique orientation under the consideration). Second: When we submitted these results to the exploratory factor analysis, we realized that process of moral thinking at the abstract level with our examinees consists of the following patterns: the Authentic and the Egoistic pattern. We emphasize again that these patterns are activated simultaneously during the process of the moral thinking (these results are related with **neurophysiological data** about simultaneous activation of different brain locations during the process of moral thinking at the abstract level). Third: Difference between our male and female subjects in the Egoistic pattern level of activation indirectly supported Gilligan`s theory about girls moral development (higher activation level of Egoistic pattern).

Based on the size and structure of the sample (1.034 respondents) it can be claimed with considerable confidence that the obtained results are a real projection of the process of moral thinking at the abstract level examined future managers of that age in Serbia, which all adds to the significance of the research. The respondents in this research were all students and it would be interesting to conduct the research among non-student managerial population. All in all, this research was just the first step towards creating a better approach to the examination of an individual's moral thinking at the abstract level and their general ethical behavior in this critical period of mankind.

Including Bandura in Story: *Potius Sero Quam Nunquam*

We found that Bandura`s sociocognitive theory and his concept of moral engagement (Bandura, 1991) is very useful for explaining an individual`s moral behavior over time. Moral action manifests itself in the power to restrain from inhuman behavior as much as in the proactive power to act human. Moral action is built in a broader sociocognitive theory that contains organization of personality, proactive, self-perceptory and self-regulatory mechanisms that are rooted in personal standards connected with self-restraint. The self-regulatory mechanisms that control our moral behavior do not express themselves unless they are activated, but there are a number of psychosocial maneuvers by which moral self-control selectively shuts down. Moral exclusion can be achieved by the cognitive restructuring of inhuman behavior into a benign one, or one worthy of moral excuse, into language euphemisms, into nonobjective comparison, into the negation of feelings of self engagement by means of mixing or shifting of responsibility, into negation or minimization of effects of inhuman behavior on others, into accusation of victims of inhuman behavior and into their dehumanization. The exclusion or cutting off of a working ethical framework through the deactivation of the mechanisms of control during inhuman behavior is a growing problem in society, both public and private. In his book everybody does it: Crime by the Public, Thomas Gabor (Gabor, 1994) documents the deactivation of the mechanisms of moral frameworks. Psychological theories of morality focus mostly on moral theory (Piaget, 1967., Kohlberg, 1973) and completely neglect moral conduct. The regulation of human behavior includes much more than mere moral reasoning. A complete moral theory of activity must combine knowledge about morality together with moral action. It demands an action centered theory of morality rather than a theory that is enclosed in thinking about morality. Such a theory would list the mechanism by which people realize that they live in harmony with their moral standards. In Bandura's sociocognitive theory (Bandura, 1986, 1991), the claim is made that moral "learning" translates into action through activation and deactivation of the mechanism of moral control, which, in turn, is rooted in moral standards and self-evaluation through which moral activity is practiced. Our moral self is included in a wider sociocognitive theory of personality, which contains the organization of a person who is proactive, self-aware and self-regulatory. Being proactive, self-aware and self regulating comprises a set of human characteristics we term "mechanisms." In early phases of development, human behavior is mostly regulated by external influences such as social standards. In the process of socialization, people adopt moral standards that shape their behavior depending on the conditions in which they find themselves. They judge moral decisions on the basis of the consequences they perceive as they make decisions. Also, people do things that give them pleasure and grade their feeling of personal value. And, conversely, people refrain from action that has shown to bring harm. Restraint from action that may cause self-regulation threatens the self's moral standards. In addition, behavior that may support or seem to support self esteem may in fact be harmful for a preexisting moral code.

In light of situational induction of inhuman behavior, people cannot simply act differently by using self-control. Self-regulation reflects behavior in line with personal standards. This manner of self-control provides meaning to moral activities. Through practicing self-control, behavior becomes motivated and regulated. The practice of moral action consists of two components: inhibitory and proactive. Inhibitory behavior manifests itself in the ability to refrain from inhuman actions. Proactive forms of morality are expressed in the power to act humane. In the later component, individuals invest their understanding of their own values in human notions and social obligations, so that they act against what they consider unjust and immoral even if their action may have harmful consequences for them personally. Investigations that show so-called "good" people acting cruelly are quite stunning. Stanley Milgram's work is an example of such findings. The research shows that for the most part people refuse to act abusive, even under an extremely authoritarian system of command. If they find themselves in a situation where they are personally responsible for their actions and when they can foresee the consequences of their actions then people in general will not be abusive or act inhumane (Bandura, et al., 1975; Milgram, 1974). The affirmation of humanity and human values can bring out the best in others. The insistence on a type of proactive morality brings to the fore a type of humanist principle of moral action. As a result of this type of action, an action based on humanist principles, people are then ready to take responsibility for their actions, which opens up the possibility of living in a better community. Humanization instigates empathy, the social obligations which then connect with moral auto censure and instigates the transcendence of selfish interests as chief motivators of conduct (Bandura, 1986). The weakening of the mechanisms of moral control is often a gradual process. A series of small losses of control begins to tighten control mechanisms. This lowering produces a larger degree of harmful behavior so that the subject gradually becomes trained. The radicalization of one's immoral behavior represents a process of the gradual weakening of one's mechanisms of moral control. The research into the development of personality shows that the weakening of mechanisms of moral control starts at an early age (Bandura, Barbanelli, Caprara, Pastorelli, 1996). The development of morality is usually investigated through the adoption of abstract moral values, which work at an abstract level. In adolescents, who differ in quantity of delinquent behavior, there do not usually exist any difference when it comes to abstract moral values. The shapeless abstraction of moral norms complicates the dynamic process of conduct of the mechanisms of moral control that are founded by the perception of personal efficiency or inefficiency in their conduct. The self-regulation of moral behavior is only a matter of intrapsyhic mechanisms (psychological term referring to internal psychological processes of the individual), but is also in line with the social reality in which we find ourselves. Sociocognitive theory accepts the interactive approach to morality and it holds that morality is a product of personal and social influences. Conflict often occurs when society punishes activities that an individual considers right and just. The answers to this conflict are, by and large, determined by auto censure, some kind of social sanctions and the manner of their application. Complete understanding demands an integrated approach where social influences act through psychological mechanisms and thus produce certain behavior (Bandura, 1997). Some of the mechanisms of the weakening of the mechanisms of moral control, such as distribution of responsibilities, are rooted in the organizational structure of social systems, while certain ideological orientations create various forms of moral excuse. People are both creators and products of social systems. Within certain established rules, their interpretation, adoption, rejection, is directly dependable on personal characteristics of the members (Burus and Dietz, in print). Neither circumstances (Milgram, 1974), nor dispositions (Gillespie, 1971) give adequate or full explanations of human moral behavior. Within sociocognitive theory, both sociocultural and personal determinants act interdependent within a common causal structure.

THE SECOND RESEARCH: *NON SCHOLAE, SED VITAE DISCIMUS*

The basic aim of this second research is to compare the University professors moral thinking at the abstract level with their real-life moral activity itself (their idea of morality linked with their moral behavior over time).Their moral thinking at the abstract level (dependent variable) was examined by an ad hoc questionnaire, created specifically for this research. It consists of eight Likert items (Likert, 1932) that we formulated according to the present theoretical concepts of the notion of morality. The activation or de-activation of their mechanism of moral control (moral behavior over time) was estimated by an item in which the examinees got a question concerning their persistence in the enforcement of their moral standing points in real life (independent variable). The research was conducted by an on-line questionnaire. A link to the questionnaire electronic form was sent to our examinees via e-mail and they returned their answers using the same method. In this way, we ensured our examinees absolute anonymity.

Sample

The sample was comprised of 257 professors at The University of Novi Sad[1]. After sending the link to the electronic form of the questionnaire 62% of the examinees responded.

---

[1] The University of Novi Sad is now the second largest among six state universities in Serbia. The main University Campus, covering an area of 259,807m², provides the University of Novi Sad with a unique and beautiful setting in the region and the city of Novi Sad. Having invested considerable efforts in intensifying international cooperation and participating in the process of university reforms in Europe, the University of Novi Sad has come to be recognized as a reform-oriented university in the region and on the map of universities in Europe. Teaching at the University and at the faculties is entrusted to professors and teaching associates who hold academic titles prescribed by law (43259 students at undergraduate studies, 2692 attained doctoral degrees, 2897 teaching staff which includes professors, teaching associates, lecturers and 1137 non-teaching staff).

Research Hypotheses

General research hypothesis **H0** is as follow: The process of the professor's moral thinking significantly differs when they consider moral at the abstract level than they consider it in the real life context (moral behavior over time). Specific research hypotheses are: the process of the professor's moral thinking at the abstract level underlies of different moral orientations of different intensity under the simultaneous consideration **H1** and that the process of the professor's moral thinking at the abstract level possesses latent structure, consists of patterns **H2**.

Results

From the Table 9 we see that, with our examinees (professors), the most intensive considered moral orientation at the abstract level of moral thinking is the theory of ethics is called "Golden Rule" (M = 4.47, SD = .91) and the distributive concept of justice (M = 4.04, SD = 1.03), while the moral orientation of egoistic nature is of the smallest consideration intensity (M = 1.58, SD = .89), as well as the orientation of subjectivist nature (M = 2.03, SD = 1.15). It should be emphasized that the examinees answered on the Likert type five level items.

Table 9. Intensity of the Professor's Moral Orientations at the Abstract Level of Moral Thinking

Items	Mean	Std. Deviation	Analysis N
Moral is that which is good for me	1.58	.89	257
I think that it is necessary to do others what we would like them to do to us	4.47	.91	257
It is enough to obey the law in order to be moral	2.09	.97	257
It is necessary to do well regardless of its consequences for me	3.61	1.08	257
Moral person takes care of the interests of others as well	4.04	1.03	257
Moral is a very subjective category, it is the matter of personal taste	2.03	1.15	257
Moral is what brings more good than evil	3.11	1.22	257
There is a universal moral truth that we should all observe	3.60	1.19	257

After this, we performed exploratory factor analysis (EFA) on this data, in order to discover observed phenomenon latent structure (**in-depth** analysis of moral thinking at the abstract level). We extracted these patterns of professor's moral thinking at the abstract level:

1) SUBJECTIVE pattern
2) FORMAL pattern
3) DEONTOLOGICAL pattern

The patterns activation level average values for all professors are presented by factor scores and our basic finding is that they are mostly SUBJECTIVE during the process of moral thinking at the abstract level.

Given the nature of the factor scores, we can say that the professors highly activated pattern during the process of their moral thinking at the abstract level is the subjective one. The least activated during their process of moral thinking at the abstract level is the formal pattern and it has a strong negative token in relation to average value. The deontological pattern level of activation is around absolute average, it is insignificantly below average. It is very important to be emphasized that during their process of moral thinking at the abstract level all patterns are activated simultaneously (Figure 5).

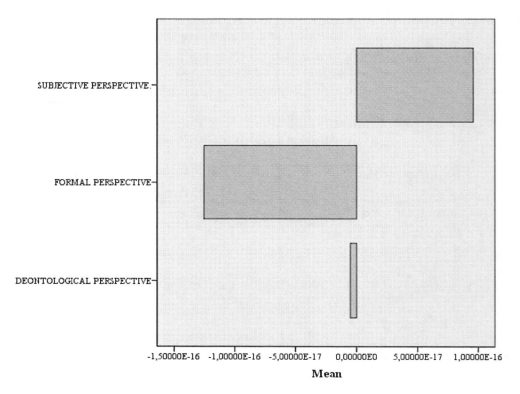

Figure 5. The Average Level of Pattern Activation When Professor`s Consider Moral at the Abstract Level.

Considering the theoretical basis of this paper (Bandura's sociocognitive moral theory), we were interested in the mechanism of moral engagement, so we showed it qualitatively, meaning that we investigated the question of orientation: the proactive one or the possibility of shutting down of the mechanism of moral control of the contextual nature (relative or absolute).

Table 10. Do you always Act with Respect to Your Moral Stance?
(Moral Behavior over Time)

		Frequency	Percent	Valid Percent	Cumulative Percent
Valid	Yes, always	75	29.2	29.2	29.2
	Yes, mostly	174	67.7	67.7	96.9
	Depends on the situation in which I find myself	8	3.1	3.1	100.0
	Total	257	100.0	100.0	

From the Table 10 (our examinee`s moral behavior over time) we see that 29.2 % of our subjects have absolutely proactive moral behavior over time, meaning that they would act in harmony with their moral standards in every situation. 67 % of those polled act in such way for most of time, meaning that there are situations in which their mechanisms of moral control shutdown, while with 3.1 % of them the activation or deactivation of their mechanisms of moral control is absolutely contextually determined.

Finally, we analyzed professor`s moral thinking patterns in their real life context (their moral behavior over time) to get final results. For that purpose, we obtained an analysis of variance (ANOVA).on our data.

Table 11. ANOVA (Influence of Moral Behavior over Time on the Moral Thinking
Patterns Activation Level)

Patterns of Moral Thinking		Sum of Squares	df	Mean Square	F ratio	p
DEONTOLOGICAL PATTERN	Between Groups	8.91	2	4.45	**4.58**	.011
	Within Groups	247.09	254	.97		
	Total	256.00	256			
FORMAL PATTERN	Between Groups	5.83	2	2.92	**2.96**	.053
	Within Groups	250.17	254	.99		
	Total	256.00	256			
SUBJECTIVE PATTERN	Between Groups	8.33	2	4.16	**4.27**	.015
	Within Groups	247.67	254	.98		
	Total	256.00	256			

From the Table 11 we see that our examinee's moral behavior over time on statistically significant level (p ≤ .05) influencing on all their three moral thinking patterns activation level. According these results we can recognize following moral behavior patterns among professors:

1) Proactive moral behavior over time with highly activated DEONTOLOGICAL pattern during the real life moral thinking, deciding and acting (see Appendix, Graph 2). This persons in real life consider moral as a duty and always decide and act according to their moral believes. They never adjusted their moral precepts to circumstances

2) Relative contextual determined moral behavior over time with highly activated SUBJECTIVE pattern during the real life moral thinking, deciding and acting (see Appendix, Graph 3). This persons in real life do not consistently thinking, deciding and acting. They often (not always) adjusted their moral precepts to circumstances.

3) Absolute contextual determined moral behavior over time with highly activated FORMAL pattern during the real life moral thinking, deciding and acting (see Appendix, Graph 4). In real life this persons always adjusted their moral thinking, deciding and acting according to their own personal interests. On the other hand, they talk about moral very nice at the abstract level as we saw in the Table3; in real life they are recognized from other people as hypocrites.

CONCLUSIONS: *ACTA, NON VERBA!*

This research offers few primary contributions.

First, that the process of professor's moral thinking at the abstract level underlie of the different moral orientations of different intensity under the simultaneous consideration (not of the unique orientation under the consideration). The results show (when we analyzed them at the descriptive level) that the most intensive considered moral orientation in the process of moral thinking at the abstract level is the "Golden Rule", while moral egoism is of the lowest consideration intensity.

Second: When we submitted these results to the exploratory factor analysis (in depth), we realized that process of moral thinking at the abstract level with our examinees consists of the following patterns: the DEONTOLOGICAL, the FORMAL and the SUBJECTIVE pattern. We emphasize again that these patterns are activated simultaneously during the process of the moral thinking. The factor scores show that with them the SUBJECTIVE pattern in the process of moral thinking is at the highest level of activation, while the **least** activated during this process in real time is the FORMAL pattern. The DEONTOLOGICAL pattern during the process of moral thinking at the abstract level is somewhere at the average level of activation. This fact implies understanding that, after all, the moral is (even at the abstract level of thinking, not linked with action), on the ground of regularity, an inherent part of human existence. Third, we can see that their concrete, real live moral behavior is not consistent:

their activation and deactivation of the moral mechanisms is by and large selective, determined by circumstances, only 29.2 % of our examinees have absolutely proactive moral attitude.

Fourth, that the relative relations between professor's patterns activation level during the process of the moral thinking dramatically changes (at the statistically significant level) when they consider moral in their real life context. These statistically significant differences of the patterns activation level during the process of moral thinking regarding activation and deactivation of moral mechanisms (moral behavior over time) speak in favor of Bandura's sociocognitive moral theory. Had we not discovered these statistically significant differences, Bandura's claiming about the importance of proactive attitude to morality in this research would not have been confirmed. The results, thus, confirmed general hypothesis of this research and showed that the investigation of moral thinking, without inclusion of dimension of activation and deactivation of the mechanism of moral control (Bandura, 1986), does not shed adequate light on this aspect of human behavior. Also, we find that proactive moral behavior over time increases the DEONTOLOGICAL pattern activation rate in the process of moral thinking.

Level of pattern activation	high	medium	low
Deontological pattern			
Subjective pattern			
Formal pattern			
MORAL BEHAVIOUR OVER TIME	Proactive	Relative contextual	Absolute contextual

Figure 6. Possible moral behavior pattern (patterns of moral thinking linked with moral behavior over time).

We assume that established relation among patterns of moral thinking activation level and moral behavior over time is reversible (e g. someone's high subjective pattern activation level during the process of moral thinking at the abstract level increases its relative contextual determinate moral behavior over time rate) but this assumption have to be an object of the future careful designed research. Also, knowing someone's moral behavior over time we shall be able to predict relative relations between its moral thinking patterns at the abstract level. Based on these discovered relations we shall be able to explain total diversity of human real life moral behavior (by the putting someone's moral thinking patterns activation levels: high, average, low together with its moral behavior over time modes: proactive, relative contextual and absolute contextual, Figure 6), describe all moral behavior patterns, explain them and at the end, predict someone's moral behavior.

Only theoretical assumptions linked with empirically obtained data are giving to us our observed phenomenon real picture. It was possible to us to stop our data analysis at the descriptive level and get nice story: Our professors consider moral at the abstract level mostly from the Golden rule position and they are not egoist. But, is it really true?

Tempus Omnia Revelat

Real life examples are often in discrepancy with our theoretical knowledge and research data, unfortunately often show us all academic powerlessness in facing with them. In this case, EFA and ANOVA, as legitimate research tools, provided to us observed phenomenon picture in depth and tied our theoretical ethics knowledge together with our real life moral behavior (moral control mechanism as missing link in complex moral behavior chain). I am deeply convinced that science major duty is to be closely tied to real life. Science has to contribute to our real life deeper understanding by description, explanation and prediction of its all manifestation kinds.

In this paper, simply, we wanted to show (with full respect to theoretical base and methodological rules together) that we can not just think and talk about moral; we have also to act morally in consistent manner. So if we want to put some facts about moral thinking and moral acting in few words we can use this Latin sentence: *DICTUM, FACTUM.*

REFERENCES

Alexander, C. S., Becker, H. J. (1978). "The Use of Vignettes in Survey Research". *Public Opinion Quarterly* 42, 93-104.

Allmon, D. E., Chen H. C. K., Pritchett, T. K., Forrest, P. (1997). "A Multicultural Examination of Business Ethics Perceptions". *Journal of Business Ethics* 16 (2), 183-188.

Bandura, A. (1986). *Social foundations of thought and action: A social cognitive theory.* Englewood Cliffs. NJ: Prentice-Hall.

Bandura, A. (1991). Social cognitive theory of moral thought and action. In Kurtines W. M. & Gewirtz, J. L., *Handbook of moral behavior and development: Theory, research and applications* (71-129). Hillsdale, NJ: Erlbaum, 1990.

Bandura, A. (1992). Social cognitive theory of social referencing. In Feinman, S., *Social referencing and the social construction of reality in infancy* (175-208). New York: Plenum.

Bandura, A., Barbaranelli, C., Caprara, G. V., Pastorelli, C. (1996). Mechanisms of moral disengagement in the exercise of moral agency. *Journal of Personality and Social Psychology.* 71, 364-374.

Bandura, A., Underwood, B., Fromson, M. E. (1975). Disinhibition of aggression through diffusion of responsibility and dehumanization of victims. *Journal of Research in Personality. 9,* 253-269.

Baron, J. (1995). A Psychological View of Moral Intuition. *The Harvard Review of Philosophy,* 70, 36-43.

Baron, J., Spranca, M. (1997). Protected Values. *Organizational Behavior and Human decision Processes,* 70, 1, 1-16.

Bass, K., Barnett, T., Brown, G. (1999). Individual Difference Variables, Ethical Judgments and Ethical Behavior Intentions. *Business Ethics Quarterly* 9, 2, 183-205.

Belknap, R.A. (2000). One woman's life viewed through the interpretive lens of Gilligan's theory. *Violence Against Women,* 6, 586-605.

Borkowski, S. C., Ugras, T. J. (1997). Business Students and Ethics: A Meta Analysis. *Journal of Business Ethics* 17, 11, 1117-1127.

Brenner, S. N. (1992). "Ethics Programs and Their Dimensions". *Journal of Business Ethics*, 11, 391-399.

Buchholz, R. A. (1989). "Fundamental Concepts and Problems in Business Ethics". In Madsen, P., & Shafritz, J. M. (107-123). *"Essentials of Business Ethics"*. New York: Penguin Books.

Carroll, A. B. (1990). "Principles of Business Ethics: Their Role in Decision Making and in Initial Consensus". *Management Decision*, 28 (8), 21-23.

Cohen, D., Nisbett, R. E. (1994). Self-protection and the culture of honor: Explaining Southern violence. Special Issue: The self and the collective. *Personality and Social Psychology Bulletin,* 20, 551-567.

Colby, A; Kohlberg, L. (1987). The Measurement of Moral Judgment Vol. 2: *Standard Issue Scoring Manual*. Cambridge University Press.

Dane, E., & Pratt, M. (2007). Exploring Intuition and its Role in Managerial Decision Making. *Academy of Management Review,* 32, 1, 35-54.

Dean, P. J. (1992). "Making Codes of Ethics 'Real'". *Journal of Business Ethics*, 11, 285-290.

Diener, E. (1977). Deindividuation: Causes and Consequences. *Social Behavior and Personality,* 5, 143-156.

Diener, E., Dineen, J., Endresen, K., Beaman, A. L., Fraser, S. C. (1975). Effects of Altered Responsibility, Cognitive Set, and Modeling on Physical Aggression and Deindividuation. *Journal of Personality and Social Psychology,* 31, 328-337.

Donaldson, T., Dunffe, T. W. (1994). "Toward a Unified Conception of Business Ethics: Integrative Social Contracts Theory". *Academy of Management Review* 19 (2), 252-284.

Forsyth, D. R. (1980). A Taxonomy of Ethical Ideologies. *Journal of Personality and Social Psychology* 39, 1, 175–184.

Forsyth, D. R. (1992). Judging the Morality of Business Practices: The Influence of Personal Moral Philosophies. *Journal of Business Ethics* 11, 5/6, 461–470.

Gabor, T. (1994). *Everybody does it: Crime by the public*. Toronto: University of Toronto Press.

Gandz, J., Bird, F. G. (1989). "Designing Ethical Organizations". *Business Ethics Quarterly*, 54 (2), 108-112.

Gillespie, W.H. (1971). Aggression and Instinct Theory. *International Journal of Psycho-analysis,* 52, 155-160.

Gilligan, C., Attanucci, J. (1988). Two moral orientations: Gender differences and similarities. *Merrill-Palmer Quarterly*, 34, 223-237.

Haidt, J. (2001). The emotional dog and its rational tail: A social intuitionist approach to moral judgment. *Psychological Review,* 108, 4, 814-834.

Haidt, J. (2007). The New Synthesis in Moral Psychology. *Science,* 316, (18 May), 998-1002.

Haidt, J., & Baron, J. (1996). Social Roles and the Moral Judgment of Acts and Omissions. *European Journal of Social Psychology,* 26, 2, 201-218.

Hauser, M., Cushman, F., Young, L., Jin, R., & Mikhail, J. (2007). Dissociation Between Moral Judgments and Justifications. *Mind & Language,* 22, 1, 1-21.

Jones, T. M. (1991). Ethical decision making by individuals in organizations: An issue-contingent model. *Academy of Management Review,* 16, 2, 366-395.

Karande, K., Rao, C., Singhapakdi, A.(2002). Moral Philosophies of Marketing Managers: A Comparison of American, Australian, and Malaysian Cultures. *European Journal of Marketing* 36, 7/8, 768–791.

Kelman, H. C. (1973). Violence without moral restraint: Reflections on the dehumanization of victims and victimizers. *Journal of Social Issues,* 29, 25-61.

Kilham, W., Mann, L. (1974). Level of destructive obedience as a function of transmitter and executant roles in the Milgram obedience paradigm. *Journal of Personality and Social Psychology,* 29, 696-702.

Kirrane, D. E. (1990). "Managing Values: A Systematic Approach to Business Ethics". *Training and Development Journal*, 53-60.

Kohlberg, L. (1971). *From Is to Ought: How to Commit the Naturalistic Fallacy and Get Away with It in the Study of Moral Development*. New York: Academic Press.

Kohlberg, L. (1973). The Claim to Moral Adequacy of a Highest Stage of Moral Judgment. *Journal of Philosophy,* 70, 630–646.

Kohlberg, L. (1981). Essays on Moral Development, Vol. I: *The Philosophy of Moral Development*. San Francisco, CA: Harper & Row.

Kohlberg, L., Levine, C., Hewer, A. (1983). *Moral stages: a current formulation and a response to critics*. Basel, NY: Karger.

Kohlberg, L., Lickona, T. (1976). Moral stages and moralization: The cognitive-developmental approach. *Moral Development and Behavior: Theory, Research and Social Issues*. Holt, NY: Rinehart and Winston.

Lefton, L. A. (2000). Child Development. In *Psychology,* (pp. 350-351), Allyn & Bacon publishing.

Loviscky, G., Trevino, L., Jacobs, R. (2007). Assessing Managers' Ethical Decision Making: An Objective Measure of Moral Judgment. *Journal of Business Ethics,* 73, 2, 263-285.

Madsen, P., Shafritz, J. M., (1990). *"Essentials of Business Ethics"*. New York: Penguin Books.

McDonald, G., Zepp, R. (1990). "What Should Be Done? A Practical Approach to Business Ethics". *Management Decision*, 28 (1), 9-13.

McIntyre, A. (2001). Doing Away With Double Effect. *Ethics,* 111, 2, 219-255.

Mikhail, J. (2007). Universal Moral Grammar: Theory Evidence and the Future. *Trends in Cognitive Science,* 15, 4, 1-10.

Mikhail, J. (2008). The Poverty of the Moral Stimulus. In W. Sinnott-Armstrong (Ed.), *Moral Psychology* (pp. 353-360). Cambridge, MA:MIT.

Milgram, S. (1974). *Obedience to authority: An experimental view*. New York: Harper & Row.

Moll, H., Tomasello, M. (2007). Cooperation and Human Cognition: the Vygotskian Intelligence Hypothesis. *Philosophical Transactions* - B, 362, 1480.

O`Fallon, M., Butterfield K. (2005). A Review of the Empirical Ethical Decision-Making Literature: 1996-2003. *Journal of Business Ethics* 59; 375-413.

Pecujlija, M., Cosic, I., Ivanisevic, V. (2011). A Professor`s Moral Thinking at the Abstract Level vs. The Professor`s Moral Thinking in the Real Life Situations (Consistency Problem). *Science and Engineering Ethics,* 17, 2, 299-320.

Petrides, K.L. (2011). A general mechanism for linking personality traits to affect, motivation, and action, *New Ideas in Psychology*, 29, 2, 64-71

Petrinovich, L., O'Neil, P., Jorgensen, M. (1993). An Empirical Study of Moral Intuitions: Toward and Evolutionary Ethics. *Journal of Personality and Social Psychology,* 64, 3, 467-478.

Piaget, J. (1932). *The Moral Judgment of the Child.* London: Kegan Paul, Trench, Trubner and Co.

Rest, J. (1980). Moral Judgment Research and the Cognitive-Development Approach to Moral Education. *Personnel and Guidance,* 58, 9, 602-606.

Rest, J. (1986). *Moral Development: Advances in Research and Theory* (New York: Praeger).

Ritov, I., Baron, J. (1999). Protected Values and Omission Bias. *Organizational Behavior and Human decision Processes,* 79, 2, 79-94.

Rummel, R. J. (1988). *Applied Factor Analysis.* Northwestern University Press.

Sims, R. R. (1991). Institutionalization of Organizational Ethics. *Journal of Business Ethics,* 10, 493-506.

Singhapakdi, A. (2004). Important Factors Underlying Ethical Intentions of Students: Implications for Marketing Education. *Journal of Marketing Education* 26, 3, 261–270.

Sonenshein, S. (2007). The Role of Construction, Intuition, and Justification in Responding to Ethical Issues at work: The Sense-Making Intuition Model. *Academy of Management Review,* 32, 4, 1022-1044.

Stone, L.D. (2010). Creating Knowledge That Makes Important Contribution to Society. *Journal of Managerial Psychology,* 25, 3, 192-200.

Strong, K. C., Meyer, G. (1992). An Integrative Descriptive Model of Ethics Decision Making. *Journal of Business Ethics,* 11, 89-94.

Thompson, T. (1991). "Managing Business Ethics". *Canadian Public Administration,* 34 (1), 153-157.

Trevino, L. K. (1986). Ethical Decision Making in Organizations: A Person-Situation Interactions Model. *Academy of Management Review,* 11, 3, 601-617.

Wark, G.R., Krebs, D.L. (1996). Gender and dilemma differences in real-life moral judgment. *Developmental Psychology,* 32, 220-230.

Warneken, F., Tomoasello, M. (2006). Altruistic Helping in Human Infants and Young Chimpanzees. *Science,* 311, 3, 1248-1249.

In: Psychology of Morality   ISBN: 978-1-62100-910-8
Editors: A. S. Fruili and L. D. Veneto   © 2012 Nova Science Publishers, Inc.

Chapter 4

Worldview Beliefs, Morality Beliefs, and Decision-Making Referents: Implications for the Psychology of Morality and Ethics Instruction

Robert G. Magee
Department of Communication, Virginia Tech

Abstract

Values have been a staple in the study of the psychology of morality, but the construct of worldview, in particular, fundamental assumptions related to personal epistemology, can also shed light on the field. In the exploratory correlational study presented in this chapter, worldview beliefs made a significant contribution, apart from morality beliefs, to explaining an individual's tendency to rely on either intrinsic or extrinsic decision-making referents. Although worldview beliefs and morality beliefs were largely independent, multivariate models that included both types of beliefs often were more predictive of an individual's preference for intrinsic or extrinsic referents. Core worldview beliefs seemed to be foundational to decision-making, and scholarship in the psychology of morality would benefit from considering the influence of worldviews. Also, effective ethics training, in addition to providing instruction in ethical skills, should engage students' worldviews and effect incremental transformation over the course of time.

Introduction

Scholars and practitioners in professional media programs agree that students require training in ethics to be effective in their craft, and most, if not all, of the best programs have implemented courses designed to teach students how to engage in ethical decision-making. Some instructors, however, have doubted the effectiveness of semester-long ethics courses. Leslie (1999), for example, surveyed students at the beginning and the end of a course in journalism ethics and found that the course did little to change students' ethical stance. Their ranking of Rokeach's (1968, 1974) terminal and instrumental values remained relatively unchanged at the end of the course. Particularly impervious to change were those associated with postmodern culture, Leslie found. Surlin (1987) conducted a similar study and was "struck by the consistency of pre-post rank mean scores and overall rankings for most values" (p. 566). Only one value, "Equality," made a statistically significant increase, although students reported having higher "ethical self-esteem."

Four years of learning is not an exercise in futility, however, as university students change during their programs of study. Guimond and Palmer (1996) surveyed students during their first and third year of studies and found that students' choice of major led to a change in epistemic beliefs regarding the cause of poverty and unemployment. In their first year of studies, students' beliefs about internal and external causes of poverty exhibited no significant relationship. After their third year of study, however, business students were more likely to attribute poverty to internal causes, and students majoring in the social sciences were more likely to cite systemic factors. The authors concluded that the choice of major, particularly through the influence of professors and curriculum, resulted in belief change.

These studies suggest that, although little change occurs after a single course, students' values and beliefs do indeed change during their university experience. How, then, do worldview beliefs and morality beliefs influence a tendency to rely on either extrinsic or intrinsic decision-making referents? A person's ethical values derive both from one's moral values and from one's worldview, which is the way a person perceives and interprets his or her experience. To explore the relationship between one's worldview beliefs, morality beliefs, and bases for making decisions among young adults, questions adapted from the General Social Survey (Davis, Smith, & Marsden, 2004) were administered to 309 undergraduate students. This study was exploratory and correlational in nature and sought to establish a foundation on which to build further research in moral psychology, particularly as it might relate to moral and ethical decisions.

MORALITY AND MEDIA ETHICS

The relationship between moral reasoning and belief systems in media ethics is certainly worthy of examination, and several researchers have worked in that direction (Black, Barney, & Van Tubergen, 1979; Harless, 1990; Leslie, 1999; Surlin, 1987; Singletary, Caudill, Caudill & White, 1990; Whitlow & Van Tubergen, 1978). However, most research in media ethics has been legal or philosophical in nature. Few social science studies have been published, and much of that research has consisted of taxonomies and descriptive studies, which, of course, is appropriate for theory building at this phase of the research area. Noteworthy steps toward complementing the larger body of research from a social science perspective include Coleman and Wilkins (2002; 2004), White and Pearce (1991), and White and Singletary (1993). Nevertheless, given the importance of this field of research, scholarship in moral psychology could complement current approaches.

Kohlberg, extending Piaget's work on childhood development, proposed three levels of moral development (Kohlberg, 1981, 1984; Crain, 2000). At the preconventional level, one is preoccupied with one's own interests, subordinating any concern for other people. A person decides a course of action based on rewards and punishment that underlie a strict adherence to rules and authority. At the conventional level of moral development, one's actions are guided by a desire or obligation to conform to societal norms. One's perspective moves beyond merely seeking one's own wellbeing to include a concern for other people. Most people remain at the conventional level of moral development. At the postconventional level, one's behavior is informed by reasoning based on universal principles. Such judgment arises from an internalized set of principles that apply to every human being, principles that can transcend societal norms and laws. Each level consists of two stages, for a total of six stages. In later studies, Kohlberg abandoned the sixth stage, saying that few people ever attained that level of moral development (Crain, 2000).

Kohlberg's work forms the basis of a notable portion of theory and research in media ethics. Black, Barney, and Van Tubergen (1979), for example, sought to classify journalists using Kohlberg's stages of moral development. Coleman and Wilkins (2002, 2004) used the Defining Issues Test, developed from Kohlberg's theory, to evaluate journalists' moral development and compare it to those of other professions.

Other theories have informed research on media ethics, as well. Scholars have incorporated Rokeach's (1968, 1974) research on terminal and instrumental values into research and pedagogy (Black, Barney, & Van Tubergen, 1979; Leslie, 1999; Surlin, 1987). A person's value system comprises two types: instrumental values, which guide conduct, and terminal values, which are desirable end-states of existence. Instrumental moral values are normative beliefs that govern interpersonal behavior, while instrumental competence values are self-oriented. Terminal values also can be divided into those that focus on social relations and those that concern the self. Values, which are few in number, and attitudes, which can number in the thousands, are organized hierarchically, with "a dozen and a half" terminal values ordering "five or six dozen" (Rokeach, 1968, p. 552) instrumental values, which, in turn, influence attitudes.

White (1996), drawing on Carter's Paradigm of Affective Relations and Kelman's Functional Theory of opinion change, examined the elements of salience and pertinence in journalists' moral reasoning. Carter's Paradigm held that the value one ascribes to an object is a function of that object's salience to that person and its pertinence in any given context. In White's research, however, those qualities pertain as much to the ethical dilemma as they do to the nature of individual differences among decision-makers, which is the focus of this present study. It is important, therefore, to separate the attributes of a particular ethical dilemma from an individual's values system, worldview, and tendency toward either extrinsic or intrinsic decision-making referents.

INTRINSIC AND EXTRINSIC REFERENTS

It is worth noting that Kelman's Functional Theory of opinion change (Kelman, 1961; White, 1996) parallels Kohlberg's three levels of moral reasoning. Kelman used the term "opinion," in the broadest sense of the word, in the context of social influence. However, in common parlance opinions are linked to attitudes, which are less enduring than values or belief systems, but Kelman used the term without regard for the mutability of a particular class of beliefs. Kelman originally outlined two processes for exerting social influence, but he subsequently proposed three processes: compliance, identification, and internalization. In compliance, one's behavior is shaped by a desire to gain rewards or avoid punishment, an orientation that resembles Kohlberg's preconventional level of moral development (Stages 1 and 2). A person accepts an idea, at least outwardly, because the source of the idea exerts some form of power over that person. In identification, one accepts an idea because he or she is attracted to the source of that idea and derives value from a particular relationship, identifying oneself with an individual or social group. This parallels Kohlberg's conventional level of moral development, in which a person's actions are guided with reference to a smaller social group such as family and friends (Stage 3), or by considering one's relationship to the larger society (Stage 4). In internalization, a person accepts an idea based on its own merits, because it is congruent with one's value system, and incorporates it into his or her way of thinking. Internalization is similar conceptually to Kohlberg's postconventional level, wherein one exercises judgment based on internalized values.

A key element underlying Kohlberg's levels of moral development, and Kelman's processes of opinion change, is the shift from external constraints that inform decision-making to a reliance on one's own intrinsic capacity for judgment using internalized principles. White and Pierce (1991) tapped the distinction between intrinsic and extrinsic referents for moral reasoning. In validating the Ethical Motivations Scale, they discovered three factors that predicted attitudes toward ethical dilemmas. Generally, instrinsic motivations were reliable predictors of ethical choices. Extrinsic referents, on the other hand, failed to predict how a person said he or she might resolve an ethical dilemma. White and Singletary (1993) suggested that for ethical principles to be employed, an individual must have some type of intrinsic motivation for relying on extrinsic guides to ethical decision-making.

The bulk of instruction in media ethics involves the learning and application of extrinsic ethical referents, such as a code of ethics. Both journalist and public relations professional organizations have developed codes of ethical behavior to guide their members, and these are rightfully studied in courses in media ethics. Lacking in media ethics scholarship is an examination of what factors might enable or hinder the likelihood that an individual would refer either to these extrinsic referents or to rely on one's own personal judgment. The present exploratory study examines the possibility that the underlying motivation for either recurring to extrinsic guides or appealing to one's internalized values is a function, in part, of one's worldview. Of the three dimensions of the Ethical Motivations Scale (White & Pearce, 1991; White, 1996), Professional Ethic, Following Ethical Guides, and Higher Ethic, only the latter would parallel the construct of worldview.

WORLDVIEWS

A worldview is a set of beliefs about physical and social reality that shapes the way a person perceives and interprets the world (Koltko-Rivera, 2004, Magee & Kalyanaraman, 2009). These core constructs, which to a large degree function in a tacit or implicit manner, form the foundation for knowing and understanding what a person experiences, and guide a person's cognition and behavior. The beliefs are not testable statements and can be characterized as a set of assumptions about reality with which a person perceives and interprets surrounding events and information. A worldview's core beliefs concern person-nature relations, a person's orientation toward time, how one makes sense of causation, and the nature of truth (Kluckhohn & Strodtbeck, 1961), all of which can influence how a person makes sense of one's experience. A sense of personal efficacy has also been identified as a core belief (Koltko-Rivera, 2004). These basic beliefs about "the way the world works" often are tacit, but they shape the way a person thinks and behaves. A worldview provides a sense of meaning to reality and guides the inferences a person draws from what he or she experiences.

The term worldview comes from the German *Weltanschauung*, which is often translated as philosophy of life. Philosopher Ludwig Wittgenstein (1972) preferred the term *Weltbild*, or "world picture," to refer to an individual's perspective on reality because by the early 20th century *Weltanschauung* had come to mean a totalizing or universal view of the world. Wittgenstein held that a *Weltbild*, or a worldview, functions at two moments. At the moment of perception, it is a lens, influencing what a person sees. Once the target has been perceived, the worldview functions as a riverbed, guiding the flow of the cognitive processes as a riverbed shapes the course of the water. That is, a worldview shapes attentional processes by filtering the perception of an object or event, but after that it constrains or enables the types of thoughts a person will have regarding that object or event.

Although a worldview is broadly stable, it does change over time, and its function can vary with other factors. The core constructs that make up a worldview guide decision rules and the formation and use of mental models, schemta, and other knowledge structures. In addition, although a worldview is chronically accessible, any number of factors can influence its accessibility in a given situation (Magee & Kalyanaraman, 2009).

WORLDVIEW BELIEFS AND MORALITY BELIEFS

A worldview is more fundamental than most value-attitudes. Worldview statements form a foundational core of assumptions that inform existential beliefs, evaluative beliefs, and prescriptive and proscriptive beliefs (Koltko-Rivera, 2004). Berzonsky (1994) called the statements "hard-core assumptions" about oneself, the nature of knowledge, and the nature of the world in which one lives. These core constructs define problems, orient the solutions to the problems, and specify the criteria by which a solution will be evaluated. Christians et al (2005) defined values as ideas that reflect "presuppositions about social life and human nature" (p.2), thereby making a tacit distinction between values and the "presuppositions" that undergird them. These presuppositions are what Potter called "fundamental ideas" and reside at the "ground of meaning" level (Potter, as cited in Christians et al, 2005, p. 26, fn. 5).

Christians et al (2005, p. 26, fn. 3) listed five categories of values: professional values (e. g., proximity, impact, and recency), moral values (e. g., truthtelling, fairness, and stewardship), sociocultural values (e. g., thrift, restraint, and hard work), logical values (e. g., consistency, competence, and knowledge), and aesthetic values (e. g., harmonious, pleasing, and imaginative). Yet these values are conceptually distinct from the epistemic assumptions that inform them. For example, for *knowledge* to be logical value, one must have certain assumptions regarding possibility of certainty and whether reality is knowable. The moral value of *self-control* depends on one's assumptions regarding the locus of control and free will. A person who values *consistency* is more likely to depend on either/or analytic thinking instead of both/and holistic thinking. Thus, values and worldviews are distinct, though not unrelated, constructs.

Values researchers maintain that values are a belief structure that shapes behavior. Schwartz and Bilsky (1990, 1994) identified five key characteristics of values. Values (a) are beliefs, (b) concern end states or behaviors, (c) transcend situations, (d) guide behavioral choices, and (e) are ordered by importance. Building on Schwartz and Bilsky, Rokeach, and other values theorists, Rohan (2000) also defined value systems as cognitive structures that serve as abstract trans-situational guides. Rohan quoted seven definitions of values to support the contention that value systems are in essence belief structures. The key thread in the definitions, however, is not merely that values are beliefs, but that they are beliefs about what is desirable or preferable as a guide to conduct.

The Schwartz value theory is organized along two motivational dimensions: individual outcomes versus social context outcomes, and focus on opportunity versus focus on organization. These dimensions suggest that certain beliefs, such as the motivational dimensions, are precursors to the values themselves. Schwartz and Bilsky (1990) found, for example, that the motivational dimensions had explanatory power for Western societies, but not for their sample from Hong Kong. The meanings of the values were identical, but the structural dimensions along which they were organized were quite distinct. Indeed, the authors noted, "Analysis of distinctive aspects of the world views of different cultures could suggest hypotheses about the dynamic structuring of motivational domains in these cultures" (p. 889).

Rohan (2000), using Tetlock's (1986) definition of ideology as political thought, distinguished ideology from a value system. Ideologies are value-laden guides, either nonconscious or explicit, that direct decision-making processes. However, ethics is a system of guides to behavior, and in that respect, the notion of ethical systems parallels that definition of ideology. For Rohan, one's value system and worldview shape one's ideology, which guides attitudes and decisions. Rohan (2000) also distinguished values, which are abstract and trans-situational, from attitudes, which are specific to a particular target. However, a greater distinction must be drawn between value-attitudes that are enduring and resistant to change, and those that are more malleable. As Chaffee (1991) noted, if social attitudes are defined as enduring predispositions, one should not expect much change or variance. Studies of attitude change, the purview of persuasion research, would be an oxymoron, if that definition were employed. Feather (1995) found that values influenced a person's attitudes (termed *valences*) toward alternative courses of action. Valences, which are situationally specific, refer to "the subjective attractiveness or aversiveness of specific objects" (p. 1135) Values are defined as hierarchically organized structures of abstract beliefs about desirable end states. Value-attitudes have a valence and an object, and what are studied here are core beliefs, sometimes referred to as core values or centrally held values.

Centrally held values will be defended vigorously when challenged, but values have a motivational role, as well, shaping what is desirable and how much effort one should put into pursuing a particular goal (Feather, 1995). Rohan (2000) placed a double arrow (p. 270) in the values model to show that worldview beliefs and values can be recursive. Although the distinction between worldview and values is not sharp, worldview beliefs are foundational to normative values or desirable end states and foundational to guides for making decisions. For the purposes of this study, then, a worldview is a set of implicit beliefs that shapes the way a person perceives and interprets one's experience. Conceptually, a worldview is distinct from values, or what one considers to be desirable, although both guide attitudes, decisions, and behavior. Worldview beliefs are also distinct from morality beliefs, long a part of the study of the psychology of morality. Morality beliefs concern normative guides to behavior, and most worldview beliefs lack a normative component. Although one logically would expect normative beliefs regarding morality to influence an individual's tendency toward intrinsic or extrinsic referents for decision making, it is quite likely that worldview beliefs, such as beliefs regarding one's sense of efficacy, a sense of purpose in life, or religious beliefs, also influence an individual's tendency toward intrinsic or extrinsic referents. Beliefs that have a religious foundation can overlap with other worldview beliefs and morality beliefs, and controlling for religious components of worldview and morality beliefs can shed light on the relationship between nonreligious beliefs and morality beliefs in the utility in predicting whether an individual will rely on intrinsic or extrinsic referents.

METHOD

The aim of this study was to explore the possible relationships among worldview beliefs, morality beliefs, and decision-making referents. It is hoped that this study will serve a heuristic function in generating hypotheses for research into moral psychology and media ethics instruction. It is important to note that the purpose here is theory research, and not application research (Calder, Phillips, & Tybout, 1981). Thus, at this stage in a research program it is unnecessary to gauge every essential component and level of a worldview, nor to assess the influence of every major moral belief, nor to examine every decision-making referent that media professionals might use. It is sufficient to document the existence of different types of core beliefs and describe the relationships among them as predictors of a reliance on either intrinsic or extrinsic decision-making referents.

Worldview Beliefs

To measure components of a person's worldview beliefs on a Likert scale, five items were drawn from the General Social Survey (GSS, Davis, Smith, & Marsden, 2004). Coleman and Wilkins (2004) used GSS items to measure professional autonomy and religiosity, along with the Defining Issues Test and other measures, in their study on journalists' moral reasoning. The items used in this study do not attempt to capture every major belief that might form part of one's worldview. Instead, these items focus on beliefs regarding self-efficacy, meaning in life, and the existence of a deity. Although their role in explaining a reliance on decision-making referents is expected to be significant, they do not comprise all of the constituent worldview beliefs, as other unmeasured assumptions of a worldview likely play a role, as well. The following items were used:

- *Theism*: God is very concerned with every human being personally.
- *Predeterminism*: The course of our lives is decided by God. The GSS label was *Predeter*.

- *Fatalism*: There is little that people can do to change the course of their lives.
- *Nihilism*: Life does not serve any purpose.
- *OwnFate*: We each make our own fate.

The first two items reflect a belief in deity, particularly the Judeo-Christian deity. *Theism* taps a belief in a God who is involved with personal reality. The second item, *Predeterminism*, taps a Judeo-Christian variant of a fatalistic view that might be associated with a low level of self-efficacy.

The remaining three items reflect a nontheistic worldview, but they differ among each other in several regards, mainly with regard to self efficacy and a sense of purpose in life. *Fatalism*, like *Predeterminism*, taps a belief associated with a low level of self-efficacy, but the item excludes any reference to a deity. *Fatalism* contrasts with *OwnFate*, which measures a high degree of self-efficacy and personal responsibility for the outcomes in life. *Nihilism* measures the extent to which the respondent says life has no meaning.

Morality Beliefs

To measure morality beliefs on a Likert scale, four GSS items were used. One item's association with a Judeo-Christian perspective was attenuated, however, to make it resemble the other measures and minimize a possible confound with a particular group of religious convictions.

- *PunSin*: Those who violate moral rules must be punished. The GSS item read: Those who violate God's rules must be punished.
- *BlkWhite*: Right and wrong are not usually a matter of black and white; there are many shades of gray.
- *RotApple*: Immoral actions by one person can corrupt society in general.
- *PerMoral*: Morality is a personal matter and society should not force everyone to follow one standard.

Although *PunSin* and *RotApple* measure different beliefs, both items reflect the degree to which one recognizes societal norms as constraints on the individual. Likewise, both *BlkWhite* and *PerMoral* measure the degree to which a respondent endorses moral relativism.

Decision-Making Referents

To measure the reported importance respondents placed on referents for decision-making, three GSS items were adapted. Again, an effort was made to broaden the items' applicability beyond the Judeo-Christian traditions. Because a number of participants did not come from a Judeo-Christian tradition, the wording of these two items was changed to broaden their relevance to the greatest possible number of participants and to minimize a potential confound with religious identity. The construct of interest was a reliance on religious referents, not necessarily Judeo-Christian ones, for decision-making.

- *Family*: How important is family in helping you to make decisions in life?
- *Social Group*: How important is a social group or organization in helping you to make decisions in life?
- *Oneself*: How important is your own personal judgment in helping you to make decisions in life?

The variable *Family* was modified from the GSS item DecOths, which read "your family and friends" and made it impossible to distinguish the role of family and peers in the decision-making process of young adults. To avoid confounding the reference to both family and peers, the item was modified to refer exclusively to one's family.

The variable *Social Group* was formed to provide a nonreligious alternative to the religious organization measured in the GSS item DecChurh, which read "How important is a religious group or organization for making decisions?" This item was modified because it was possible that nonreligious social organizations also play a role in helping people make decisions.

The variables Family and Social Group measured extrinsic referents for making decisions. The variable *Oneself* was used to measure an intrinsic referent, namely one's own judgment. Together, the variables measured the importance of three decision-making resources: family, a social organization, and one's own judgment.

RESULTS

The items comprising worldview beliefs, morality beliefs, and decision-making referents were administered via paper and pencil to 309 university students, who received course credit for their participation. Of the participants, 70% were female, and 83% were white, which reflected the composition of the pool from which the students were recruited. Mean age was 20.7 years.

A significance level of .05 was used as a reference point rather than a cut-off point (Cohen, 1990), and because this study was exploratory in nature, *p* values that were greater than .05 were examined, although any observations or interpretations, of course, remained more tentative. Further, single-item measures of a construct are less reliable than multi-item measures, so greater allowance was made for the role of random error. Nevertheless, the single-item measures were taken from the GSS (Davis, Smith, & Marsden, 2004) and should be sufficiently reliable for exploratory research.

CORRELATIONS OF WORLDVIEW BELIEFS AND MORALITY BELIEFS

Correlations of worldview beliefs and morality beliefs (Table 1) supported the contention that they are largely separate, though related, types of beliefs. Understandably, a belief in the existence of a deity correlated highly with a belief that a deity decided the course of a person's life. A belief in a deity correlated negatively with the belief that life had no purpose or that a person was able to decide his or her life's course, but the magnitude of the coefficients was modest. The theistic worldview beliefs correlated with the morality beliefs, with seven of eight correlations statistically significant, but none exceeded .30, and only one coefficient exceeded .20, that of *Theism* and *BlkWhite*, $r(309) = -.24$, $p < .001$.

Importantly, the nontheistic worldview beliefs causation and purpose in life exhibited no significant relationship with most of the morality beliefs. Of the twelve coefficients, only two were statistically significant, and the magnitude of these correlations was only .12. This pattern suggests that some worldview beliefs are largely orthogonal to morality beliefs. Therefore, in addition to examining beliefs regarding morality, scholarship in the psychology of morality and the development of ethics instruction should include worldview beliefs regarding religion, a sense of purpose, and one's efficacy. These types of beliefs should provide additional insight into the foundations of a person's moral and ethical decision-making behavior.

UNIVARIATE TESTS OF WORLDVIEW BELIEFS

Worldview beliefs were tested as single predictors of extrinsic and intrinsic bases for making decisions. *Theism* was a significant positive predictor of a reliance on *Family*, $\beta = .24$, $p < .001$ [$CI = .08, .21$], and on a *Social Group*, $\beta = .13$, $p = .025$ [$CI = .01, .18$], but it was not a significant predictor of a reliance on *Oneself*, $p = .58$ [$CI = -.03, .04$]. *Nihilism* was a significant negative predictor of a reliance on *Family*, $\beta = -.32$, $p < .001$ [$CI = -.59, -.29$], on a *Social Group*, $\beta = -.16$, $p = .004$ [$CI = -.46, -.09$], and on *Oneself*, $\beta = -.20$, $p < .001$ [$CI = -.21, -.06$].

Upon first reflection, one might think of *Nihilism* as being directly opposed to *Theism*, particularly given their negative correlation, $r = -.27$, $p < .001$, but the measures tap two separate, though related dimensions. A positive score on the *Theism* measure taps a belief in the existence of a deity, and a negative score taps the belief that a deity does not exist, or atheism. *Nihilism*, which concerns a belief that life has a purpose, would more closely approximate agnosticism, which does not take a stance one way or the other on the existence of a deity. It is reasonable for a respondent who indicated a high score on *Theism* to report disagreement with *Nihilism*, but the converse is not necessarily true; a respondent who reported not believing in a deity would not necessarily also express the belief that life has no purpose. Therefore, a model that includes both worldview dimensions should yield more insight and have more explanatory power.

Beliefs concerning personal efficacy also should predict a tendency to rely on extrinsic or intrinsic bases for making decisions. *Predeterminism* was a significant positive predictor of a reliance on *Family*, $\beta = .21$, $p < .001$ [$CI = .06, .19$], and on a *Social Group*, $\beta = .18$, $p = .002$ [$CI = .05, .21$]. *Predeterminism* was not a significant predictor of a reliance on *Oneself* ($p = .79$). *Fatalism* was not a significant predictor of a reliance on *Family*, $p = .27$ [$CI = -.15, .04$], on a *Social Group* ($p = .72$), or on *Oneself*, $\beta = -.08$, $p = .17$ [$CI = -.08, .01$]. *OwnFate* was not a significant predictor of a reliance on *Family* ($p = .99$), or on a *Social Group*, although the latter test was inconclusive, $\beta = -.08$, $p = .146$ [$CI = -.18, .03$]. *OwnFate* was a significant positive predictor of a reliance on *Oneself*, $\beta = .16$, $p = .004$ [$CI = .02, .10$].

Table 1. Correlations among worldview beliefs and morality beliefs

	1	2	3	4	5	6	7	8	9
1. Theism	1.00								
2. Predeter	0.60***	1.00							
3. Fatalism	0.13*	0.22***	1.00						
4. Nihilism	-0.27***	-0.15**	0.16**	1.00					
5. OwnFate	-0.21***	-0.33***	-0.19**	0.01	1.00				
6. PunSin	0.14*	0.09	0.02	0.03	0.03	1.00			
7. BlkWhite	-0.24***	-0.18**	-0.01	0.05	0.12*	-0.12*	1.00		
8. RotApple	0.18**	0.18**	0.12*	-0.02	-0.06	0.19***	-0.12*	1.00	
9. PerMoral	-0.20***	-0.11*	0.08	0.07	0.03	-0.27***	0.15**	-0.09	1.00

Note. * = p > .05, ** = p > .01, *** = p > .001.

The results of the tests suggest that different worldview beliefs influence either extrinsic or intrinsic of decision-making referents, but not necessarily both. Belief regarding the existence of a deity predicted a reliance on extrinsic bases but not intrinsic ones. Likewise, a belief that a deity decides the course of one's life predicted a dependence on extrinsic referents and not intrinsic ones. A belief regarding purpose in life predicted both extrinsic and intrinsic referents. A fatalistic belief was not a clear predictor of either extrinsic or intrinsic referents, but a belief that one is responsible for the outcomes in one's life predicted the likelihood of relying on an intrinsic referent but not on extrinsic referents. Therefore, it is possible that a combination of these beliefs influence a person's tendency to rely on either extrinsic or intrinsic decision-making referents. This possibility will be examined in the multivariate tests.

UNIVARIATE TESTS OF MORALITY BELIEFS

Morality beliefs were tested as single predictors of extrinsic and intrinsic decision-making referents. *PunSin* appeared to be a positive predictor of a reliance on *Family*, but the test was inconclusive, $\beta = .09$, $p = .12$ [$CI = -.05, .45$]. *PunSin* also appeared to be a positive predictor of a reliance on a *Social Group*, $\beta = .10$, $p = .081$ [$CI = -.03, .58$], but it was not a significant predictor of a reliance on *Oneself* ($p = .83$). *RotApple* appeared to be a significant predictor of a reliance on others, but the test was inconclusive, $\beta = .10$, $p = .08$ [$CI = -.02, .43$]. *RotApple* was a significant positive predictor of a reliance on a *Social Group*, $\beta = .12$, $p = .044$ [$CI = .01, .56$], but it was not a significant predictor of a reliance on *Oneself* ($p = .45$).

Both *BlkWhite* and *PerMoral* concern beliefs regarding moral relativism. *BlkWhite* was not a significant predictor of a reliance on *Family* ($p = .26$), or on a *Social Group* ($p = .99$). *BlkWhite* appeared to be a significant predictor of a reliance on *Oneself*, but the test was inconclusive, $\beta = .09$, $p = .13$ [$CI = -.02, .20$]. *PerMoral* appeared to be a significant predictor of a reliance on *Family*, but the test was inconclusive, $\beta = -.09$, $p = .12$ [$CI = -.36, .04$]. *PerMoral* was not a significant predictor of a reliance on a *Social Group* ($p = .88$), or on *Oneself* ($p = .52$).

In contrast to the tests of worldview beliefs, only one test of morality beliefs exceeded conventional levels of significance, that of *RotApple* predicting a reliance on a *Social Group*, and extrinsic referent. This belief also appeared to predict the other extrinsic referent. A belief that violations of moral rules must be punished appeared to predict a reliance on extrinsic, but not intrinsic, decision-making referents. A belief that clear moral standards do not exist did not predict a reliance on extrinsic referents, but it appeared to predict a reliance on an intrinsic referent. The belief that morality is a personal matter exempt from societal standards did not predict a reliance on an intrinsic referent; it did not predict a reliance on a social group, but there might be an association with a reliance on one's family members. Compared with worldview beliefs, these morality beliefs were less likely to predict a reliance on extrinsic or intrinsic decision-making referents.

MULTIVARIATE TESTS OF WORLDVIEW BELIEFS

Beliefs regarding the existence of a deity and the existence of purpose in life, taken together, should produce a clearer model than either belief alone. *Family* was regressed on a model of *Theism, Nihilism,* and their interaction term, which produced a significant model, $F(3, 304) = 17.44$, $p < .001$, Adj. $R^2 = .14$. *Theism* was a significant predictor, $\beta = .16$, $p = .004$ [$CI = .03, .17$], as was *Nihilism,* $\beta = -.19$, $p = .003$ [$CI = -.44, -.09$]. Their interaction term was also significant, $\beta = .16$, $p = .010$ [$CI = .02, .12$]. Compared to the univariate tests, the standardized slope of *Theism* dropped from .24 to .16, while the slope of *Nihilism* dropped from -.32 to -.19. A post hoc probe of the interaction (Table 2) revealed that the simple-simple slope of *Nihilism* was stronger given higher levels of *Theism,* but weaker, yet still significant given lower levels of *Theism.* Higher levels of Theism, in conjunction with a greater sense of purpose in life, predicted a greater likelihood of conferring with family in making decisions. Conversely, people who believed in the existence of a deity, but felt life had no purpose, were less likely to consult with family. Among respondents who doubted the existence of a deity, this relationship, though still significant, was weaker.

A model predicting a reliance on a *Social Group* also was significant, $F(3, 304) = 3.63$, $p = .013$, Adj. $R^2 = .03$. In this model, the slope for *Theism* was nonsignificant, $\beta = .09$, $p = .125$ [$CI = -.02, .16$], while the slope for *Nihilism* was significant, $\beta = -.14$, $p = .034$ [$CI = -.47, -.02$]. The interaction term was nonsignificant ($p = .89$). It is important to note, however, that the slope for *Theism* in the univariate test was significant and positive ($\beta = .13$, $p = .025$), but controlling for a nihilistic belief resulted in a nonsignificant slope for *Theism.* The test of the slope of *Nihilism* produced a similar slope, but the test of significance weakened somewhat. Given the suppression evident in the multivariate test, the relationship merited examination despite the nonsignificant interaction term. A post hoc probe (Table 2) revealed that *Nihilism* appeared to predict a reliance on a *Social Group* only at low levels of *Theism.*

Table 2. Slope analysis of Nihilism and Theism

Theism	Family		Group		Self	
	β	p	β	p	β	p
+1 *SD*	-.64	< .001	-.12	.456	-.12	.468
-1 *SD*	-.39	< .001	-.13	.084	-.18	.022

Note. The coefficient is the simple-simple slope of *Nihilism.*

A model predicting a reliance on *Oneself* also was significant, $F(3, 303) = 4.38$, $p = .005$, Adj. $R^2 = .03$. In this model, only the slope for *Nihilism* was significant, $\beta = -.22$, $p < .001$ [$CI = -.24, -.06$], while the slopes for *Theism* ($p = .68$) and the interaction term ($p = .54$) were nonsignificant. These results were not a substantive change from the univariate tests reported above. However, a post hoc probe (Table 2) revealed that the simple-simple slope of *Nihilism* was significant at low levels of *Theism* but nonsignificant at high levels of *Theism*. Taken together, the slope analyses suggested, except for predicting a reliance on one's family, that Nihilism was not a predictor of decision-making referents when respondents had high levels of *theism*.

Efficacy Beliefs

Univariate tests of *Fatalism* were nonsignificant, but controlling for *Predeterminism*, a theistic form of fatalism, produced a significant model, $F(3, 304) = 6.47$, $p < .001$, Adj. $R^2 = .05$, of respondents' reliance on *Family* for making decisions. *Predeterminism* was a significant positive predictor, $\beta = .25$, $p < .001$ [$CI = .08, .21$], and *Fatalism* was a significant negative predictor, $\beta = -.14$, $p = .03$ [$CI = -.22, -.01$]. The univariate test of *Fatalism* was nonsignificant, but controlling for *Predeterminism* produced a significant coefficient. The terms' interaction term was nonsignificant, $p = .40$, but given the change in *Fatalism*, the interaction merited further examination. A post hoc probe (Table 3) of the interaction revealed that Fatalism was a significant predictor of a reliance on one's Family among respondents who tended not to believe that the course of their lives was governed by a deity. In other words, controlling for the influence of theism revealed that a fatalistic belief was a negative predictor of a tendency to rely on one's *Family*. This result suggests that higher fatalistic beliefs, apart from theistic beliefs, are associated with a lower likelihood to rely on *Family* for assistance in making decisions.

A model predicting a reliance on a *Social Group* was significant, $F(3, 304) = 3.84$, $p = .01$, Adj. $R^2 = .03$, but controlling for *Predeterminism* , $\beta = .20$, $p < .001$ [$CI = .06, .23$],did not markedly improve the utility of *Fatalism*, $\beta = -.07$, $p = .23$ [$CI = -.21, .05$], to predict a reliance on a *Social Group*. The interaction term also was nonsignificant ($p = .56$), but a slope analysis (Table 3) revealed that the simple-simple slope of *Predeterminism* was significant at low levels of *Fatalism* but nonsignificant at high levels of *Fatalism*.

A model predicting a reliance on *Oneself* was nonsignificant, $F(3, 303) = 1.93$, $p = .12$, Adj. $R^2 = .01$, but the coefficient for *Fatalism* improved in its predictive utility. *Predeterminism* was not a significant predictor, $p = .38$, but *Fatalism* was a significant negative predictor, $\beta = -.14$, $p = .04$ [$CI = -.11, -.01$], a considerable improvement over the univariate test. The interaction term neared the conventional level of significance, $\beta = .12$, $p = .06$ [$CI = -.00, .04$], and a post hoc probe (Table 3) revealed that the simple-simple negative slope of fatalism was stronger among respondents who reported a higher belief in *Predeterminism*. In other words, respondents with a strong belief in *Predeterminism*, and who did not believe that the course of their life was decided by fate, were more likely to trust their own judgment when making decisions. The significance tests for both simple-simple slopes are a marked difference considering that the significance of the univariate test of *Fatalism* was inconclusive. Further, the simple-simple slope of *Predeterminism* at low levels of *Fatalism* was 0, which suggested that respondents attributed greater weight to the theistic portion of the item. The correlation between *Theism* and *Predeterminism*, $r(309) = .60$, $p < .001$, is evidence of this relationship.

Taken together, the post hoc probes of the terms' interaction revealed that *Fatalism* was a significant predictor of a reliance on *Family* or a *Social Group* given low levels of *Predeterminism*. This pattern did not hold for a reliance on *Oneself*. That is, among respondents who did not believe the course of their lives was decided by fate, Predeterminism was a positive predictor of a reliance on one's *Family* or *Social Group*. With regard to a reliance on *Oneself*, *Predeterminism* negatively predicted a reliance on one's own judgment among respondents who reported a high degree of *Fatalism*. Thus, parsing out religiously founded worldview beliefs from other beliefs can yield a more precise view of the relationship between worldviews and extrinsic and intrinsic decision-making referents.

Table 3. Slope analyses of Predeterminism and Fatalism

Fatalism	Family		Group		Self	
	β	p	β	p	β	p
+1 *SD*	.12	.392	.12	.422	-.22	.137
-1 *SD*	.22	< .001	.18	.003	.00	.999

Note. The coefficient is the simple-simple slope of *Predeterminism*.

Predeterminism	Family		Group		Self	
	β	p	β	p	β	p
+1 *SD*	-.27	.163	-.17	.402	-.45	.027
-1 *SD*	-.17	.055	-.10	.269	-.22	.017

Note. The coefficient is the simple-simple slope of *Fatalism*.

Predeterminism and *Own Fate* exhibited a modest significant correlation, r (309) = .33, p < .001, and controlling for *Predeterminism* in *OwnFate* produced a significant model, F(3, 304) = 6.54, p < .001, Adj. R^2 = .05, of respondents' reliance on *Family* for making decisions. *Predeterminism* was a significant positive predictor, β = .25, p < .001 [*CI* = .08, .22], and *OwnFate* appeared to be a positive predictor, β = .10, p = .08 [*CI* = -.01, .17]. The slope of *OwnFate* was a substantial change from the nonsignificant univariate slope (p = .99) reported above. The terms also appeared to interact, β = -.09, p = .08 [*CI* = -.06, .01]. At high levels of *Predeterminism*, a belief that one was responsible for the outcomes one's life was a significant predictor of a reliance on family for advice when making decisions (Table 4). That belief was also a predictor at lower levels of *Predeterminism* but the magnitude of the slope was weaker. The same pattern held true when viewed from the opposite perspective, as the simple-simple slope of *Predeterminism* was significant at high and low levels of *OwnFate*, with a stronger magnitude at high levels of *OwnFate*.

A model predicting a reliance on a *Social Group* was significant, F(3, 304) = 3.66, p = .013, Adj. R^2 = .03. Controlling for *Predeterminism*, β = .18, p = .004 [*CI* = .04, .21], did not produce a significant slope for *OwnFate* (p = .81), which was a marked change from the univariate test reported above (β = -.08, p = .146). The interaction term also was nonsignificant (p = 38), but the simple-simple slope of *Predeterminism* was significant at low levels of *OwnFate* (Table 4).

A model predicting respondents' reliance on *Oneself* was significant, $F(3, 303) = 3.99$, $p = .008$, Adj. $R^2 = .03$. Although *Predeterminism* was not a significant predictor, $\beta = .09$, $p = .15$ [$CI = -.01, .06$], *OwnFate* was a significant predictor, $\beta = .21$, $p < .001$ [$CI = .03, .13$]. The interaction term was nonsignificant, $\beta = -.08$, $p = .17$ [$CI = -.03, .01$]. A post hoc probe (Table 4) revealed that, although the simple-simple slope of *OwnFate* was significant at both high and low levels of *Predeterminism*, the magnitude was greater among respondents who reported a higher endorsement of *Predeterminism*.

Table 4. Slope analysis of Predeterminism and OwnFate

Predeterminism	Family		Group		Self	
	β	p	β	p	β	p
+1 *SD*	.36	.035	.12	.503	.41	.018
-1 *SD*	.18	.028	.02	.782	.27	.001

Note. The coefficient is the simple-simple slope of *OwnFate*.

OwnFate	Family		Group		Self	
	β	p	β	p	β	p
+1 *SD*	.62	.006	.36	.113	.38	.096
-1 *SD*	.43	< .001	.29	.017	.23	.069

Note. The coefficient is the simple-simple slope of *Predeterminism*.

MULTIVARIATE TESTS OF MORALITY BELIEFS

Tests of correlations among nontheistic worldview beliefs and morality beliefs suggested that these different types of beliefs exist separately. Most of the univariate tests of morality beliefs were nonsignificant, but it might be that explaining variance associated with worldview beliefs might yield a clearer picture of relationships between morality beliefs and decision-making referents. Therefore, worldview beliefs were included in multivariate tests of morality beliefs.

With regard to *PunSin*, controlling separately for *Fatalism* and *OwnFate* did not produce any substantive change in either the slopes or tests of significance. Univariate tests of this morality belief were only marginally significant for extrinsic decision-making referents.

However, controlling for *Nihilism* produced a significant model, $F(3, 305) = 12.78$, $p < .001$, Adj. $R^2 = .10$, of respondents' reliance on *Family* for making decisions. *Nihilism* was a significant negative predictor, β = -.33, p < .001 [CI = -.60, -.30], while the test of *PunSin* approached conventional levels of significance, β = .11, p = .052 [CI = -.00, .48]. The interaction term was nonsignificant (p = .46).

Table 5. Slope analysis of PunSin and Nihilism

PunSin	Family		Group		Self	
	β	p	β	p	β	p
+1 *SD*	-.57	.096	-.90	.012	-1.57	< .001
-1 *SD*	-.48	.030	-.63	.006	-1.06	< .001

Note. The coefficient is the simple-simple slope of *Nihilism*.

Nihilism	Family		Group		Self	
	β	p	β	p	β	p
+1 *SD*	-.01	.968	-.20	.202	-.58	< .001
-1 *SD*	.09	.122	.07	.231	-.07	.207

Note. The coefficient is the simple-simple slope of *PunSin*.

A model predicting respondents' reliance on a *Social Group* also was significant, F(3, 305) = 5.50, p = .001, Adj. R^2 = .04. *Nihilism* was a significant negative predictor, β = -.19, p < .001 [CI = -.51, -.13], and *PunSin* was a significant positive predictor, β = .13, p = .025 [CI = .04, .65]. In addition, the interaction term was significant, β = .12, p = .037 [CI = .02, .64]. A slope analysis (Table 5) revealed that a belief that life has a purpose was a stronger negative predictor among respondents who believed that moral violations should be punished. That is, respondents who believed that life has a purpose and that moral violations should be punished were more likely to rely on a social group for decision-making.

A model predicting respondents' reliance on their own judgment was significant, F(3, 305) = 9.80, p < .001, Adj. R^2 = .08. *Nihilism* was a significant negative predictor, β = -.24, p < .001 [CI = -.24, -.09], but the test of *PunSin* was nonsignificant (p = .51). Nevertheless, their interaction term was significant, β = .23, p < .001 [CI = .13, .37]. A post hoc probe (Table 5) revealed that *PunSin* was a significant negative predictor of a reliance on *Oneself*, at high levels of *Nihilism*, but it was nonsignificant at low levels of *Nihilism*. That is, respondents who believed that moral violations should be punished and who believed that life had no purpose were more likely to rely on their own personal judgment. The univariate test of this morality belief (p = .83) was nonsignificant, but when controlling for *Nihilism*, it was a predictor of an intrinsic decision-making referent only among respondents who believed that life had no purpose. In this instance, the inclusion of a worldview belief permitted a clearer test of this morality belief as a predictor of an intrinsic basis for making decisions in life.

Black and White

In none of the univariate tests reported above was *BlkWhite* a statistically significant predictor. Controlling for *Fatalism* did not produce any substantive change in the slopes or tests of significance of *BlkWhite*.

However, controlling for *Nihilism* produced a significant model, $F(3, 305) = 12.78, p < .001$, Adj. $R^2 = .10$, of respondents' reliance on *Family* for making decisions. *Nihilism* was a significant negative predictor, $\beta = -.33, p < .001$ [$CI = -.60, -.31$], while the test of *BlkWhite* was nonsignificant, $p = .53$. However, their interaction term appeared noteworthy, $\beta = .10, p = .08$ [$CI = -.02, .43$]. *BlkWhite* was a significant negative predictor at high levels of *Nihilism*, but not at low levels of *Nihilism* (Table 6).

A model that predicted a reliance on a *Social Group* also was significant, $F(3, 305) = 2.83, p = .039$, Adj. $R^2 = .02$. However, only the slope for *Nihilism* was significant, $\beta = -.16, p = .005$ [$CI = -.46, -.08$], with nonsignificant tests for *BlkWhite* ($p = .92$) and their interaction term ($p = .83$). Controlling for a sense of purpose in life did not change the utility of this moral belief in predicting a reliance on a social group for making decisions.

However, a model that predicted a reliance on *Oneself* was significant, $F(3, 304) = 7.13, p < .001$, Adj. $R^2 = .06$. The slope for *Nihilism* was significant, $\beta = -.22, p < .001$ [$CI = -.23, -.08$], as was the slope for *BlkWhite*, $\beta = .12, p = .037$ [$CI = .01, .23$], which was a notable change in the univariate test of *BlkWhite* ($\beta = .09, p = .13$). In addition, their interaction term was significant, $\beta = .13, p = .023$ [$CI = .02, .25$]. At high levels of *BlkWhite*, the simple-simple slope of *Nihilism* (Table 6) was remarkably strong, and the magnitude weakened somewhat given lower levels of *BlkWhite*. Respondents who believed that clear moral standards did not exist, and who tended to believe that life had a purpose, were more likely to trust their own judgment compared with respondents who tended to espouse the existence of clear moral standards. Or put another way, a sense the life has a purpose predicted a greater likelihood of relying on *Oneself* in making decisions. The pattern of univariate and multivariate results for BlkWhite suggested that worldview beliefs can make a substantial contribution, apart from morality beliefs, in understanding people's bases for decision-making and behavior.

The belief that a person is in control of the fate of his or her life was tested, as well. A model of that regressed a reliance on *Family* on the variables *OwnFate*, *BlkWhite* and their interaction term was nonsignificant, $F(3, 305) = .68, p = .56$. Likewise, a similar model with a reliance on a *Social Group* as the criterion was nonsignificant, $F(3, 305) = .81, p = .49$.

However, a model with a reliance on *Oneself* as the criterion was significant, $F(3, 304) = 5.89, p < .001$, Adj. $R^2 = .05$. The variable *OwnFate* was significant, $\beta = .12, p = .032$ [$CI = .01, .09$], while *BlkWhite* remained nonsignificant ($p = .36$). However, their interaction term was significant, $\beta = -.16, p = .006$ [$CI = -.11, -.02$]. A post hoc probe was conducted at 1 *SD* above and below the mean of *BlkWhite*, and the simple-simple slopes of *OwnFate* ($\beta_{+1SD} = .83, p = .001$, vs. $\beta_{-1SD} = .57, p < .001$) suggested that among respondents who subscribed to moral relativism, a belief that people are responsible for the outcomes in their own life was a stronger predictor of a reliance on one's own judgment than among respondents who did not subscribe to moral relativism. Or viewed from the opposite perspective, with a probe at 1 *SD* above and below the mean of OwnFate, the simple-simple slopes of BlkWhite ($\beta_{+1SD} = .57, p = .003$, vs. $\beta_{-1SD} = .31, p = .003$) suggested that among respondents who held that each person is responsible for his or her own fate, a belief in moral relativism was a stronger predictor of a reliance on *Oneself* than among those who did not believe that people make their own fate.

Table 6. Slope analysis of BlkWhite and Nihilism

BlkWhite	Family		Group		Self	
	β	*p*	β	*p*	β	*p*
+1 *SD*	-.95	.010	-.08	.833	-1.06	.005
-1 *SD*	-.72	.003	-.11	.655	-.74	.002

Note. The coefficient is the simple-simple slope of *Nihilism*.

Nihilism	Family		Group		Self	
	β	*p*	β	*p*	β	*p*
+1 *SD*	-.31	.049	.04	.802	-.25	.120
-1 *SD*	-.08	.146	.01	.843	.05	.383

Note. The coefficient is the simple-simple slope of *BlkWhite*.

Rotten Apple

With regard to *RotApple*, controlling separately for *Nihilism* and *OwnFate* did not produce any substantive change in either the slopes or tests of significance. Controlling for *Fatalism*, though, produced noteworthy interactions with *RotApple*.

However, controlling for *Fatalism* yielded a model of respondents' reliance on *Family*, $F(3, 305) = 2.57$, $p = .056$, Adj. $R^2 = .02$, that produced a significant coefficient for *RotApple*. The test of *Fatalism* was inconclusive, $β = -.10$, $p = .083$ $[CI = -.19, .01]$, despite the strong univariate test, but *RotApple* was a significant positive predictor, $β = .12$, $p = .033$ $[CI = .02, .48]$, an improvement over the univariate test of *RotApple*. Their interaction term also appeared noteworthy, $β = .10$, $p = .093$ $[CI = -.02, .25]$. Although the tests of the simple-simple slopes of *Fatalism* (Table 7) were nonsignificant, the coefficients changed sign, with $β = -.47$ at high levels of *RotApple* and $β = .27$ at low levels of *RotApple*. The sign of the simple-simple slopes of *RotApple* also changed at high and low levels of *Fatalism*.

A similar model of respondents' reliance on a *Social Group* for making decisions was nonsignificant, $F(3, 304) = 2.02$, $p = .112$, and yielded no substantive change in *RotApple*.

A model of respondents' reliance on *Oneself*, however, was significant, $F(3, 303) = 2.64$, $p = .049$, Adj. $R^2 = .02$. *Fatalism* was a significant predictor, $β = -.12$, $p = .039$ $[CI = -.10, -.01]$, while the slope of *RotApple* was nonsignificant, $β = .07$, $p = .213$ $[CI = -.04, .18]$. Nevertheless, their interaction term was significant, $β = .13$, $p = .023$ $[CI = .01, .15]$. The test of the simple-simple slope of *RotApple* (Table 7) neared conventional levels of significance at low levels of *Fatalism* but was nonsignificant at high levels of *Fatalism*. Among respondents who tend to have low levels of efficacy, a belief that a person's moral behavior can affect society predicts greater tendency to rely on one's own judgment in making decisions, but this belief is nonsignificant among those who believe they are responsible for the outcome of their life.

Table 7. Slope analysis of RotApple and Fatalism

RotApple	Family		Group		Self	
	β	*p*	β	*p*	β	*p*
+1 *SD*	-.47	.187	.36	.346	.21	.555
-1 *SD*	.27	.234	.20	.373	.10	.651

Note. The coefficient is the simple-simple slope of *Fatalism*.

Fatalism	Family		Group		Self	
	β	*p*	β	*p*	β	*p*
+1 *SD*	.17	.304	.16	.344	.21	.195
-1 *SD*	-.03	.674	.03	.684	.11	.086

Note. The coefficient is the simple-simple slope of *RotApple*.

Personal Morality

Controlling separately for *Nihilism* or *Fatalism* did not produce any substantive change in either the slopes or tests of significance of *PerMoral*.

Controlling for a belief that one is responsible for the outcomes in life, however, produced a significant model of respondents' reliance on *Oneself*, $F(3, 304) = 3.99$, $p = .008$, Adj. $R^2 = .03$. *OwnFate* was a significant predictor, $\beta = .17$, $p = .003$ $[CI = .02, .10]$, while the slope of *PerMoral* was nonsignificant, $p = .52$. Nevertheless, their interaction term merited probing, $\beta = .10$, $p = .087$ $[CI = -.01, .09]$. A post hoc probe was conducted at 1 *SD* above and below the mean of *PerMoral*, and the simple-simple slopes of *OwnFate* ($\beta_{+1SD} = -.19$, $p = .372$, vs. $\beta_{-1SD} = -.01$, $p = .925$) suggested that among respondents who expressed that morality was a personal matter not subject to social standards, the belief that that people are responsible for the outcomes in their own life was not a significant predictor of a reliance on *Oneself*. Or viewed from the opposite perspective, with a probe at 1 *SD* above and below the mean of *OwnFate*, the simple-simple slopes of *PerMoral* ($\beta_{+1SD} = -.40$, $p = .065$, vs. $\beta_{-1SD} = -.22$, $p = .063$) suggested that the belief that social moral standards should apply to everyone was a stronger predictor among respondents who held that each person is responsible for his or her own fate. The negative sign indicated that these respondents were more likely to rely on their own judgment to the extent that they believed that society has moral standards.

DISCUSSION

Worldview beliefs and morality beliefs were largely independent, and the only modest correlations that were observed tended to occur between religion-based worldview beliefs and morality beliefs. The lack of associations between those worldview beliefs that concerned efficacy and meaning and the morality beliefs supports the contention that they are distinct sets of beliefs. The association between morality beliefs and decision-making referents is more complex than a simple univariate relationship. Jointly, the worldview beliefs and morality beliefs predicted some dependent variables but not others. Although morality beliefs only occasionally predicted the decision-making referents, controlling for worldview-related beliefs permitted a clearer picture of the relationship between morality beliefs and decision-making referents. In general, different types of worldview beliefs were associated with either extrinsic or intrinsic bases of reference for decision-making. A belief that a deity provides meaning in life was positively associated with a reliance on extrinsic referents, but was not predictive of a reliance on an intrinsic referent. Likewise, a belief that a deity governs the course of one's life predicted a reliance on extrinsic, but not intrinsic, referents. A belief regarding a sense of purpose in life was predictive of both extrinsic and intrinsic bases for making decisions. Univariate tests of fatalistic and efficacy beliefs were inconclusive. Most univariate tests of morality beliefs, likewise, were inconclusive. It bears noting, however, that the dependent variables employed in the present study, which were drawn from the GSS, concern "decisions in life" in general, and not specifically moral or ethical decisions. Future research can focus more specifically on an individual's intrinsic and extrinsic referents for making moral or ethical choices.

A person's core beliefs are complex, however, and multivariate tests that controlled for different beliefs yielded clearer insight on the factors that might influence an individual's tendency to rely on either extrinsic or intrinsic referents. The predictive utility of a belief that life has a purpose depended, in part, on a person's belief regarding the existence of a deity. Although the univariate tests of a fatalistic belief were nonsignificant, this belief was a significant predictor when controlling for predeterminism, a religious form of fatalism. Fatalism predicted a reliance on extrinsic referents largely when preterminism was low. A belief that a person makes his or her own fate, though nonsignificant as a univariate predictor, was a significant predictor when controlling for predeterminism.

Likewise, even though the univariate tests of morality beliefs were nonsignificant, these beliefs were significant when controlling for different worldview-related beliefs. For example, a belief that moral violations should be punished was a significant predictor of extrinsic, but not intrinsic, referents, when controlling for a belief that life has a purpose. A belief in moral relativism predicted a reliance on an intrinsic referent when respondents believed that life had a purpose. Likewise, moral relativism predicted a reliance on intrinsic, but extrinsic, referents when controlling for a belief in personal efficacy. The belief that moral actions have social consequences was a significant predictor when controlling for a fatalistic belief. This morality belief predicted a reliance on one's family but not on a social group, both of which are extrinsic referents. This morality belief interacted with fatalism in predicting a reliance on one's own judgment, an intrinsic referent, as it appeared to be predictive only among respondents who believed that an individual was not responsible for the outcome of his or her life. A belief that morality was subject to personal, and not social, standards, predicted a reliance on one's own judgment, but only when controlling for a person's sense of efficacy.

The morality beliefs parallel Kohlberg's levels of moral development. The belief that morality is a personal matter not subject to social norms parallels the conventional level, as does the belief that there are no clear standards of morality. The beliefs that moral actions have social consequences and that they deserve punishment might tap the postconventional level of development. If so, then the items can be used to further examine moral development and decision-making referents, especially in conjunction with Kelman's notion of internalized standards of judgment.

These findings, though tentative, may reconcile the apparent conflicting findings of Leslie (1999) and Guimond and Palmer (1996). The findings suggest that a relationship exists between one's worldview and the factors that are involved in making decisions. Changes in approaches to making decisions appear negligible because developments in worldviews occur slowly, evolving in incremental ways that are imperceptible over time. Values, likewise, appear to derive from worldviews and are strongly tied to them, and because worldviews change slowly over time, any corresponding substantive change in values would be perceptible only after the passage of time.

The influence of worldview beliefs might help explain Braun's (1999) finding that students in media ethics courses said that the instruction should emphasize pluralistic principles more than universal principles. Such a preference would reflect the students' epistemic assumptions regarding the certainty of universal knowledge. More to the point, though, the students likely were asking for instruction that was congruent with their existing worldview and morality beliefs. The perceived ethicality of any given set of standards is based on worldview assumptions regarding the nature of truth and objectivity (Magee & Kalyanaraman, 2010).

Longitudinal studies would be a valuable means of exploring the development of worldview beliefs and morality beliefs. In addition, such future research should ensure that the measures are sensitive enough to capture nuanced differences in worldviews and ethical values. The findings thus far suggest several research questions: What are the components of the worldviews of media students? Does locus of control influence ethical decision-making? Does a sense of purpose in life result in greater ethicality? How do normative values regarding relativism or universalism influence the development of ethical skills? What is the relationship between worldviews and the value placed on codes of ethics and other extrinsic bases of ethical behavior?

The results can contribute to greater effectiveness in instruction in media ethics and moral reasoning, thereby aiding in filling a need for such research (Christians & Lambeth, 1996). If subsequent research provides further evidence that worldview beliefs are foundational to moral psychology and ethical decision-making, effective efforts to instill ethical values in media students, in addition to providing instruction in ethical skills, would engage students' worldviews and effect incremental transformation throughout the course of study. Zull (2002), integrating insights from pedagogy and neuroscience, maintained that teaching is the "art" of changing the synapses in the brain. A teacher begins with a student's prior knowledge and from there helps create changes in the brain's "neuronal network." By having a student engage the material, a continual stretching of students' knowledge should occur over time. Ethical decision-making, then, should be incorporated into every course in the media curriculum, not merely as a stand-alone course, or even as a module in a series of courses, but woven throughout four years of instruction.

Further, ethics instructors should continue to adapt pedagogical techniques to students' epistemic assumptions. Or, as Zull argued, they should build on students' existing neuronal networks, particularly those in implicit memory. For students who maintain that each person provides meaning to one's world and who rely on instrinsic referents for making choices, for example, ethics should be taught, not as a system of rules for making decisions, but as a way of imbuing meaning to one's world as a media professional. For ethics training to be most effective, the craft of the media professions and their values should be incorporated into a person's larger sense of identity and perspective on the world.

The construct of worldview was shown to make a significant contribution, apart from value-attitudes, to explaining a reliance on decision-making referents. Therefore, the construct should be considered for inclusion in the design of ethics research and pedagogy. The results of this study have yielded insight into the relationships among worldviews, values, and decision-making. This study has also served a heuristic purpose in generating a number of research questions and testable hypotheses. Additional efforts should yield a fruitful line of research for both the psychology of morality and ethics instruction.

REFERENCES

Berzonsky, M. D. (1994). Individual differences in self-construction: The role of constructivist epistemological assumptions. *Journal of Constructivist Psychology, 7*, 263-81.

Braun, M. J. (1999). Media ethics education: A comparison of student responses. *Journal of Mass Media Ethics, 14*, 171-182.

Calder, B. J., Phillips, L. W., & Tybout, A. M. (1981). Designing research for application. *Journal of Consumer Research, 8*, 197-207.

Chaffee, S. H. (1991). *Communication Concepts 1: Explication*. Newbury Park, CA: Sage.

Cohen, J. (1990). Things I have learned (so far). *American Psychologist, 45*(12), 1304-1312.

Christians, C. G., Rotzoll, K. B., Fackler, M., McKee, K. B., & Woods, Jr., R. H. (2005). *Media Ethics: Cases and Moral Reasoning*. (7th ed.) Boston, MA: Allyn and Bacon

Christians, C. G., & Lambeth, E. B. (1996). The status of ethics instruction in communication departments. *Communication Education, 45*, 236-243.

Davis, J. A., Smith, T. W., & Marsden, P. (2004). General Social Survey 1972-2000 Cumulative Codebook. Retrieved from the World Wide Web at http://www. icpsr.umich.edu:8080/GSS/homepage.htm

Feather, N. T. (1995). Values, valences, and choice: The influence of values on the perceived attractiveness and choice of alternatives. *Journal of Personality and Social Psychology, 68*, 1135-1151.

Guimond, S., & Palmer, D. L. (1996). The political socialization of commerce and social science students: Epistemic authority and attitude change. *Journal of Applied Psychology, 26*(22), 1985-2013.

Harless, J. D. (1990). Media ethics, ideology, and personal constructs: Mapping professional enigmas. *Journal of Mass Media Ethics, 5*(4), 1-17.

Kelman, H. C. (1961). Processes of opinion change. *The Public Opinion Quarterly, 25*(1), 57-78.

Kluckhohn, F. R., & Strodtbeck, F. L. (1961). *Variations in Value Orientations*. Evanston, IL: Row, Peterson.

Kohlberg, L. (1981). *The philosophy of moral development: Moral stages and the idea of justice*. San Francisco: Harper & Row.

Kohlberg, L. (1984). *The psychology of moral development: The nature and validity of moral stages*. San Francisco: Harper & Row.

Koltko-Rivera, M. E. (2004). The psychology of worldviews. *Review of General Psychology, 8*, 3-58.

Leslie, L. Z. (1999, August). Value system changes resulting from a media ethics course: A postmodern perspective. Paper presented at the Media Ethics Interest Group of the Association for Education in Journalism and Mass Communication.

Magee, R. G., & Kalyanaraman, S. (2009). Effects of worldview and mortality salience in persuasion processes. *Media Psychology, 12*, 171-194.

Magee, R. G., & Kalyanaraman, S. (2010). The perceived moral qualities of Web sites: Implications for persuasion processes in human-computer interaction. *Ethics and Information Technology, 12*, 109-125.

Rohan, M. J. (2000). A rose by any name? The values construct. *Personality and Social Psychology Review, 4*(3), 255-277.

Rokeach, M. (1968). The role of values in public opinion research. *The Public Opinion Quarterly, 32*(4), 547-559.

Rokeach, M. (1974). Change and stability in American value systems, 1968-1971. *The Public Opinion Quarterly, 38*(2), 222-238.

Schwartz, S., & Bilsky, W. (1987). Toward a theory of the universal content and structure of values. *Journal of Personality and Social Psychology, 53*, 550-562.

Schwartz, S., & Bilsky, W. (1990). Toward a theory of the universal content and structure of values: Extensions and cross-cultural replications. *Journal of Personality and Social Psychology, 58*, 878-891.

Schwartz, S., & Bilsky, W. (1994). Values and personality. *European Journal of Personality, 8*, 163-181.

Singletary, M. W., Caudill, S., Caudill, E., & White, A. (1990). Motives for ethical decision-making. *Journalism Quarterly, 67*(4), 964-972.

Surlin, S. H. (1987). Value system changes by students as a result of media ethics course. *Journalism Quarterly, 64*(2/3), 564-568.

White, H. A. (1996). The salience and pertinence of ethics: When journalists do and don't think for themselves. *Journalism and Mass Communication Quarterly, 73*(1), 17-28.

White, H. A., & Pearce, R. C. (1991). Validating an ethical motivations scale: Convergence and predictive ability. *Journalism Quarterly, 68*(3), 455-464.

White, H. A., & Singletary, M. W. (1993). Internal work motivation: Predictor of using ethical heuristics and motivations. *Journalism Quarterly, 70*(2), 381-392.

Whitlow, S. S., & Van Tubergen, G. N. (1978). Patterns of ethical decisions among investigative reporters. *Mass Communication Review, 6*(1), 2-9.

Wittgenstein, L. (1972). *On Certainty*. G. E. M. Anscombe & G. H. von Wright (Eds.) D. Paul & G. E. M. Anscombe (Trans.). New York: Harper and Row.

Zull, J. E. (2002). *The art of changing the brain: Enriching the practice of teaching by exploring the biology of learning*. Sterling, VA: Stylus Publishing.

In: Psychology of Morality
Editors: A. S. Fruili and L. D. Veneto

ISBN: 978-1-62100-910-8
© 2012 Nova Science Publishers, Inc.

Chapter 5

RATIONAL CHOICE, CAPABILITIES AND THE MORALITY OF HUMAN WELL-BEING: THE THIRD WAY

Claudio Corradetti
University of Rome "Tor Vergata"

ABSTRACT

Recently the idea according to which well-being is to be valued in view of the maximization of self-utility, has been challenged by several economic theories as in particular by Sen's capability approach. This has amounted to the view according to which the "rationality" of the rational choice is something much more complex and diverse than what is a mere criterion of self-advantage. With the present essay I try to capture first the limits of rational choice theories in order to point to a more complex view of rationality. I will also discuss the role that psychology plays in such criticism and particularly in the problematization of the notion of "utility." I will then criticize two extreme and mutually exclusive interpretations that consider the capabilities either as an unconstrained list of yet to be defined human potentialities or, alternatively, as a fixed set of capabilities (Nussbaum 2006, 76-78). I will suggest that, differently from Sen's and Nussbaum's views, a third way can be defended as something based on a constrained characterization of the normative role of political judgment in conjunction with the notion of "pluralist universalism." In view of the fact that variation can be placed both across different configurations of functionings – when related to one single capability – as well as across the definition of the same list of capabilities, it follows that any list of capabilities should be contextually relevant without turning into mere relativism.

1. FROM RATIONAL CHOICE TO THE CAPABILITY APPROACH

Amartya Sen is certainly one of the best renowned economists of these times. His views have not simply contributed to economic theory itself but have also broadened the spectrum of moral (and psychological) motivations characterizing the behavior of the *homo oeconomicus*. One of the main targets of Sen is the criticism of an oversimplified view of rationality in economics and social behavior. In general, rational choice theorists claim that all rationality of human behavior consists on a strict cost-benefit analysis. According to this view, human behavior is strictly governed by the principle of maximization of self-interest and by a lack of mutual coordination with other fellow citizens. The model of classical rational choice theory, in other words, considers that what is rationally necessary amounts to the optimization of personal profit for the achievement of a collective objective *despite* any form of cooperation with other fellow citizens. When applied to the economic sphere, rational choice provides a restrictive interpretation of rational behavior "as if" it consisted solely of the optimization of personal profit. Sen criticizes to a large extent this model of behavioural explanation known also as "behavioural decision theory" (Sen 1977), and provides both psychological and moral arguments in support of a more complex reconstruction of a rationality model.

Behavioral decision theory and in particular the explanation provided by welfare economics considers that choices are rational or irrational on the basis of the egoistic or non-egoistic determinants of a decision. What makes agents to prefer X rather than Y? Following behavioural decision theory one should chose X if and only if X maximizes a personal interest. In view of this line of reasoning utilitarianism places itself in the opposite side of the spectrum since, as a certain version of utilitarianism considers, choices maximizing the total aggregate of individual benefits are to be preferred to lower aggregate of welfare aggregate. Differently from rational choice theory, utilitarianism protects the maximization of the greatest collective utility. When highest utility for totality is maximized, then the good for collectivity is achieved. On the contrary, rational choice theory, as the one defended by Adam Smith, claimed, in a famous passage of the *Wealth of Nations* [1776], that only through the maximization of individual benefit each individual is led as if by an 'invisible hand' to produce the maximum wealth for a society of individuals.

Following Smith's wordings:

> By preferring the support of domestic to that of foreign industry, he intends only his own security; and by directing that industry in such a manner as its produce may be of the greatest value, he intends only his own gain, and he is in this, as in many other cases, led by an *invisible hand* [emphasis added] to promote an end which was no part of his intention. Nor is it always the worse for the society that it was not part of it. By pursuing his own interest he frequently promotes that of the society more effectually than when he really intends to promote it. I have never known much good done by those who affected to trade for the public good. (Smith, 2009, [1776], book IV chap. II para. IX).

Smith's view on the self-ordering of markets through free rational (egoistic) choices, is critizable precisely on the basis of the presumed rationality of the individual choice itself. One of the main lines of criticism is that individual rationality does not have necessarily as an outcome that of collective rationality and that the latter is not necessarily the result of the former. This possible form of exclusivity between the two dimensions is clearly illustrated by the non-cooperative output of the prisoner's dilemma. The story runs in the following way:

> Two prisoners are accused of committing two crimes together, one big and a small one. The police does not have enough evidence to convict them for the big crime, but they can put them behind bars for the small crime. In order to get them convicted for the big crime, they

have to get at least a confession from one of the prisoners. A police officer puts both of them in separate rooms, which makes it impossible for the prisoners to communicate. The officer gives them a choice: if they both confess, then they will be convicted for the big crime, but because they confessed, they would be convicted for ten years of prison, instead of the twenty years. If neither confessed they will be convicted for the small crime and they will go in prison for only two years. If only one prisoner confesses, he betrays his companion. The consequence is that he will get no punishment, because he helped the police. Instead the other one, who did not confess, will get the maximum punishment, twenty years in jail. The options, which the two prisoners have, are shown in the matrix below. In every box the first number is related to the punishment of prisoner 1 and the second for prisoner 2. Since the numbers refer to punishment and thus represent negative benefits, a minus sign is added in this matrix showing the benefits of the different options for action (Wolters and de Graf, 2005, 385-7).

Table 1. Matrix of the prisoner's dilemma

Confesses		Prisoner 2	
		Confesses	Confesses not
Prisoner 1	Confesses	-10 -10	0 -20
	Confesses not	-20 0	-2 -2

Matrix of the prisoner's dilemma.

There are different options that must be considered in order to reconstruct the various available options. The point is: how can each prisoner maximize the best possible result for him/her? Let's consider the following possibilities: if both prisoners do not cooperate with each other but only with the police they both get -10, whereas if they mutually support each other and do not confess obtain -2. Finally, if one of the two confesses and the other does not the result is 0 against -20 or, -20 against 0, according to whom "betrays" whom. Strictly speaking, it is not possible to talk about real "betrays," since this model is designed for people who are not able to speak to each other, so that they can be seen at most as "free riders." What can be rationally foreseen is that both prisoners will confess and that therefore it will not be possible to achieve a collective optimum for both. The conclusion which can be drawn from this story is that rational acts at the individual level do not lead to rational outcomes at the collective level. Indeed, they do lead to the opposite since rational choice does not even achieve a collective form of rationality.

Sen's criticism of the prisoner's dilemma targets precisely this collective level of rationality which is in its turn a missing aspect in pure rational choice theory. Indeed in the latter no general equilibrium can be achieved (1977, 321). For instance if one takes, as Sen does, the hypothesis of a mass migration towards an hypothetical rich country, then it would be easy to obtain as a consequence that from rational choice premises one would incur into irrational outcomes where no collective rational equilibrium is achieved. In such case one would achieve the opposite affects from those wished, since he would probably impoverish himself even more.

Sen's general criticism of the −utilitarian− identification of well-being with utility, including also the most extreme version of maximization of egoistic preferences (as a one horn of welfarism), is incapable of explaining the psychological phenomenon of "adaptive preferences." This phenomenon considers that there is always a psychological adaptation to achievable preferences and that desires and feelings of well-being and happiness are contingent to situations. This implies that people are capable of adapting themselves to external conditions of extreme poverty reducing in this way the scope and the ambition of their desires. The result is a sort of artificial equilibrium between what is *believed* as relevant and what *is actually* obtained, so that those people who are permanently deprived will never be able to desire something more and better than what they actually have.

To the problems involved into the psychological adaptation of preferences Harsanyi (1977) has suggested to distinguish between "real" and "expressed" preferences. The first are preferences that someone *would have if* she had all relevant information for the achievement of a rational choice, whereas the second are the preference one *actually expresses* in the context of inadequate and partial information. To this proposal Sen has objected (1985, 191) that in order to draw such distinction one cannot focus just on those information concerning "utility," but also on other kinds of information. To the "informational monism" of utilitarianism and welfarism, Sen opposes an irreducible idea of pluralism of the goods. The notion of utility is an inadequate measure of evaluation also for another relevant reason which is connected to the psychological state of "desiring something." The point is that to define something as good, the desire of that something as something good, does not make it good, whereas to judge something as good does provide a reason to desire that something as something good. If this is true then what is implied is that a certain "consensus" on the good and the well-being is to be agreed as a form of procedural standard of evaluation. The extremely subjective form of rationality as the one defended by utilitarianism, in as far as it considers well-being as a concept exhausted by the notion of mental states, requires a more reliable and stable form of justification capable of value attribution.

It follows from this that the "rationality" of rational choice is to be subordinated to a *collective* form of rationality and that this collective form of rationality, in order to take place, must comply with a *universal standard of moral action* (1977, 344). In what follows I will discuss how Sen's most renown innovation in economics and social theory −the Capability Approach− presupposes for its functioning a system of agents' mutual coordination.

2. THE CAPABILITY APPROACH: PLURALIST UNIVERSALISM AS A THIRD WAY TO DEVELOPMENT AND WELL-BEING

Sen's Capability Approach has placed itself as one of the most promising paradigms among the contemporary models of development economics and social theory (1979, 1980; 1984; 1985; 1987, 1992; 1999). Sen's views arise not only from Smith's confrontation, as before indicated, but also from Aristotle's notion on "eudemonia" and Rawls' view on "primary goods," and in particular from Rawls' notion on "self-respect" as presented in *A Theory of Justice* (1971). In all these cases, including the interconnections between the Capability Approach and the Basic Need Approach (see for instance Streeten, 1984), the point is that the same notion of "Capability" cannot even be conceived outside a system of mutual cooperation. Sen's criticisms to traditional welfare economics consist in showing the error of equating well-being with the accumulation of commodities. Sen certainly acknowledges that the augment of goods is an element of human development. Nevertheless, he insists on the different capacity of "conversion" of goods for the same functionings required by people belonging to different societies or by different people within the same society, as for instance in the curious example Sen provides, such as that of "appearing in public without shame" (Sen 1985, 25-26; 1999, 70-71). By insisting on the capacity to "convert" a commodity into a functioning, Sen wants to highlight the fact that a simple comparison of the well-being of people is uninformative if based only upon a confrontation of possession of commodity. What is to be understood consists rather in determining how people convert such goods and how much goods are comparatively necessary for the same functionings. A second strand of criticism, which I will later re-address, considers how also the utility approach based on desire-fulfillment is an inadequate measure for evaluating well-being. According to Sen people normally do not or cannot make choices in accordance to their own preferences (Sen 1985, 18-20) and utility theories do not distinguish between morally worthy and morally unworthy taste. Finally, utility approach is an unreliable criterion since not only it ignores other intrinsically relevant values such as rights and liberties but it remains subordinated to adaptive expectations.

It seems, thus, that the best strategy for measuring human well-being is that of addressing more straightforwardly the capability to achieve a certain set of valuable functionings. Before entering into a more detailed discussion, it is worth providing a number of conceptual clarifications. Sen defines as "functionings" what a person can achieve in terms of doing or being something (Sen 1985, 10). For instance being adequately nourished, that is achieving a specific functioning, is not simply subjected to the allocation of a certain number of commodities but it depends on a wide number of factors, both personal and social which together contribute to define the capability for a certain person to convert goods in functionings. The notion of "functioning" refers therefore to the actual use a person makes of commodities at her disposal. Connected to this, as anticipated, is the notion of "capabilities." This refers to a person's ability to obtain a certain functioning, as for instance the capability to be healthy and conduct a healthy life, or the capability not to be literate. To these notions, it must be added the "functioning n-tuple," that is, the combination of doings and beings constituting a person's conduct of life. Each n-tuple represents a certain life-style and the capability set refers to the attainable functioning n-tuples that can be achieved. Sen's framework on the kind and number of available capabilities is quite flexible and it admits a large degree of pluralism allowing a wide possibility of application. Since Sen does not claim that there is a fixed list of capabilities, the same set of necessary capabilities depends on evaluative judgments taking into account the relevant contexts of application (Sen 1993, 47; Qizilbash 2002). The refusal to provide a definite list of capabilities has attracted various criticisms (Williams 1987, 96; Nussbaum 1988, 176; Qizilbash 1998, 54), but the value of Sen's proposal remains strictly connected to the possibility of allowing only to *public reasoning* the possibility of defining which capabilities are necessary to a specific context. The political force of public reasoning seems therefore to hold the main weight of Sen's proposal but this represents also a potential limit for those development countries characterized by either non-democratic or not-fully democratic political systems.

Towards a closed list of capabilities based on a theory of objective goods is directed the work of Nussbaum (1990; 1995; 2000, 11-15; 2003, 43-4). Nussbaum's theory lists, without providing adequate justification, a set of essential human capabilities that include the following categories: (1) *Life;* (2) *Bodily health;* (3) *Bodily integrity;* (4) *Senses, imagination and thought;* (5) *Emotions;* (6) *Practical reason;* (7) *Affiliation;* (8) *Other species;* (9) *Play;*

and (10) *Political and material control over one's environment* (Nussbaum, 2000, 72-5). According to Nussbaum, this list is non-negotiable, that is, it must be seen as required for any sort of life oriented to well-being. Nevertheless, if Nussbaum is right, then, the capacity of public reasoning to assess case by case the required capabilities is strongly reduced, as well as it is lowered the relevance of dialogical exchange in the public realm.

Notwithstanding the unavoidable "non-political" outcome of Nussbaum's closed list, it must be recognized that at least category number 10) concerning the "Political and material control over one's environment" configures itself as a meta-condition for the achievement of other capabilities. Given the special status of this category a third way can be found between Sen's insistence on the role of public deliberation and judgment and Nussbaum's requirement of core areas at the basis of the capability approach.

Accordingly, hereafter, I will develop an alternative strategy aimed at highlighting the role of a constrained form of deliberation and public judgment. As a matter of fact, the point is that a deliberation conducted in order to establish required capabilities can function only if, as a procedure, it gets constrained by categories of human rights.

According to my views (Corradetti 2009), a justification of a deliberative procedure constrained by human rights claims that, from the perspective of a reformulated theory of communicative action, one can derive necessary background conditions for the normative validity of speech-acts by referring to the fundamental conditions of recognition of a generalized otherness. What is meant by this is that, in order to achieve normative rightness, illocutive speech-acts must respect, first, the intersubjective condition of recognition. For the sake of clarification, one might distinguish between a metalinguistic function of speech acts and a properly linguistic function, and then state that the political activity of human rights discourses represents a linguistic activity oriented to a metalinguistic reflection upon those same normative validity conditions of our speech-acts. The discursive "filtering" function of a formal system of recognized liberties is reformulated and enriched by community-situated discourses of human rights producing the backward effect of resetting those same metalinguistic rules of our political grammar.

In the following section I will canvass upon the second-mentioned legitimacy claim raised by illocutionary speech-acts, that is, the claim of exemplar validity they raise once a formal compliance to an intersubjective dimension of recognition is fulfilled. In particular, I will explain how the formal system of liberty rights can be related to the notion of 'judgment' according to Kantian premises and how reflective judgment can explain the construction of specific human rights legal provisions from within socio-political contexts.

It is only if one presupposes this model of deliberation and judgment that it becomes then possible to obtain valid and appropriate capabilities for the specific contexts in which they are called to contribute.

Going back to the model, the transition from human rights as conditions of purposive agency to the exemplar validity of reflective judgments, does establish the transition from a formal system of freedoms to a substantive one. Indeed if, on the one hand, the presupposition of mutual recognition fixes the conditions of formal liberties for the individuals, on the other hand, their specific configurations and situated validity achievable through the use of reflective judgments, translate such formal constraints into substantive political principles capable of providing motivation to action for socially and politically embedded subjects.

From this it follows that through reflection on the necessary implied conditions for the realization of purposive agency ⁻understood as elements of a coherent life plan⁻ the agent becomes the depository of a sphere of liberties as political necessary conditions for the realization of reasonable plans of life. Inasmuch as these requirements represent *political enabling* conditions for purposive agency, the so-called liberties of the ancients and those of the moderns become concurrent elements, and not competing candidates, of one single system of rights.

Turning to the specific contribution afforded by the reflective judgment, one can claim, in general, that all judgments, according to Kant are dependent on both the conditions posed by the determinant and by the reflective judgment without (at least in theory) this entailing the impossibility of distinguishing between a pure determinant and a pure reflective judgment[1]. If determinant judgment, given the transcendental laws of the intellect, subsumes the particular within an already given universal category[2], reflective judgment must supply itself with a principle for functioning as a judgment and this operation is assisted by an *a priori* principle represented by the regulative idea of the finality or purposiveness of nature.[3] That this represents, for Kant, a *functional* and not a *structural* distinction can be understood by reference to the three-fold partition of judgments into the categories *a priori*, *a posteriori*, the analytic and the synthetic distinctions.[4]

Analytic judgments, inasmuch as they do not need to find a law for themselves, are *a priori* judgments, which belong to the domain of the determinant judgment. Nevertheless, they are not typical determinant judgments since, for analytic judgments, the problem of the subsumption of the particular to a universal is easily solved by the fact that the particular already contains the universal within itself, so that the process is that of manifesting their mutual relationship, rather than of subsuming one within the other. But whereas synthetic *a priori* judgments must also be linked to the function played by determinant judgment since, in their case, a universal is given and is *a priori* in the case of *a posteriori* judgments, one must recognize a connection to the activity of reflective judgment. For *a posteriori* judgments, indeed, a particular is given but a universal concept under which the particular is to be subsumed still needs to be found.[5] It is precisely the *a posteriori* judgments that, for Kant, possess the status of judgments of knowledge, both in their more empirical-descriptive version, as in the case of the judgment of experience, and in their more paradigmatic versions, such as in the case of scientific-normative judgments constructed on synthetic *a priori* judgments.

---

[1] According to Kant, there are two categories of purely reflective judgments: aesthetic judgments (the judgment of taste and the judgment of the sublime) and teleological judgment.

[2] Kant (1953 [1790], section 4).

[3] «Kant indicates the true nature and function of this principle [the principle of the finality of nature] when he claims that through it, "judgment prescribes, not to nature (which would be autonomy) but to itself [my emphasis] (which is heautonomy), a law for the specification of nature" (KU 5: 185-6; 25). Thus, even though the principle concerns nature as the object of investigation, its prescriptive force is directed back to judgment itself. In order to emphasize the purely reflexive, self-referential nature of this principle, Kant coins the term "heautonomy." To claim that judgment is "heautonomous" in its reflection is just to say that it is both source and referent of its own normativity. In fact, this is what distinguishes judgment's a priori principle, from those of the understanding, which legislates transcendental law to nature, and of (practical) reason, which prescribes the objectively necessary laws of a free will» Allison (2001,41).

[4] The notion of structural and functional distinction among judgments is defended by Garroni (1976) who also saw a connection with the functional activity of reflective judgment within synthetic a posteriori judgments.

[5] This does not rule out that the possibility that a posteriori synthetic judgments are connected also to determinant judgment, since the condition for their possibility implies that they contain a synthetic a priori judgment, as for instance, in the case of experiential judgment.

Scientific judgments are not, therefore, constituted only by synthetic *a priori* conditions, since the latter provide simply the *a priori* conditions for those judgments. Synthetic *a posteriori* judgments on the other hand, require the functional conditions provided by the reflective judgment and thus a specific principle, that of the finality of nature, subsuming the particular under the universal.

Proceeding from such Kantian premises, my analysis here seeks to extend Kantian epistemological observations to the practical domain of human rights judgments (a reformulated notion of the "capability approach"), through deduction of a guiding principle which can mediate between the particular and the formal system of human rights. This principle is what can be defined as the principle of 'finality of rights' which, by anticipating the consensus of a universal community, allows reflective judgment to find a form of exemplar universality. The principle of 'finality of rights' provides reflective judgment with a regulative idea which is logically antecedent to reflective judgment (in our case, specifically the reflective composite judgment), and which orients it to the construction of a frame which would maximally extend rights internal balancing.

Reflective judgments, starting from the assumption of a formal system of liberty, interpret the latter in a context where the universal rule is not given but still to be found. Inasmuch as reflective judgments play a role, according to their functionality, within *a posteriori* judgments, the notion of exemplar universality takes the form of a universality which can be reviewed and reformulated with reference to different contexts. Distinctly from synthetic *a priori* judgments, which can derive the particular from the universal *independently* of any situated horizon of understanding, *a posteriori* judgments are always constructed on the basis of a contingent frame of informational data which prompt a search for universal criteria of validity.[6]

The constructive function of the reflective judgment, thus, takes its move from the unrejectable presuppositions of purposive agency in terms of constitutive rules of a game, and it works reflectively by constructing within the open space of "grammatical" possibility left open by such constitutive rules, its exemplar forms of capabilities, as according to Sen's. But reflectivity is not only involved in the construction of such principles through the interpretive activity of the reflective judgments of the background conditions of purposive action. Reflectivity is also involved in the application of such rights particularly when there are conflicts of rights, as it will be later discussed.

Since the notion of universal validity of reflective judgment is sensitive to its capacity of expressing a criterion of normative validity particular to a specific context, the same form of universality formulated through the orienting principle of the 'finality of rights'[7] must be sensitive to the specific cultural and situational conditions for which it aims to be valid. This amounts to saying that the *a posteriori* status of human rights judgments advances a model whose universal validity, while trespassing on context, is measured against the temporally and

---

[6] Even without drawing all the necessary implications, Habermas seems to recognize the limits of abstract universalism when he writes: «The application of norms calls for argumentative clarification in its own right. In this case, impartiality of judgment cannot again be secured through a principle of universalization; rather, in addressing questions of context-sensitive application, practical reason must be informed by a principle of appropriateness (*Angemessenheit*). What must be determined here is which of the norms already accepted as valid is appropriate in a given case in the light of all the relevant features of the situation conceived as exhaustively as possible». Habermas (1993, 13ff).
[7] The notion of 'finality of rights' will be later used in the idea of deontological goal-oriented theory.

experientially determined *locus* of reflection. This does not rule out the possibility that while the normativity of reflective judgment rests upon the *a priori* principle of the 'finality of rights,' as a synthetic judgment it must be validated from *within* a given experience where the particular can either prompt or impede a feeling of 'furthering life'.[8] While the accord between the particular and the universal is guided by an *a priori* principle, the judgment is situated within *a posteriori* conditions of reflection.

Of central significance, here, is the idea that there is no rule which tells us how to apply the use of reflective judgement to the substantivisation of the formal system of liberties in any objective way within a specific context. If this were not so, it would be necessary to supply a description of grounds on which it would be possible to introduce an interpretive rule requiring, in turn, a further rule providing an objective interpretation of the rule itself, in infinite regress. In particular, the principle of 'finality of rights' plays the same role, within the practical ethical-political domain, as Kant's principle for the finality of nature stated in section 11 of *The Critique of Judgment*. Paraphrasing Kant, one could say that the principle of 'finality of rights' is bound, subjectively, to the representation of a socio-political construction embedding a system of human rights legal provisions which provides, through a universally communicable sentiment, *sensus communis*, a pleasure, a motivation for judgment.

In Kantian terms, that the universality of a pure judgment of taste rests on a notion of *sensus communis* means that what can be universally communicated presupposes the possibility of a 'sense' shareable by all human beings. Such a 'sense,' in order to be normatively cogent, must lie between a naturalistic reduction, on one hand, and a complete cultural embedding of our possibilities. According to this reading, when engaged in the activity of reflection, the faculty of judgment presupposes *a priori* the modalities of representation of all others. The notion of 'common sense,' as applied to the notion of aesthetic anticipation and accordance between imagination and intellect, can therefore be explained as an *a priori* delimitation of the horizon within which any possible problem of specification of human rights provisions, either at the national or at the regional and international level, can be validly postulated.

This notion of exemplar validity of human rights judgments brings with it an element of 'exemplar necessity', meaning here the necessity of agreement of all with a judgment considered as the rule of a universal principle which cannot be provided as something already given, but as something still to be constructed.[9] The 'example' becomes thus the only possible representation of the rule itself, allowing, on one hand, the 'exhibition' of empirical concepts showing their closeness to empirical judgments, and on the other, representing the 'rule' itself by showing, in this case, its closeness to the pure judgment of knowledge.[10]

---

[8] On the purposive active character of this notion and its link with the notion of pleasure, Allison observes: «Underlying this characterization is the definition of life given in the Critique of Practical Reason as "the faculty of a being by which it acts according to the faculty of desire", with the latter being the "faculty such a being has of causing, through its ideas, the reality of the object of these ideas". In the same context, he defines pleasure as "the idea of the agreement of an object or an action with the subjective conditions of life" (Kp V 5: 9n; 9-10)» (Allison, 2001, 69).

[9] Kant (1953 [1790], section 18).

[10] See Kant (1953 [1790], section 59). This point helps clarify why Kant sometimes uses the term 'objective' when referring to the role that the presupposition of common sense brings to the subjective necessity of the judgment of taste, for example, in section 22, Kant (1953, [1790]).

Finally, according to the perspective defended here, the principle of 'finality of rights' guides and orients the principles of human rights in the creative construction of an exemplar universal model, through the construction and the evaluation of the experience on the basis of an endless interpretive effort and from within a contextualized point of observation.

Interconnected to this point is the concern of this theory on how, through the use of reflective judgments, it is possible to close the gap between, on the one hand, state-evaluation independent of rights proper of the so-called "welfarist instrumentalists" who see rights in terms of their consequences for *right-independent* goals and, on the other hand, the so-called "constraint-based deontologists" who assign relevance to rights without taking into consideration any *consequential justification* as a possible constraint on action.[11]

So, similarly, if rights conflicts (stemming from conflicting duties) prevent the global satisfaction of individuals' rights, then evaluation of the overall consequences on a global system of rights may more adequately justify the temporary weakening of a right (in terms of its connected non-primary duties), if supported by clear evidence of extent and severity than inaction consequent on inability to defend both at the same time. This paves the way for an idea of the finality of rights within a deontological argument and activates the notion of situated judgment as something capable of assessing those circumstances and solutions which better advance overall protection of human rights. General human rights principles seen in terms of capabilities, cannot determine by themselves their most appropriate specifications for any possible situation. They can only attempt to do this through an aesthetic understanding of the specific experiences at stake on the basis of imaginative projections of possible consequences brought forth by different options. This means that human rights principles, that is capabilities, in order to be translated into specific political decisions, in terms of both constitutional articles and of the balancing of right-configurations along judicial sentences, need the support of a situated judgment which, through imaginative thinking, evaluates and derives specific capabilities configurations from more general constraints. Due to the plurality of configurations of valid judgments satisfying the general implicit commitments of purposive agency, I would define this approach as a form of *pluralistic universalism* (Corradetti 2009). Such form of pluralistic universalism embraces two different levels of reflection which articulate the activity of the reflective judgment both to its *external function*, that is, the hermeneutic interpretation of the transcendental conditions of liberty which, through the reflective judgment does establish the political formulation of capabilities, and its *internal* function, that is, the reflective activity of the judgment deployed *case by case* through the judicial activity of each capability configuration. If in the first case, the reflective judgment confronts moral transcendental liberty rights with capabilities autonomously deliberated by and for a community of political beings, in the latter case the terms of confrontation concern the juridical-political relevance of social facts as such. It is precisely in accordance to its *internal function* that reflective judgments do explicate the function of providing exemplarily justified thresholds of quantitative allocation of basic goods in order to satisfy, on social basis, the right to basic well-being, and with this, the possibility of individuals to accede to civil and political freedoms. The so-called "liberty from hunger", "deprivation," "illness" etc. while formally established through a formal system of liberties in terms of an implied contract, can receive an adequate fulfillment and proportionate allocation of required services and goods, only when conceived from a situated point of reflection.

---

[11] For the gap left unsolved by both approaches see Sen (1988, 190).

As it has been previously noticed, Sen's insistence on the opportunity to leave the public space open to discussion for the definition of which capabilities are to be considered necessary, leads to the formulation of a deliberative threshold from which human rights precommittments contribute to the definition of human capabilities. This form of precommittment cannot suffice in itself to avoid a pluralism of perspectives and views. Pluralism is indeed radically inevitable in modern societies and constitutes the essential core of vibrant democratic discourse. The point of pluralist variation does not concern simply the variation of the different circumstances of given data for the exercise of judgment and, thus, the variation of the balancing of rights provided by the judgment in relation to the change of the circumstances. Pluralism is, instead, concerned with the idea that the relevance of the considered data is dependent upon the cultural images that each interpretive domain has in its own context, so that judgmental pluralism is always mediated by the pre-cultural understanding of the evidences to be submitted to balancing and to their same optimal balancing itself.

One important implication of the deliberative right-based process here defended, indeed, is that a "radial" pervasiveness of human rights, as well as of their extensive application for the achievement of a normatively justified process of capabilities selection and definition, is a crucial element. Public statements must always be legitimated, at least indirectly, on the basis of the effects human rights bring forth for a proposed public plan. Taking into account the interests of all the affected that are put at stake by a governmental action, contrasting views can be assessed and evaluated for compliance with fundamental interests. Indeed, dialectical mediation can occur between conflicting parties only within an institutional framework that guarantees the reasonableness of political outcomes which, when so constrained, can deliver results acceptable to all parties on the basis of the guarantee of the non-infringement of the conditions of purposive agency.[12] Institutional designs strictly affect the democratic interplay among parties and the possibility that they reach a compromise within a morally justified frame: while precluding *a priori* predictability of the results themselves, fundamental rights nevertheless configure essential guarantees for the expectation of the reasonable outcomes that do not infringe those same basic interests of the competing parties.

CONCLUSIONS

In the two-step argument for the formulation of capabilities through a constrained form of deliberation, I proposed an understanding of the use of the reflective judgment as subordinated to certain inescapable formal conditions derived from the notion of mutual recognition. In so doing, the creative use of the reflective judgment has been normatively constrained to invariable performative conditions for the production of both publicly valid claims and specific articulations of human rights principles. This means that contrary to a

---

[12] As recently observed: «[…] No compromise could ever be purely substantive: some institutions exist even if they are not the object of negotiations. The model of "substantive" compromise is based on the assumption that no decisions have been yet made about the institutional framework or that the institutions are such that the probability of a substantive compromise holding is quite low […] democracy can be established only if there exist institutions that would make it unlikely that the competitive political process would result in outcomes highly adverse to anyone's interests given the distribution of economic, ideological, organizational and other relevant resources» Przeworski (1997, 66).

fixed, but not adequately justified, list of capabilities presented by Nussbaum (2000), one can justify a restricted range of human rights categories on the basis of the idea of performative contradiction, and only then proceed to a public assessment of what is required in a specific context of certain capabilities.

From such view it follows that the same notion of public reason can be pluralized and viewed as fragmenting itself into competing positions, which are in turn submitted to the scrutiny of the public opinion itself. In order to achieve public agreement, we do not need to search for a general support springing from the dividing and incommensurable views of the goods characterizing modern pluralistic societies. We must, instead, look for a *second-order judgmental construction* of an internally articulated reflective judgment that, from the plurality of those views passing the test of performative contradiction posed by the conditions of purposive action, overcome interpretive conflicts and mis-recognitions through the construction of a yet new exemplar universal configuration as a result of a *dialectically mediated form of recognition* among the reasonable position of the concurring parties.

The third way here presented, consists in trying to find an equilibrium between a free floating deliberative activity which cannot remain undetermined if it wants to achieve normatively relevant results, and the refusal to adopt an arbitrary and too rigid definition of moral constraints which would only frustrate the public definition of contextually relevant human capabilities.The path which has been followed then, consisted in providing an argument both for the definition of basic human rights preconditions of public deliberation which can only orient, on the basis of the principle of finality, the direction of the judgment, but cannot at all exhaustively define a close list of capabilities to be adopted once and for all in every occasion.

REFERENCES

Allison, H.E. (2001), *Kant's Theory of Taste. A Reading of the Critique of Aesthetic Judgment*, Cambridge University Press, Cambridge, MA.

Corradetti, C. (2009), *Relativism and Human Rights. A Theory of Pluralist Universalism*, Dordrecht, Springer.

Garroni, E. (1976), *Estetica ed Epistemologia*. Riflessioni sulla Critica del Giudizio, Bulzoni, Roma.

—— (1986), *Senso e paradosso*, Laterza, Roma-Bari.

Harsanyi, J.C. (1977), Morality and the Theory of Rational Behaviour, Social Research, vol.44, n.4.

Kant, I. (1953 [1790]), *The Critique of Judgment*, Meredith, J.C. (trans.), Oxford University Press, Oxford.

—— (1970a, [1795]), "Perpetual Peace: a Philosophical Sketch", in, Reiss, H. (ed.), *Kant's Political Writings*, Cambridge University Press, Cambridge MA.

—— (1970b, [1784]), "Idea for a Universal History with a Cosmopolitan Purpose", in, Reiss, H. (ed.), *Kant's Political Writings*, Cambridge University Press, Cambridge MA.

—— (1983a [1797]), "Metaphysics of Morals", in, *Ethical Philosophy*, Hackett, Indianapolis IN.

—— (1983b [1785]), "Grounding for the Metaphysics of Morals", in, *Ethical Philosophy*, Hackett, Indianapolis IN.

—— (1999 [1781]), *Critique of Pure Reason*, Guyer, P. and Wood, A.W. (eds.), Cambridge University Press, Cambridge MA.

Lewin, L. (1988), Utilitatianism and rational choice. *European Journal of Political Research*, 16, 29-49.

McQuaig, L. (2001) *All you can eat: Greed, Lust and the New Capitalism*. Penguin Books, New York

Nussbaum, M. C. (1988), "Nature, Function and Capability: Aristotle on Political Distribution", in *Oxford Studies in Ancient Philosophy*, Suppl. Vol., 145-84.

Przeworski, A. (1997), "Democracy as a Contingent Outcome of Conflicts", in, Elster. J. and Slagstad, R. (eds.), (1988), *Constitutionalism and Democracy*, Cambridge University Press, Cambridge MA, 59–80.

Qizilbash, M. (1998), "The Concept of Well-Being", in *Economics and Philosophy*, 14, 51-73.

Rawls, J. (1971), *A Theory of Justice*, Boston Mass.: Harvard University Press.

Sen, A.K. (1977), Rational Fools: A Critique of the Behavioural Foundations of Economic Theory, reprinted in *Choice, Welfare and Measurement*, Oxford: Blackwell, 1982.

—— (1979), "Equality of What?", in The *Tanner Lecture*, Stanford: Stanford University Press.

—— (1983), Development: Which Way Now?, *Economic Journal*, 93, 745-62.

—— (1984), *Resources, Values and Development*, Oxford: Basil Blackwell.

—— (1985a), Well-being, Agency and Freedom: the Dewey Lectures, *Journal of Philosophy*, 82(4), 169-221.

—— (1985b), *Commodities and Capabilities*, Oxford: Elsevier Science Publishers.

—— (1987), *The Standard of Living: The Tanner Lectures*, Cambridge: Cambridge University Press.

—— (1988), "The Concept of Development", in H. Chenery and Thirukodikaval N. Srinivasan (ed.), *Handbook of Development Economics*, Vol.1, North Holland: Elsevier Science Publishers, 10-26.

—— (1990), "Development as Capability Expansion", in K. Griffin and J. Knight (eds.), *Human Development and the International Development Strategy for the 1990s*, London: Macmillan, 41-58.

—— (1992), *Inequality Re-examined*, Oxford: Clarendon Press.

—— (1993), Capability and Well-being, in M. C. Nussbaum and Amartya K. Sen (eds), *The Quality of Life*, Oxford: Clarendon Press, 30-53.

—— (1994), "Well-Being, Capability and Public Policy", *Giornale Degli Economisti e Annali di Economia*, 53, 333-47.

—— (1997), "Editorial: Human Capital and Human Capability", *World Development*, 25(12), 1959-61.

—— (2004), "Capabilities, Lists and Public Reason: Continuing the Conversation", *Feminist Economics*, 10(3), 77-80.

—— (2005), "Human Rights and Capabilities", *Journal of Human Development*, 6(2), 151-66.

Smith, A. (2009 [1776]), *The Wealth of Nations*, Digireads.com Publishing.

Streeten, P. (1984), "Basic Needs: Some Unsettled Questions", *World Development*,12(9), 973-8.

Williams, B. (1987), The Standard of Living: Interests and Capabilities, in Hawthorn G. (ed.), *The Standard of Living*, Cambridge: Cambridge University Press, 94-102.

Wolters, W.G. and de Graf, N.D. (2005), *Maatschappelijke problemen; beschrijvingen en verklaringen*. Amsterdam: Boom onderwijs.

In: Psychology of Morality
Editors: A. S. Fruili and L. D. Veneto

ISBN: 978-1-62100-910-8
© 2012 Nova Science Publishers, Inc.

Chapter 6

TRAIT ATTRIBUTIONS
WITHIN THE MORALITY DOMAIN

Holly R. Hackett and David Trafimow
New Mexico State University

ABSTRACT

Based on general attribution principles, much research has focused on the processes involved in making morally relevant trait attributions. For example, it has long been thought that the process by which people make trait attributions is different in the moral domain than in other domains. However, more recent research demonstrates that the story is much more complex than that; there exist multiple attribution processes even in the moral domain. The present chapter reviews both the relevant empirical findings and theoretical developments that have contributed to our present understanding.

Understanding the processes involved in making trait attributions has been of vital interest to researchers in the past several years. Initially, researchers investigated trait attributions under the assumption that a single process was used in a variety of attributional domains. However, some inconsistencies lead to the conclusion that the process used for trait attributions differed across different domains. For instance, Reeder and Brewer (1979) argued that different schemas were applied to attributions pertaining to different kinds of trait dimensions. More recent research suggests that trait attribution processes are even more complex than that. The present chapter reviews the relevant research.

Early research in the field of attribution treated the concept of attribution as a single process. Research focused heavily on identifying factors within this process that governed whether individuals' behaviors were attributed to dispositional or situational causes. Researchers were primarily interested in identifying under what conditions individuals would infer others' dispositions or traits from their behaviors. Throughout this research, a few prominent and influential factors emerged, which included situational context, consensus or base rate information, and behavioral consistency.

Heider (1958) suggested that individuals have a strong tendency to undervalue, or even disregard, the influence of environmental or situational relevant factors on behavior, while overrating the influence of dispositional or trait relevant factors when attributing behavior. Even in the presence of strong situational constraints on behavior, people often do not consider these constraints when explaining one's behavior (Jones and Harris, 1967) and tend to make strong trait attributions or infer enduring traits from one's behavior (Jones, 1979). Thus, one overarching rule that emerged in terms of the attribution process was that when observing and explaining behavior, dispositional or trait attributions are much more prominent than situational attributions.

Another factor that received a lot of attention in the area of attribution was consensus or base rate information. Consensus or base rate information refers to whether or not most other individuals would engage in similar behaviors under similar situations. High base rate information would indicate that most others would perform the behavior in question, whereas low base rate information would indicate that most others would not perform the behavior in question. Observed behavior of a low base rate as compared to a high base rate should lead people to attribute the behavior more to dispositional factors than situational factors (Kelley, 1967). Furthermore, enduring traits should be inferred from the observed behavior to a greater extent when the behavior is of low versus high base rate (Jones and Davis, 1965). The reasoning lies in the idea that if most people would not perform the behavior under similar situations, then the behavior must demonstrate some dispositional characteristic of the target person.

Attribution researchers argued that base rate information would influence the attribution process across all domains, even within the morality domain. Kelley (1973) stated that morality judgments should not differ from other domains. Therefore, as an overarching rule people should make stronger correspondent inference when an individual engages in a behavior that would not be expected from most others as compared to a behavior that would be expected from most others, regardless of whether or not the trait in question possesses a moral component.

Research investigating base rate information produced some inconsistent results. Some researchers did, in fact, find that people use base rate information when attributing observed behavior (Kulik and Taylor, 1980; Lay, Burron, and Jackson, 1973). Individuals attributed behavior more to situational factors when the observed behavior was similar to most others' behaviors, and attributed behavior more to dispositional factors when the observed behavior was not similar to most others' behaviors (Hansen and Stonner, 1978). However, other researchers found that people did not use base rate information when categorizing (Kahneman and Tversky, 1973) or when making specific judgments about others (Nisbett and Borgida, 1975). Even more specifically, others found that base rate information may influence the attribution process depending on the causal factors of the observed behavior (Ajzen, 1977) and the size of the base rate comparison group (Ajzen and Fishbein, 1975). Clearly, when considering the overarching rule of base rate information on the attribution process inconsistencies appear to exist across different domains.

Another overarching rule that emerged in early attribution research was behavioral consistency. Kelly (1967) suggested that whether or not an individual behaves consistently toward specific targets and across situations influences trait attributions. The argument made was that if an individual responds in a manner that is consistent with their previous behavior, the observed behavior would be attributed more to dispositional factors than situational factors. However, if an individual does not respond in a manner that is consistent with their previous behavior, then the observed behavior would be attributed more to situational factors than dispositional factors (Kelley, 1967). Research supported this claim by demonstrating that high prior probability that an individual has the specific trait in question and that the individual would engage in the behavior in question increased trait attributions (Ajzen, 1971).

As researchers continued to investigate the attribution process, findings began to suggest that the process was more dependent upon the specific characteristics of the traits being evaluated than on overarching rules applied to all trait domains. For instance, the attribution process is influenced by factors such as desirability (Ajzen, 1971) and extremity of the behavior being performed (Birnbaum, 1973). Furthermore, one highly influential discovery was that the process by which people make attributions in the moral domain differed from that of other domains. For example, performing a single immoral behavior outweighed the performance of several moral behaviors (Birnbaum, 1973). These findings began to suggest the possibility of a unique process used when making attributions in regards to moral behaviors. While the previous research provided valuable information regarding attributions, such as the tendency to make more dispositional versus situational attributions and that some specific factors can influence the attribution process under some conditions, no substantial explanation was available which could fully account for the differences found for attributions among specific types of traits.

Prior to Reeder and Brewer (1979) little attention was paid to the idea that the processes used when making trait attributions may be influenced by the specific dispositional trait in question. Instead, as previously discussed, a set of rules regarding attributions were generalized to all domains, suggesting that a single process was used for all trait attributions regardless of the specific trait at hand. Reeder and Brewer (1979) took a unique approach by suggesting that different processes might exist depending on the traits that are being inferred from a person's behavior. These different processes, in turn, may impact the status of the previously investigated rules, such that context, base rate information, and consistency may or may not be relevant depending on the specific trait in question.

According to Reeder and Brewer (1979), there are two different types of trait dimensions. For partially restrictive (PR) trait dimensions, individuals are expected to have a somewhat fixed position along the dimension; however, their behavior is expected to vary from the average position depending on specific situations. In other words, PR trait dimensions are so termed because individuals' behaviors are only somewhat restricted within their position along the dimension. For example, if an individual is characterized as being extremely friendly, then it would not be unexpected if under some situations the individual behaved moderately friendly. However, behavior in accordance with the other extreme end of the continuum (i.e. extremely unfriendly) would be unexpected and could lead to greater trait attributions. Thus, given the fact that a specific position on a PR trait dimension can be associated with variable behaviors, a positive expectancy is not easily changed with the performance of a single inconsistent behavior.

The other trait dimension was termed hierarchically restrictive (HR). Similar to PR trait dimensions, individuals are expected to have a somewhat fixed position along the dimension. The difference between the two trait dimensions lies within the extreme ends of the dimensions. While positions at the lower extreme of HR trait dimensions are not restrictive, similar to PR trait dimensions, positions at the upper extreme are restrictive. Individuals' behaviors are expected to vary from their average position depending on specific situations when at the lower end of the trait dimension; however, individuals' behaviors are not expected to be in accordance with the lower end of the dimension when at the upper end of the dimension. For example, an individual who is characterized as being somewhat dishonest is expected to engage in behaviors that are both honest and dishonest. Yet, an individual who is characterized as honest is not expected to perform dishonest behaviors, and such behaviors would lead to strong trait attributions. Thus, a single negative HR behavior (e.g., dishonest behavior) carries a large amount of attributional weight.

The distinction between PR and HR trait dimensions quickly gained empirical support. For instance, one claim was that HR trait dimensions require few behavioral inconsistencies to elicit strong trait attributions (Reeder and Brewer, 1979). Fittingly, researchers found that traits that were characterized as HR required only a single behavior in accordance with the lower end of the dimension to disconfirm the trait (e.g., Rothbart and Park, 1986).

Another claim regarding HR trait dimensions that gained support was that the lower end of the trait dimensions were not restrictive, whereas the upper end of the trait dimensions were restrictive. When an individual was characterized as being immoral and then performed a moral behavior, he or she was not subsequently judged as being moral. However, when an individual was characterized as being moral and then performed an immoral behavior, he or she was subsequently judged as being immoral (Reeder and Coovert, 1986). In other words, with HR trait dimensions only one inconsistent behavior with the upper end of the trait dimension led to a change in trait attributions, whereas one inconsistent behavior with the lower end of the trait dimension did not lead to a change in trait attributions.

While this initial research was influential and greatly supported the claims made regarding HR trait dimensions, research failed to investigate the distinction between HR and PR trait dimensions in their entirety. Furthermore, the initial supportive research did not investigate claims regarding how people use situational information when making trait attributions within the two types of trait dimensions. Trafimow and Schneider (1994) addressed these issues.

In Trafimow and Schneider's (1994) research, participants were first presented with information about a target individual. To investigate the differences between PR and HR trait dimensions, two types of target traits were selected in accordance with the two types of trait dimensions. Participants were also presented with information about the target individuals' current situation and a behavior the target individual performed. The behavior was either consistent with the target trait or its opposite. Finally, participants were asked the extent to which they believed the target individual possessed the target trait (i.e. trait attribution).

The results of this research demonstrated that person, situation, and behavior information all influenced trait attributions. Participants made stronger trait attributions when the target individual performed a behavior consistent versus inconsistent with the target trait and when the target individual was portrayed as possessing the target trait. Of more vital importance, the results greatly supported the need to distinguish between the two types of trait dimensions. The behavior manipulation was found to have a greater effect, and person and situational information were found to have a lesser effect on HR than PR trait dimensions.

As reviewed, the distinction between HR and PR trait dimensions and how specific factors influence trait attributions within these types of trait dimensions had gained tremendous support. However, one critical question had not yet been addressed; what is the underlying principle that causes this distinction among trait dimensions? Reeder and Brewer (1979) argued that negative behaviors associated with HR trait dimensions demonstrated immorality because moral people would not ever engage in such behaviors. In line with this claim, researchers suggested that trait dimensions related to morality were HR, whereas trait dimensions related to ability were PR (Schneider, 1991; Trafimow and Schneider, 1994). Therefore, attribution researchers assumed that the underlying factor that distinguished PR and HR trait dimensions was due to a moral component. However, Trafimow and Trafimow (1999) suggested that this distinction was much more complicated than previously assumed.

Trafimow and Trafimow (1999) drew upon the philosophy of Immanuel Kant to explain why there is a distinction made between morality dimensions. According to Immanuel Kant's (1797/1991) Categorical Imperative, there is actually a two-part distinction within the area of morality, *perfect* and *imperfect* duties. Moral individuals always perform perfect duties and never violate them. However, although moral individuals are expected to fulfill some imperfect duties, there are conditions under which moral individuals can violate them. Some perfect duties include honesty and loyalty whereas some imperfect duties include being charitable and friendly. Thus, for example, under Kant's moral system, a moral person can be uncharitable on occasion but can never be dishonest.

Trafimow and Trafimow (1999) suggested that the distinction between perfect and imperfect duties provides an a priori principle for why some trait dimensions are HR and some are PR. According to Trafimow and Trafimow (1999), violations of perfect duties carry a large amount of attributional weight and lead to strong correspondent inferences. For example, a dishonest behavior leads to strong trait attributions that the person who performed the behavior is dishonest. In contrast, violations of imperfect duties do not carry much attributional weight and do not lead to strong correspondent inferences. For example, an unfriendly behavior does not necessarily lead to strong trait attributions that the person who performed the behavior is unfriendly. Relating the distinction between perfect and imperfect duties to the HR-PR distinction, Trafimow and Trafimow (1999) suggested that perfect duties pertain to HR trait dimensions whereas imperfect duties pertain to PR trait dimensions.

One nice characteristic of the theorizing by Trafimow and Trafimow (1999) is that it implied a new prediction. Recall that before this article, attribution researchers accepted that all trait dimensions pertaining to morality were HR. The distinction between perfect and imperfect duties implies that there should also be some PR morality dimensions. These PR morality trait dimensions should be the traits that pertain to imperfect duties (e.g., friendliness, charitableness, and cooperativeness). Consistent with predictions, when Trafimow and Trafimow (1999) tested these imperfect duties against the prefect duty of honesty, imperfect duty violations resulted in much weaker trait attributions than did the perfect duty violation.

Several other empirical studies also supported the distinction between perfect and imperfect duties. For instance, violations of perfect duties were found to lead to stronger correspondence inferences than violations of imperfect duties (Trafimow, Reeder, and Bilsing, 2001). Also, Trafimow et al. suggested that base rate information should not be used for violations of perfect duties, because even high base rates do not justify violating a perfect duty. However, base rate information should be used for violations of imperfect duties, because there are less clear restraints on violating imperfect duties. In fact, base rate information was found to have a greater effect on attributions about violations of imperfect than perfect duties (Trafimow et al., 2001).

Brown, Trafimow, and Gregory (2005) provided yet stronger evidence that the perfect versus imperfect duty distinction was valuable, by demonstrating that the morality of an act, or the morality attached to the act that is being performed, rather than the behavior itself influences trait attributions. In other words, if an immoral behavior (e.g. being dishonest) is performed in a situation that would result in that immoral behavior being perceived as moral (e.g. saving a life) then positive expectancies of a person are not changed. Furthermore, those immoral behaviors are not expected to generalize to other situations. However, in less extreme contexts, violating a perfect duty did result in strong correspondent inferences and were expected to generalize.

Trafimow (2001) extended this research by specifically testing for the generality of violations of perfect or imperfect duties. In a set of three experiments, Trafimow showed that if participants were exposed to a violation of a perfect duty (e.g., a dishonest behavior), participants expected that the person who performed the behavior would have the trait across situations (e.g., the person would be dishonest across situations). However, if the target person violated an imperfect duty, then participants did not expect the person to exhibit the trait in other situations. Thus, perfect duty violations generalize much more than do imperfect duty violations.

An implication of the distinction between perfect and imperfect duties is that the well-known fundamental attribution error or correspondence bias, whereby people ignore information about situations, should not apply well to trait dimensions pertaining to imperfect duties. Trafimow (1998) suggested that one reason why people seem to ignore information about the situation is because attribution dependent measures typically mention the relevant trait. This primes people to focus on the trait and ignore the situation. In fact, one aspect of the Trafimow and Schneider (1994) paper was that when participants were asked to make external attributions as opposed to internal attributions, there was a reverse error whereby participants paid more attention to situational information than trait information. A nice solution to the problem of the dependent measure priming the use of trait or situation information would be if it were possible to not ask any question at all, and thereby avoid the priming effects of questions.

One way of not asking a question is to use a person memory paradigm. Researchers have known for quite some time that people recall information that is incongruent with their trait expectancies better than congruent information, and congruent information is better recalled than irrelevant information (e.g., Hastie and Kumar, 1979; Srull, Lichtenstein, and Rothbart, 1985). Trafimow (1998) exploited this "incongruity effect." He presented participants with prior information that a target person was kind or unkind either at home, at work, or in general. Subsequently, participants heard about 36 behaviors; these behaviors were kind, unkind or irrelevant, and were performed at work or at home. To understand the predictions, let us consider the general trait expectancy first. If participants expect the target person to be kind or unkind in general, then it does not matter whether the congruent, incongruent, or irrelevant behaviors are performed at home or at work. In all cases, incongruent behaviors should be best recalled and irrelevant behaviors worst recalled. The interesting predictions concern the at home and at work expectancies.

Let us first consider the expectancies that the target person is kind or unkind at home. If the standard social psychology assumption that people ignore situation information is correct, then it does not matter whether the behaviors are performed at home or at work. Incongruent behaviors should be best recalled and irrelevant behaviors should be worst recalled. But if people do pay attention to the situation, then there should be a situation-specific incongruity effect. That is, incongruent behaviors should be best recalled only if the behaviors were performed at home. Behaviors performed at work are not particularly relevant to the expectancy about the target person being kind or unkind at home and so there should be no incongruity effect pertaining to "work" items.

Or, if we consider the expectancies in the work condition, then an incongruity effect should be obtained only for "work" behaviors and not for "home" behaviors. The findings precisely matched predictions. In the general expectancy conditions, there was an incongruity effect for behaviors performed at work and behaviors performed at home. However, in the home and work expectancy conditions, only situation-specific incongruity effects were obtained. If the behaviors were performed in the same situation as the expectancy, then incongruity effects were obtained. But if the behaviors were performed in a situation not relevant to the expectancy, then incongruent, congruent, and irrelevant items were recalled equally well. Thus, at least with respect to an imperfect duty, people pay strong attention to the situation and there is no fundamental attribution error or correspondence bias.

Utilizing Kant's (1797/1991) distinction between two types of moral trait dimensions offered a lot to the area of attribution research. The distinction provided an a priori principle underlying HR and PR trait dimensions. It also led to a new prediction not only about the existence of PR morality dimensions but even about precisely what these dimensions would be. It also put the fundamental attribution error or correspondence bias in its proper perspective and made correct predictions about the generalization of immoral behaviors. Nevertheless, despite all of these successes, there remained a problem. Specifically, what causes some duties to be perfect whereas other duties are imperfect?

Kant proposed a highly sophisticated and complicated procedure for distinguishing between perfect and imperfect duties. First, according to Kant, moral duties are based on a standard of rationality. These moral duties may be established as being either perfect or imperfect depending on whether violations, when universalized, cause practical or logical contradictions. Universalizing means imagining that everyone performs the violation. If universalizing a duty violation would result in a logical contradiction, then that duty would be established as a perfect duty. If a specific duty violation can be universalized without logical contradiction, although it is unlikely that any rational person would wish the duty to be universal law, then the duty would be established as an imperfect duty.

In order to better understand Kant's distinction between perfect and imperfect duties, let us consider specific examples. As previously discussed, a dishonest behavior violates the perfect duty to be honest. According to Kant's reasoning, honesty is a perfect duty because if everyone performed dishonest behaviors as a matter of routine, nobody would be believed, and dishonest behaviors would not fool people. Because the purpose of being dishonest is to fool people, and universalizing dishonest behaviors implies that people would be unlikely to be fooled by them, universalizing causes a contradiction between the behavior and its purpose. In contrast, consider the imperfect duty to be charitable. According to Kant, a world where being uncharitable was universal is logically possible; if everyone were uncharitable then being uncharitable would still result in people keeping more of their money. Thus, although a world where no one helps others would not be desirable by any rational person, universalizing does not cause a contradiction between the behavior and its purpose.

Although it is unlikely that the typical person utilizes Kant's highly complex procedure during the attribution process, people still appear to follow the rationale behind the procedure when making trait attributions. Trafimow, Bromgard, Finlay, and Ketelaar (2005) proposed that affect might be involved in the attribution process, which accounts for why people appear to make a distinction between perfect and imperfect duties. This claim was based on two arguments. First, Trafimow et al. assumed that violations of perfect duties result in greater negative affect than does violations of imperfect duties. Second, they argued that the affect that is elicited by violations of perfect and imperfect duties is the main determinant of the attributional weight the violation carries. In other words, violations of perfect duties generate greater negative affect compared to violations of imperfect duties which, in turn, explains why perfect duty violations lead to stronger trait attributions. These claims were extensively investigated over a series of five studies.

In the first study, participants were presented with a target person characterized with either a perfect duty (i.e. honest/dishonest) or imperfect duty (i.e. charitable/uncharitable, cooperative/uncooperative, or friendly/unfriendly). Participants were asked to indicate both the number of incongruent behaviors required for expectancy change and how negatively or positively they would feel if the target person engaged in such incongruent behaviors. Not surprisingly, fewer violations of a perfect duty versus imperfect duty were required to change a positive expectancy. Also, a greater number of positive behaviors were required to change a negative expectancy for perfect duties as compared to imperfect duties. More importantly, violations of a perfect duty lead to greater negative affect than violations of imperfect duties; however, similar results were not found in regards to positive affect induced from positive behaviors. Furthermore, correlational results indicated that as negative affect increased, fewer duty violations were needed to override a positive expectancy. Thus, Study 1 provided the first support for an association between negative affect and attributional weight.

Where Study 1 focused on general violations of perfect/imperfect duties, Study 2 investigated specific behaviors while ensuring that the perfect and imperfect duty behaviors were equally rated. Each participant was presented with four honest/dishonest behaviors and four friendly/unfriendly behaviors and asked about trait attribution and affect. As expected, the type of behavior predicted both affect and trait attributions, with both being stronger for dishonest than unfriendly behaviors. Even more interesting, the relationship between behavior type and trait attributions was mediated by affect. In other words, when affect was controlled, the relation between behavior and trait attribution was not significant.

Study 1 and 2 both provided strong correlational support for the association between violations of duties and attributional weight; however, in order to support the claim that affect induced by duty violations determines the attributional weight carried by these violations, an experiment was required. As previously stated, Trafimow et al. (2005) claimed that perfect duty violations induce a great deal of negative affect, whereas violations of imperfect duties do not induce much negative affect. Thus, if negative affect was induced by other means when making trait attributions, attributional weight could potentially increase for imperfect duty violations. However, because violations of perfect duties already induce great negative affect, inducing negative affect by other means should not influence attributional weight. This claim was addressed in Study 3.

In Study 3, participants were randomly assigned to a control condition where affect was not influenced or an experimental condition where negative affect was induced. After the mood manipulation, participants were presented with duty violations and asked to indicate the number of violations required to override a perfect or imperfect duty. As expected, the duty by affect interaction was significant. The number of imperfect duty violations required to change a positive expectancy was less in the negative affect condition than the control condition; however, the number of perfect duty violations required to change a positive expectancy was not influenced by the affect manipulation. Thus, Study 3 demonstrated a causal relationship between affect and attributional weight.

If adding negative affect increases the attributional weight of imperfect duty violations while not influencing the attributional weight of perfect duty violations, then it would be reasonable to assume that removing affect would have the opposite effect. For instance, violations of imperfect duties do not induce much negative affect, so removing affect should not influence the attributional weight carried by the violations. However, violations of perfect duties induce a great deal of negative affect. Removing negative affect during the attribution process should decrease the attributional weight of perfect duty violations. Study 4 investigated this claim.

Study 4 was designed to provide an outlet whereby negative affect could be attributed to another source other than duty violations. First, participants were shown an image and told that the image was either designed to produce negative affect or no emotional response. Participants then responded to scenarios of a target person who violated either perfect or imperfect duties. Trafimow et al. assumed that in the misattribution condition, participants would attribute their negative affect induced by the duty violations to the image. As expected, there was a misattribution by duty violation interaction. More violations of perfect duties were required for expectancy change in the misattribution condition than the no attribution condition; however this was not the case for imperfect duty violations. In summary, consistent with Trafimow et al.'s reasoning, using a misattribution paradigm to take away negative affect in Study 4 reversed the two-way interaction obtained by inducing negative affect in Study 3.

Finally, Study 5 addressed the research findings that all negative emotions do not always produce similar effects on judgment (Lerner and Keltner, 2000). This study investigated whether the general feeling of negative affect causes attributional weight, or if specific negative emotions influence attributional weight. Using the Study 3 paradigm, participants were randomly assigned to a fear, disgust, sadness, or control condition, where such emotions were induced. Participants then responded to scenarios of people violating either perfect or imperfect duties. Similar to the previous studies, fewer violations of perfect duties than of imperfect duties were required to override a positive expectancy. Also, as in Study 3, the number of imperfect duty violations required to change a positive expectancy was less when negative affect was induced than when it was not; however there was no such effect with respect to perfect duty violations. Most important, this two-way pattern generalized across all three of the negative affect conditions (i.e. fear, disgust, or sadness). This generalization indicates that it is the negative affect all three negative emotions have in common rather than the idiosyncratic cognitions associated with fear, disgust, or sadness, respectively.

As reviewed, research in the field of attribution has made great strides over the past several years. However, the possibilities for future research still remain vast. One future research possibility could be to investigate whether perfect duty violations influence trait attributions on imperfect duties, and vice versa. For example, if someone engages in a dishonest behavior, would that indicate anything about the person's friendliness? Or, if someone engages in an unfriendly behavior, would that indicate anything about the person's honesty? According to the halo and reverse halo effect, people have the tendency to believe that a person possesses a variety of positive or negative traits as a result of observing one major positive or negative trait (Nisbett and Wilson, 1977). Based on this effect, it would be reasonable to assume that violations of perfect or imperfect duties could influence attributions on imperfect and perfect duties, respectively. However, given the attributional weight differences between violations of the two duties, it may be highly likely that the effect would be more pronounced for perfect versus imperfect duty violations.

Another future research possibility could be to investigate whether duty violations influence observers' subsequent behavior. For example, would an observer's subsequent behavior (e.g. punishment, social exclusion) be more extreme toward a person who violates a perfect versus an imperfect duty? In other words, would observers' behavior differ depending on the type of moral duty being violated? Extending the perfect/imperfect duty distinction to predict actual behavior or behavioral intentions could prove to be quite valuable.

Finally, another interesting topic that could be addressed in the future is the idea of "guilty by association." Would similar trait attributions be made for two people, if one person was associated with another person who violated a perfect or imperfect duty? Furthermore, would it depend upon the type of duty being violated? For example, say there was a scenario where two close friends were in a department store, and one friend stole an item from the store. Strong trait attributions should be made for the person who stole the item; however, it is not as clear whether strong trait attributions would be made for the other person. Furthermore, if trait attributions were made for the other person, then what caused these trait attributions? It may be possible that the negative affect induced by the duty violation simply extended onto the other person due to the association. However, it might also be possible that the other person's inactions against the violation lead to strong trait attributions. Research could extensively investigate this topic in the future.

As reviewed, research in the field of attribution has made progress over the past few years marked by a few substantial contributions. First, Reeder and Brewer (1979) introduced the claim that the processes used in attribution differed depending on the specific trait in question by identifying HR and PR trait dimensions. Second, Trafimow and Trafimow (1999) challenged the assumption that the distinction between HR and PR trait dimensions was due to a morality component by applying Kant's perfect and imperfect duty distinction to include moral behaviors as both HR and PR traits. Finally, Trafimow et al. (2005) demonstrated that the attributional weight carried by duty violations was due to the negative affect induced by such violations. While advancements have been made, we hope that many more will be made in the future.

REFERENCES

Ajzen, I. (1971). Attribution of disposition to an actor: Effects of perceived decision freedom and behavioral utilities. *Journal of Personality and Social Psychology, 18*(2), 144-156.

Ajzen, I. (1977). Intuitive theories of events and the effects of base-rate information on prediction. *Journal of Personality and Social Psychology, 35*(5), 303-314.

Ajzen, I., and Fishbein, M. (1975). A bayesian analysis of attribution processes. *Psychological Bulletin, 82*(2), 261-277.

Birnbaum, M.H. (1973). Morality judgments: Test of an averaging model with differential weights. *Journal of Experimental Psychology, 99*(3), 395-399.

Brown, J., Trafimow, D., and Gregory, W.L. (2005). The generality of negative hierarchically restrictive behaviours. *British Journal of Social Psychology, 44*, 3-13.

Hansen, R.D., and Stonner, D.M. (1978). Attributes and attributions: Inferring stimulus properties, actors' dispositions, and causes. *Journal of Personality and Social Psychology, 36*(6), 657-667.

Hastie, R., and Kumar, P.A. (1979). Person memory: Personality traits as organizing principles in memory for behaviors. *Journal of Personality and Social Psychology, 37*(1), 23-38.

Heider, F. (1958). *The psychology of interpersonal relations*. New York: Wiley.

Jones, E.E. (1979). The rocky road from acts to dispositions. *American Psychologist, 34*, 107-117.

Jones, E.E., and Davis, K.E. (1965). From acts to dispositions: The attribution process in person perception. In L. Berkowitz (Ed.). *Advances in experimental social psychology* (Vol. 2). New York: Academic Press.

Jones, E.E., and Harris, V. (1967). The attribution of attitudes. *Journal of Experimental Social Psychology, 3*, 1-24.

Kahneman, D., and Tversky, A. (1973). Subjective probability: A judgment of representativeness. *Cognitive Psychology, 3*, 430-454.

Kant, I. (1991). *The metaphysics of morals*. (M.Gregor, Trans.). Cambridge, UK: Cambridge University Press. (Original work published in 1797).

Kelley, H.H. (1967). *Attribution theory in social psychology*. In D. Levine (Ed.). Nebraska Symposium on Motivation (Vol. 15). Lincoln: University of Nebraska Press.

Kelley, H.H. (1973). The process of causal attribution. *American Psychologist, 28,* 107-128.

Kulik, J.A., and Taylor, S.E. (1980). Premature consensus on consensus? Effects of sample-based versus self-based consensus information. *Journal of Personality and Social Psychology, 38*(6), 871-878.

Lay, C.H., Burron, B.F., and Jackson, D.N. (1973). Base rates and information value in impression formation. *Journal of Personality and Social Psychology, 28*(3), 390-395.

Lerner, J.S., and Keltner, D. (2000). Beyond valence: Toward a model of emotion-specific influence on judgment and choice. *Cognition and Emotion, 14*, 473-493.

Nisbett, R.E., and Borgida, E. (1975). Attribution and the psychology of prediction. *Journal of Personality and Social Psychology, 32*(5), 932-943.

Nisbett, R.E., and Wilson, T.D. (1977). The halo effect: Evidence for unconscious alterations of judgments. *Journal of Personality and Social Psychology, 35*(4), 250-256.

Reeder, G.D., and Brewer, M.B. (1979). A schematic model of dispositional attribution in interpersonal perception. *Psychology Review, 86*(1), 61-79.

Reeder, G.D., and Coovert, M.D. (1986). Revising an impression of morality. *Social Cognition, 4,* 1-17.

Rothbart, M., and Park, B. (1986). On the confirmability and disconfirmability of trait concepts. *Journal of Personality and Social Psychology, 50,* 131-142.

Schneider, D.J. (1991). Social cognition. *Annual Review of Psychology, 42,* 527-561.

Srull, T.K., Lichtenstein, M., and Rothbart, M. (1985). Associative storage and retrieval processes in person memory. *Journal of Experimental Psychology: Learning, Memory, and Cognition, 11*(2), 316-345.

Trafimow, D. (1998). Situation-specific effects in person memory. *Personality and Social Psychology Bulletin, 24,* 314-321.

Trafimow, D. (2001). The effects of trait type and situation type on the generalization of trait expectancies across situations. *Personality and Social Psychology Bulletin, 27*(11), 1463-1468.

Trafimow, D., Bromgard, I.K., Finlay, K.A., and Ketelaar, T. (2005). The role of affect in determining the attributional weight of immoral behaviors. *Personality and Social Psychology Bulletin, 31,* 935-948.

Trafimow, D., Reeder, G.D., and Bilsing, L.M. (2001). Everybody is doing it: The effects of base rate information on correspondent inferences from violations of perfect and imperfect duties. *The Social Science Journal, 38,* 421-433.

Trafimow, D., and Schneider, D.J. (1994). The effects of behavioral, situational, and person information on different attribution judgments. *Journal of Experimental Social Psychology, 30,* 351-369.

Trafimow, D., and Trafimow, S. (1999). Mapping perfect and imperfect duties onto hierarchically and partially restrictive trait dimensions. *Personality and Social Psychology Bulletin, 25,* 687-697.

In: Psychology of Morality
Editors: A. S. Fruili and L. D. Veneto

ISBN: 978-1-62100-910-8
© 2012 Nova Science Publishers, Inc.

Chapter 7

HOW SIMILAR IS THE INTERACTION BETWEEN LOW SELF-CONTROL AND DEVIANT MORAL BELIEFS IN THE EXPLANATION OF ADOLESCENT OFFENDING? AN INQUIRY IN SUB GROUPS BY GENDER AND IMMIGRANT BACKGROUND

Lieven Pauwels
Ghent University

ABSTRACT

This study examines the effects of self-control and morality on adolescent offending. It is well known that low self-control and low morality increase the risk of offending. The question whether low levels of morality and low self-control *interact* in the explanation of offending, has been recently examined in a test in three countries (Svensson, Pauwels and Weerman, 2010). As outlined by Wikström's Situational Action Theory (Wikström, 2006), it is assumed that self-control has a stronger effect on offending for individuals with low levels of morality than for individuals with high levels of morality. No previous study has demonstrated the stability of these findings in sub groups by gender and immigrant background. To test how similar this interaction effect is, data are used from a sample of young adolescents in Antwerp, Belgium ($N = 2,486$). These data provide strong support for the hypothesis that the effect of self-control on offending is dependent on the individual's level of morality. The results are almost identical in all subgroups by gender and immigrant background. It seems that causal mechanisms of offending operate rather similar than dissimilar for Belgian immigrant and non-immigrant boys and girls.

Keywords: Self-control, morality, adolescent offending, interaction, Situational Action Theory

INTRODUCTION

One of the most influential criminological theories at present is the *Self-Control Theory,* presented by Gottfredson and Hirschi (1990) in *A General Theory of Crime.* The central assumption of this theory is that low self-control, increases the risk of offending together with other deviant and imprudent behaviors. According to Gottfredson and Hirschi, low self-control is the primary cause of crime. A large number of studies have tested this proposition (see Pratt and Cullen, 1998, for an overview), and empirical research shows that low self-control is associated with offending among different samples (e.g., youth, college students, non-students adults, males vs. females, criminals, among people in different countries) and in different types of studies (cross-sectional, longitudinal and experimental studies) (e.g. Antonaccio and Tittle, 2008; Shoepfer and Piquero, 2006; Ribeaud and Eisner, 2006; Burton et al., 1998; Vazsonyi et al., 2001; Longshore, 1998; Wikström and Butterworth, 2006; Chapple, 2005; Finkel and Campell, 2001).

However, though self-control seems to be highly correlated to offending, it is possible that self-control has a different impact on offending for individuals with different characteristics and backgrounds. This notion has been rarely discussed within the literature on self-control theory. Gottfredson and Hirschi themselves argue that the effect of self control is only dependent on the opportunities for crime but neglect the possibility that there are interaction effects with other risk factors for offending (which are not important as a cause in their reasoning). As a result, there is also a lack of research on interaction effects between self-control and other personal characteristics.

A theory of crime causation that explicitly states that the effect of self-control is strongly depending on one's level of morality the *Situational Action Theory* (SAT) (Wikström, 2004; Wikström, 2005; Wikström, 2006; Wikström and Treiber, 2007). SAT states, basically, that offending is the outcome of how individuals perceive their alternatives for action (influenced by their morality) and make their choices (influenced by their ability to exert self-control) when confronted with different types of settings. Morality (values and emotions) is seen as the main factor in offending, and offending is assumed to be primarily a question of morality and not of low self-control (Wikström, 2006; Wikström and Treiber, 2007). Social (or human) ecology may be broadly defined as the analysis and study of the social and behavioural consequences of the interaction between human beings and their environments. Situational Action Theory (SAT) is a general theory that seeks to integrate person and environmental explanatory perspectives within the framework of a situational action theory. The theory is specifically designed to address the role of the interaction between people and their social environments in crime causation (see Wikström, 2004; 2005; 2006; 2010; Wikström and Treiber, 2007; 2008; 2009).

According to SAT, crimes are moral actions and therefore should be analysed and explained as such. Acts of crime are breaches of moral rules of conduct (defined in law). Moral rules are rules that stipulate what it is right or wrong to do in a particular circumstance. What a theory of crime causation ultimately should explain is thus why people follow and breach moral rules. SAT argues that there is, in principle, no difference between explaining acts of crime and moral rule-breaking more generally because the situational process that determines any moral action is the same. According to SAT, self-control is only a relevant factor in offending when an individual actively considers committing a crime as an action alternative (thus having low levels of morality). Against this background, we hypothesize that there is an interaction effect between morality and self-control with regard to the explanation of offending. More precisely, we expect that self-control has a more important effect on offending for individuals with low levels of morality than for individuals with high levels of morality.

The question whether morality and self-control *interact* in the explanation of offending has been been examined in the research to date. As far as we know, only two studies have explicitly tested this interaction (Shoepfer and Piquero, 2006; Antonaccio and Tittle, 2008). Another study, De Li (2004) has examined whether self-control interacts with different factors of social bonds, which also included interactions with moral beliefs.

Shoepfer and Piquero (2006) used vignettes (scenarios) about behavorial intentions among 382 students to study the interaction effect. They found that both moral beliefs and self-control are related with intentions to steal and intentions to fight. Regarding the interaction, they found that low self-control was related with intentions to steal for individuals with low morals but not for individuals with high morals. However, such an interaction effect was not found for intentions to fight. Antonaccio and Tittle (2008) used face-to-face interviews among 500 eligible adults. They found that both morality and self-control are related with projections of future crime and that the effect of morality seems to be stronger than the effect of self-control. They also found a weak interaction effect between morality and self-control on predicting variety in delinquent behavior. No interaction was found with regard to property and violent offending. De Li (2004) also found a clear interaction effect between moral beliefs and self-control on the prediction of general offending. Svensson, Pauwels and Weerman tested the interaction between morality and self-control in three different urban samples: a Swedish youth survey, a Dutch youth survey and a Belgian youth survey. They report similar results, controlling for a number of background characteristics.

In short, the four studies reveal that there are indications of an interaction effect between morality and self-control on the explanation of offending. However, these studies have their limitations. First, the two studies that have focused on the interaction used intentions to commit crimes, but not actual offending. To say that you have the intentions to commit a crime, doesn't necessarily mean that you actually will do it. Shoepfer and Piquero (2006:68) acknowledged this, and pointed out that "*future research should strive to replicate our results using actual behavior*". Second, all four studies are limited in their sampling strategies. Antonaccio and Tittle (2008) point out themselves that there are some limitations of their data and that they "cannot be sure of the accuracy of the data" (p. 503). Shoepfer and Piquero (2006) used a rather small sample of university students of a mean age of 22. Svensson, Pauwels and Weerman (2010) used cross-sectional data of students. Differences in sample size did not allow for a more detailed study of the invariance of the interaction effect in sub groups by gender (biological sex) and immigrant background.

This study tests the *interaction* between self-control and morality and its effect on individuals' offending using self-reported offending and using data from a large Belgian youth survey that allows for a detailed analysis in four different sub groups: Belgian boys, immigrant boys, Belgian girls, immigrant girls.. In line with the *Situational Action Theory*, we hypothesize that there is an interaction between morality and self-control with regard to the explanation of individuals' involvement in crime. More specifically, self-control is assumed to have a stronger effect on offending for individuals with low levels of morality than for individuals with high levels of morality. Our goal is not to compare the four different sub groups but to test a theoretical argument in different sub groups. When the results are replicated and similar across all sub groups, this will provide a strong and more robust basis for drawing conclusions on the strength and stability of the interaction effect.

CONFOUNDING THE ROLE OF IMMIGRANT BACKGROUND AND GENDER WITH CAUSES OF OFFENDING

It is well established that males and immigrants commit more offences and more serious offences than females and natives in bivariate and multivariate studies of both self-reported and officially recorded delinquency (e.g. Junger-Tas et al., 1994; Loeber and Farrington, 1998). One important task facing criminology is that of developing theoretical frameworks in which both gender and immigrant background differences may be understood and explained. Most traditional theories focus explicitly on male delinquency (Bartush and Matsueda, 1996) and several researchers have concluded that more research is needed to test the gender gap in these theories (e.g., Bruinsma and Lissenberg, 1987; Liu and Kaplan, 1999; Svensson, 2003). When the gender gap in the aetiology of offending has been discussed, it is often assumed that differences in the socialization of males and females within the family are responsible for gender differences (e.g. Moffitt et al., 2001; Giordano and Cernkovich, 1997; Lanctôt and LeBlanc, 2002). Other researchers focused on differences in self-control (Burton et al., 1998; Blackwell and Piquero, 2004) and morality (Svensson, 2004) to account for gender differences. Immigrant background is often a more complex definable concept than the biological gender of respondents. Ethnic differences are often defined as racial differences in U.S. studies (Sampson and Laub, 1993), while this is usually not the case in Europe. European studies often differentiate between first, second and third generation immigrant background (e.g., Martens, 1997; Torgersen, 2001). However, regardless of the definition used, immigrant background is a rather stable bivariate correlate of delinquency in general, while its strength largely depends on the data used for analysis (e.g., Martens, 1997; Vazsonyi and Killias, 2001).

Junger and Haen-Marshall (1997) conclude that concepts from social control theory explain much of the variance among different ethnic groups, thereby focusing on the major ethnic minorities of the Netherlands such as Turkish and Moroccan adolescents. It is however often ignored that gender and immigrant background, although they may be important structural conditions setting the stage for behavioural outcomes, never can be seen as real causes, as neither gender nor immigrant background can bring about behavioural effects. Structural background variables may be important because they place adolescents in different social segments of the population, each of which generates different restrictions for living standards (Skarðhamar, 2005). It is not uncommon in criminological inquiries for attributes like sex and race to be included as predictors. In the case of sex some researchers even (wrongly) claim that it is the best predictor of criminal involvement. The problem with the common practice of including attributes as predictors is that they may confuse our search for causes and explanation of crime, and even more worryingly, they may make people think that the fact, for example, that someone is male or black could be a cause of their crime involvement.

We argue that it is important to distinguish between causes and correlates and instead focus on the general nature of an assumption of how causal processes affect offending. We have already established that prediction does not equal causation, and that for a factor to qualify as a cause we need to make a case that it has some kind of powers to initiate a causal process that produces the effect (e.g., an act of crime). It is difficult to see, for example, how being male or black could constitute a cause of crime (i.e., be a factor that initiates a causal process resulting in an act of crime). This does not mean that characteristics or experiences that are relevant in crime causation might not be more prevalent, for example, amongst males (such as, for example, poor ability to exercise self-control) but the point is that it is these characteristics or experiences that we should focus on as causal factors in our explanations rather than the fact that the person is male. In principle, if we can measure the real causative factors (e.g., the ability to exercise self-control and morality) there is no need to include attributes such as gender and immigrant background. Such characteristics are at best are 'markers' of the real causative factors among the predictors in our studies. This is a surplus rationale for studying the main and interaction effects of morality and self-control on offending in the aforementioned sub groups.

The main point is that while the correlation between attributes and crime involvement can be explained, attributes cannot explain why people commit acts of crime. We can, for example, explain why males commit more crimes overall than females, or why certain ethnic groups are more or less involved in crime, but an individual's sex or ethnic status cannot explain why he or she commits an act of crime (i.e., it cannot be a cause of crime). In the former case differences in offending by attribute is the outcome while in the latter case attributes can (mistakenly be treated as potential causes of offending.

This very important insight has significant implications for how research should be conducted and what conclusions for policy and practise can be drawn from research findings about correlations between attributes and crime involvement. The fact that a person's sex or immigrant background to some degree may predict his or her crime involvement does not mean that his or her sex or race causes his or her crime involvement.

To summarize, the unique focus of this research lies in looking at the effect of deviant moral beliefs and low self-control in combined sub samples by gender and immigrant background.

METHOD

The Antwerp Youth Survey used a traditional classroom "paper and pencil" strategy, including the provision of an envelope to ensure the respondents' confidentiality. Antwerp, one of the largest cities in Belgium has a population of approximately 500,000 inhabitants (including suburbs). With regard to levels of income and the proportion of immigrants in the population, Antwerp is not comparable to the Belgian average. Antwerp is instead characterised by higher levels of poverty and has a higher proportion of immigrants. The Antwerp school survey included all first grade students that both lived in the city of Antwerp *and* went to school in Antwerp. The survey thus constitutes a census of 2,486 first-graders attending 23 secondary schools in Antwerp. The average age of this population is thirteen years at the time they enter the first grade and fourteen years when they leave the first grade.

The study was conducted between January and June of 2005. The questionnaires were distributed by researchers and the students completed the questionnaires during lesson time in the presence of the researcher. The non-response rate for the Antwerp sample was 7.5%. Following list wise deletion of missing values, the analyses below are based on 2,317 respondents. The Antwerp sample consisted of 49.4% boys and 50.6% girls. Almost half of the respondents had a fully native background (both parents of Belgian descent), ten percent of the respondents had one parent with an immigrant background, while 45.5% of the respondents had two parents with an immigrant background. This represents an overrepresentation of students with an immigrant background, which is due to a higher level of participation among schools in inner city areas. Almost three quarters of the respondents were aged 12-14 years, while 26.2% of the respondents were aged 15-17. Fifteen per cent of the respondents lived in a single parent / caregiver family and 85% of the respondents lived with two parents or caregivers.

Measures

Self-Reported Offending

Self-reported offending is measured by a scale summing the respondents' offending frequencies across nine different criminal offenses. The delinquency scales are of the Likert-type with scale Alphas of .81 Detailed information on the index and the wording of the items is provided in Appendix 1.

Self-Control

Self-control is an additive index primarily based on the items used and developed by Grasmick et al. (1993). The construct taps into whether an individual has the ability to resist temptations and provocations. The scale is based on seven items in the Antwerp study with a scale Alpha of .78. High values on the measure indicate a low level of self-control.

Deviant Moral Beliefs

Deviant moral beliefs is an additive scale measuring moral values. The deviant moral beliefs scale used in Antwerp is adapted from the Sampson and Bartusch (1998) legal cynicism scale and is based on four items. The deviant moral beliefs scale has an alphas of .78.

Background Variables

All analyses are conducted in sub groups by gender and immigrant background. *Gender* is coded as zero for girls and one for boys. *Immigrant background* is coded zero when both parents are native and one if at least one of the parents was born abroad.

Before moving on to the results section, we start by presenting a correlation matrix and descriptive statistics for the variables included in the analysis. Table 1 presents a correlation matrix for all the variables included. Deviant moral beliefs and self-control are significantly correlated with one another in Antwerp ($r = .58$, $p = .001$).

Table 1. Correlation matrix (Pearson *r*) and descriptive statistics for Antwerp (*N*=2,317)

	1.	2.	3.	4.	5.	6.
Antwerp:						
1. Gender	-					
2. Immigrant background	.00	-				
3. Family structure	-.05*	.03	-			
4. Low self-control	.11***	.07**	.05*	-		
5. Low morality	.18***	.14***	.02	.58***	-	
6. Overall delinquency	.20***	.13***	.03	.45***	.51***	-
Range	0-1	0-1	0-1	11-55	-3-3	0-18
Mean	.49	.55	.15	31.09	-1.48	1.80
SD	-	-	-	9.49	1.33	2.96

* $p < .05$; ** $p < .01$; *** $p < .001$.

FINDINGS

The object of the analysis is to study whether there is an interaction between low self-control and deviant moral beliefs in the explanation of adolescent offending in all sub groups. To answer this question the analysis was conducted in the form of *Ordinary Least Squares* (OLS) regression models. Because of to the skewness of the offending variables, we reran the analyses using square root transformed dependent variables, and obtained similar conclusions to the findings reported in the text.

In the *first* model both self-control and morality were included as independent variables. In the *second* model the interaction term of self-control and morality was added to the first model. The problem of multicollinearity was dealt with by mean centering the variables prior to their inclusion in the interaction term (Jaccard, Turrisi, and Wan, 1990). However, multicollinearity diagnostics (i.e. the V.I.F.) suggested that there was no problem at all with multicollinearity (all VIF's were lower than 2). Table 2 and 3 present the findings that result from the regression analyses. Table 2 presents the results for Belgian non-immigrant and immigrant boys. Table 3 presents the results for Belgian non-immigrant and immigrant girls.

Table 2. OLS regression analysis using self-control and morality predicting overall offending Antwerp.
Unstandardized (b) and standardised (β) regression coefficients

	Model 1		Model 2	
	Immigrant boys	Belgian boys	Immigrant boys	Belgian boys
	B/beta (SE)	B/beta (SE)	B/beta (SE)	B/beta (SE)
Constant	2,395 ** (0,131)	1,676** (0,102)	2,208** (0,141)	1,1381** (0,115)
Low self-control	0,167/0,282*** (0,024)	0,091/0,197*** (0,021)	0,151/0,256*** (0,024)	0,104/0,224*** (0,020)
Deviant moral beliefs	0,288/0,343*** (0,034)	0,272/0,409*** (0,030)	0,252 /0,300*** (0,035)	0,239/0,360*** (0,030)
Low self-control X deviant moral beliefs			0,015/0,131*** (0,004)	0,021/0,190*** (0,004)
R^2	0,302	0,298	0,316	0,332
Adj. R^2	0,300	0,295	0,313	0,329
Change in F value	134,848***	108,231***	12,227***	26,319***

*: $p<0,05$, **: $p<0,01$, ***: $p<0,001$.

Table 3. OLS regression analysis using self-control and morality predicting overall offending Antwerp. Unstandardized (*b*) and standardised (β) regression coefficients

	Model 1		Model 2	
	Immigrant girls	Belgian girls	Immigrant girls	Belgian girls
	B/beta (SE)	B/beta (SE)	B/beta (SE)	B/beta (SE)
Constant	1,403** (0,084)	1,492** (0,084)	1,108** (0,094)	1,246** (0,099)
Low self-control	0,101/ 0,273** (0,015)	0,065/ 0,179*** (0,016)	0,110/ 0,296*** (0,015)	0,099/0,274*** (0,018)
Deviant moral beliefs	0,172/0,294*** (0,024)	0,223/ 0,411*** (0,025)	0,151/0,258*** (0,024)	0,187/ 0,345*** (0,025)
Low self-control X deviant moral beliefs			0,018/ 0,210*** (0,003)	0,015/ 0,178*** (0,003)
R^2	0,252	0,288	0,295	0,313
Adj. R^2	0,250	0,285	0,292	0,309
Change in F value	107,973***	107,483***	39,317***	19,740***

*: $p < 0,05$, **: $p < 0,01$, ***: $p < 0,001$.

The first model shows that both self-control and morality are significantly correlated with overall offending for Belgian non-immigrant and immigrant boys (Table 2). This indicates that individuals with low levels of self-control have higher risks of offending and that having low levels of morality is also correlated with higher levels of offending. In the second model, the interaction term of self-control and morality is introduced. The interaction term is significantly correlated with higher levels of offending in all sub groups in Antwerp, indicating that the effect of self-control is substantially conditional on an individual's morality to offend. The results indicate that self-control has a relatively weak effect on offending for individuals with high levels of morality. The relationship between self-control and offending is stronger for Belgian immigrant and non-immigrant boys with low levels of morality. This indicates, as hypothesized, that self-control only has an effect on offending in the presence of an individual's morality to offend and that the relationship between self-control and offending is dependent on the level of an individual's morality. The same pattern is found for both sub groups.

DISCUSSIONS AND CONCLUSIONS

The main objective of this study was to examine whether self-control and morality interact in the explanation of offending. The question of whether morality and self-control may *interact* in the explanation of offending, has only rarely been examined in the research to date. The question how invariant this interaction effect is, has as far as we know never previously been demonstrated. We assumed that self-control will have a stronger effect on offending for individuals with low levels of morality, whereas for individuals with high levels of morality the effect of self-control would be weaker. To test these hypothesis data are drawn from a sample of young adolescents in Antwerp.The results of this study show that both morality and self-control are related with adolescent offending. That both of these factors are related with offending is something that it is line with previous research (Jan Stams et al., 2006; Pratt and Cullen, 2000). Furthermore, the main findings of this study are that there is a statistical interaction between morality and self-control in the explanation of adolescent offending in all sample segments. This interaction means that self-control especially has a strong effect on offending in the presence of the level of morality. The relationship between self-control and offending seems to be rather weak for individuals with high level of morality and the effect are substantially stronger for individuals with low levels of morality.

The evidence of the interaction effect are in line with the theoretical argument by the SAT (Wikström, 2006; Wikström and Treiber, 2007) that self-control only comes into play when an individual considers engaging in an act of crime (i.e. have low morality). The findings from this study also give support of the SAT in terms of that morality seems to be a more important predictor of offending than self-control.

This study used cross-sectional data, and, it is always a limitation using this kind of data and we argue that it is important that further research test for this interaction using longitudinal data. Finally, we argue that it is important to further develop measures of morality and including the dimension of emotion, in testing for this interaction.

APPENDIX 1:
MEASURES EMPLOYED IN THE ANTWERP SAMPLE

Offending: Vandalism / graffiti / buying stolen property / shoplifting / serious theft / threatening / hit on purpose / fighting outside school / burglary   Last year frequencies: never / once or twice /three times or more
Morality (antisocial values):   Rules are made to be broken / ok to break rules, as long as do not get caught / fighting ok when provoked / if honest ways to achieve something fail, then use dishonest ways   Five point scale: totally agree/ agree/ neither agree nor disagree/ disagree/ totally disagree
Self-control: I often do things without thinking first / when angry, others had better stay away from me / I have fun when I can, even if I get into trouble afterwards / when I am angry, I'd rather hit than talk / I say what I think, even if its not smart / I often do what I want to / get angry very fast   Five point scale: totally agree/ agree/ neither agree nor disagree/ disagree/ totally disagree

REFERENCES

Antonaccio, O., and Tittle, C. R. (2008). Morality, self-control, and crime. *Criminology, 46,* 479-510.

Burton, V. S. Jr., Cullen, F. T., Evans, T. D., Alarid, L. F., and Dunaway, R. G. (1998). Gender, self-control, and crime. *Journal of Research in Crime and Delinquency*, *35,* 123-147.

Chapple, C. L. (2005). Self-control, peer relations, and delinquency. *Justice Quarterly*, 22, 89-106.

De Li, S. (2004). The impacts of self-control and social bond on juvenile delinquency in a national sample of mid-adolescents. *Deviant Behavior, 25,* 351-373.

Finkel, E. J., and Campell, W. K. (2001). Self-control and accommodation in close relationships: An interdependence analysis. *Journal of Personality and Social Psychology, 81,* 263-277.

Gottfredson, M. R., and Hirschi, T. (1990). *A general theory of crime.* Stanford, C.A: Stanford University Press.

Grasmick, H. G., Tittle, C. R., Bursik, R. J. Jr., and Arneklev, B. J. (1993). Testing the core empirical implications of Gottfredson and Hirschi's General Theory of Crime. *Journal of Research in Crime and Delinquency, 30,* 5-29.

Hay, C., and Forrest, W. (2008). Self-control theory and the concept of opportunity: The case for a more systematic union. *Criminology*, 46, 1039-1072.

Jaccard, J., Turrisi, R., and Wan, C. K. (1990). *Interaction effects in multiple regression.* Newbury Park, CA: Sage.

LaGrange, T.C., and Silverman, R. A. (1999). Low self-control and opportunity: testing the general theory of crime as an explanation for gender differences in delinquency. *Criminology*, *37*, 41-72.

Longshore, D. (1998). Self-control and criminal opportunity: A prospective test of the General Theory of Crime. *Social Problems, 45*, 102-113.

Meldrum, R. C., Young, J. T. N., and Weerman, F. M. (2009). Reconsidering the effects of self-control and delinquent peers: Implications of measurements for theoretical significance. *Journal of Research in Crime and Delinquency*, *46*, 353-376.

Pauwels, L., and Svensson, R. (2008). How serious is the problem of item nonresponse in delinquency scales and aetiological variables? A cross-national inquiry into two classroom PAPI self-report studies in Antwerp and Halmstad. *European Journal of Criminology*, 5, 289-308.

Pauwels, L., and Svensson, R. (2009). Individual differences in adolescent lifestyle risk by gender and ethnic background: Findings from two urban samples. *European Journal of Criminology, 6*, 5-23.

Pratt, T. C., and Cullen, F. T. (2000). The empirical status of Gottfredson and Hirschi's general theory of crime: A meta-analysis. *Criminology, 38*, 931-964.

Ribeaud, D., and Eisner, M. (2006) The 'drug-crime' link from a self-control perspective: An empirical test in a Swiss youth sample. *European Journal of Criminology, 3*, 33-67.

Shoepfer, A., and Piquero, A. R. (2006). Self-control, moral beliefs, and criminal activity. *Deviant Behavior, 27,* 51-71.

Sampson, R. J., and Bartush, D. J. (1998). Legal Cynicism and (Subcultural?) Tolerance of deviance: The neighborhood context of racial differences. *Law and Society Review, 32,* 777-804.

Svensson, R., and Pauwels, L. Is a risky lifestyle always "risky"? The interaction between individual propensity and lifestyle risk in adolescent offending: A test in two urban samples. *Crime and Delinquency*. Prepublished September 24, 2008, DOI: 10.1177/0011128708324290.

Vazsonyi, A. T., Pickering, L. E., Junger, M., and Hessing, D. (2001). An empirical test of a general theory of crime: A four nation comparative study of self-control and prediction of deviance. *Journal of Research in Crime and Delinquency, 38*, 91-131.

Weerman, F. M., and Bijleveld, C. C. J. H. (2007). Birds of different feathers: School networks of serious delinquent, minor delinquent and non-delinquent boys and girls. *European Journal of Criminology*, *4*, 357-383.

Weerman, F. M., Harland, P., and van der Laan, P. H. (2007). Misbehavior at school and delinquency elsewhere: A complex relationship. *Criminal Justice Review* (special issue on School Crime and Disorder), *32*, 358-379.

Wikström, P-O. H. (2004). Crime as alternative. Towards a cross-level situational action theory of crime causation. In J. McCord (Ed.), *Beyond empiricism: Institutions and intentions in the study of crime. Advances in criminological theory, vol. 13*. New Brunswick, NJ: Transaction.

Wikström, P-O. H. (2005). The social origins of pathways in crime: Towards a developmental ecological action theory of crime involvement and its changes. In D. P. Farrington (Ed.), *Integrated developmental and life course theories of offending. Advances in criminological theory, vol. 14*. New Brunswick: Transaction.

Wikström, P-O. H. (2006). Individuals, settings and acts of crime. Situational mechanisms and the explanation of crime. In P-O. H. Wikström and R. J. Sampson (Eds.), *Crime and its explanation: Contexts, mechanisms and development.* Cambridge: Cambridge University Press.

Wikström, P-O H. (2009). Crime propensity, criminogenic exposure and crime involvement in early to mid adolescence. *Monatsschrift fur Kriminologie und Strafrechtsreform, 92,* 253-266.

Wikström, P-O. H., and Butterworth, D. A. (2006). *Adolescent crime: Individuals differences and lifestyles.* Collumpton: Willan Publishing.

Wikström, P-O H. and Svensson, R. (2005). *The interaction between morality and self-control in the explanation of adolescent offending.* Paper presented at the 5 Annual Conference of the European Society of Criminology, Krakow, Polen, 31 August – 3 September 2005.

Wikström, P-O H. and Svensson, R (2008). Why are English youths more violent than Swedish youths? A comparative study of the role of crime propensity, lifestyles and their interactions. *European Journal of Criminology,* 5, 309-330.

Wikström, P-O H., and Treiber, K. (2007). The role of self-control in crime causation: Beyond Gottfredson and Hirschi's General Theory of Crime. *European Journal of Criminology, 4,* 237-264.

INDEX

N

O

P

University Centre at
Blackburn
College

Telephone: 01254 292165

Please return this book on or before the last date shown